Ellison Banks Findly

SONGS OF ECSTASY

Songs of Ecstasy

Tantric and Devotional Songs
from Colonial Bengal

Hugh B. Urban

OXFORD
UNIVERSITY PRESS

2001

OXFORD
UNIVERSITY PRESS

Oxford New York
Athens Auckland Bangkok Bogotá Buenos Aires Cape Town
Chennai Dar es Salaam Delhi Florence Hong Kong Istanbul Karachi
Kolkata Kuala Lumpur Madrid Melbourne Mexico City Mumbai Nairobi
Paris São Paulo Shanghai Singapore Taipei Tokyo Toronto Warsaw

and associated companies in
Berlin Ibadan

Published by Oxford University Press, Inc.
198 Madison Avenue, New York, New York 10016

Library of Congress Cataloging-in-Publication Data
Urban, Hugh B.
Songs of ecstasy: Tantric and devotional songs from colonial Bengal / Hugh B. Urban.
p. cm.
Includes bibliographical references and index.
ISBN 0-19-513900-3
1. Kartābhajā—Prayer-books and devotions—English. I. Title.
BL1276.86 .U73 2001
294.5'432—dc21 00-061156

9 8 7 6 5 4 3 2 1

Printed in the United States of America
on acid-free paper

Acknowledgments

In my translation of these songs and in my—at least partial—interpretation of their meaning, I am deeply indebted to a number of people, both in India and at home. Because I have already thanked them more specifically in *The Economics of Ecstasy,* I will simply mention them by name here, without going into the details of all their painstaking help: all the Kartābhajā devotees who so kindly offered me their time, patience, and hospitality; my mentors at Chicago, Wendy Doniger and Bruce Lincoln; my Sāheb-gurus in the art of translating Bengali, Ed Dimock and Clint Seely; my fellow *sādhakas* and *sādhikās* in the study of Bengali Tantra, Jeff Kripal, Rachel McDermott, Carol Salomon, Glen Hayes, and Tony Stewart; my invaluable research consultant and guide through the back alleys of old Calcutta, Hena Basu; my Ma and Pa; and, perhaps most important of all, my best pal, Nancy, and my dog, Shakti.

Contents

A Note (or Apology) on Transliteration

Unfortunately, there is no standard or satisfactory system for transliterating Bengali script into Roman characters; indeed, there seem to be as many different systems as there are scholars of Bengali. After asking numerous authorities, both Western and Indian, I have found nothing but a wild diversity of idiosyncratic systems, nor have I ever come across a work that was entirely consistent within itself. On one side, authors who wish to emphasize the Sanskritic origins of Bengali use the same transliteration system as for *devanāgarī*: they distinguish between *v*'s and *b*'s and between different sibilants (*ś, ṣ, s*) and render all final open vowels. This purely Sanskritic system is perhaps the only truly "consistent" one, though it results in some rather bizarre constructions that have no real place in either the Sanskrit or Bengali languages (e.g., rendering the final vowel of a Bengali genitive inflection, such as *bhāvera,* which does not exist in Sanskrit and is not pronounced in Bengali). On the other side, those who wish to capture the actual sound of the Bengali language adopt a basically phonetic system: hence, all *v*'s turn into Bengali *b*'s, all sibilants become the Bengali aspirated *sh*'s, all final vowels drop off, and so on. This, too, produces some weird constructions—for example, *boishnab* for the Sanskritic *vaiṣṇava*—which are unrecognizable to most non-Bengali specialists. In sum, a purely Sanskritic system ultimately does violence to the uniquely Bengali character of the language, while a purely Bengali system is basically unintelligible to scholars of most non-Bengali traditions.

For my part, I have chosen to adopt a compromise system similar to that used by Jeffrey Kripal. As Kripal points out, Bengali writers, in their own self-representations, typically use a mixed system of transliteration, slipping easily back and forth between a Sanskritic and a vernacular:

> Because the culture itself rocks back and forth between venacular and Sanskritic transliterations, I too will alternate between the two options, trying as best I can to approximate the self-representation of the culture. . . . Such a system will no doubt strike the linguistically sensitive reader as a confused melange of broken rules and inconsistencies. I can only admit my compromises, note that they are at least partly a function of the culture's own history. (Jeffrey J. Kripal, *Kālī's Child: The Mystical and the Erotic in the Life and Teachings of Ramakrishna* [Chicago: University of Chicago Press, 1995], xxxii)

No one, for example, ever writes the name "Ramakrishna" the way it is actually pronounced (i.e., "Ramkrishno"). Instead, the tradition frequently Sanskritizes itself, though usually only partially, and often quite incorrectly. Moreover, this eclectic compromise method is itself a reflection of the complex and syncretic history of the Bengali people—a people who wish to identify themselves with the rich traditions of Sanskrit literature while asserting the uniquely "Bengali" quality of their own very rich history and literary creations. This may strike most specialists as inconsistent and contradictory; but one could argue equally that a purely "consistent" and rigidly governed system would do an injustice to this tradition, which is itself highly diverse, pluralistic, and often (like every language) quite inconsistent. However, I adopt a few basic ground rules:

1. The basic system is fundamentally Sanskritic, though tailored to the peculiarities of the Bengali language. This is intended, first, to make this book reasonably accessible to scholars of Sanskrit and other Indian languages, and, second, to preserve as much of the feel of the Bengali language as possible.
2. Therefore I follow the Sanskrit distinction between *v*'s and *b*'s and between different sibilants, and I render vowels in their Sanskrit form (*a* and *ā* instead of the Bengali *o* and *uh*).
3. Final *a*'s on genitive or locative constructions are not rendered, because this produces a form that makes no sense in either Bengali or Sanskrit. Thus, I use *Bhāver,* not *Bhāvera.*
4. Words of clearly Perso-Arabic origin are not Sanskritized: thus Pīr does not become Pīra, and terms like *gorib* ("poor") are not rendered as *goriva.*
5. Proper names are left more or less as pronounced and not Sanskritized unless that person has rendered his own name Sanskritically in English publications. Thus I refer to "Āulcāṅd" and "Dulālcāṅd" rather than "Āulacāṅda" and "Dulālacāṅda." This will no doubt produce a number of unsatisfactory contradictions—but no more than most native Bengalis produce when they attempt to render their own names into English.

Abbreviations

Citations in *The Economics of Ecstasy* and in this book refer, first, to the original text and page number (e.g., KG 1 or BG 66) and, second, to the section and song number in this book. Hence, BG 160; II.1 refers to *Bhāver Gīta*, 160, translated in this volume, chapter II, song number 1.

BG	*Bhāver Gīta,* ed. Śāntirañjan Cakravartī. Calcutta: Indralekha Press, 1399 B.S. (1992).
BG (1882)	*Bhāver Gīta,* ed. Romeścandra Ghoṣe. Calcutta: Aurora Press, 1289 B.S. (1882).
EE	Hugh B. Urban. *The Economics of Ecstasy: Tantra, Secrecy, and Power in Colonial Bengal.* New York: Oxford University Press, 2001.
KDA	Manulāl Miśra. *Kartābhajā Dharmer Ādi Vṛttānta Vā Sahajatattva Prakāśa.* Calcutta: Author, 1925.
KG	*Kartābhajā Gīta.* Bengali manuscript no. 964, Bāṅgīya Sāhitya Pariṣat Library (Calcutta), 1228-33 B.S. (1821–26 CE).
SS	*Sahajiyā Sāhitya*, ed. Manidra Mohan Bose. Calcutta: University of Calcutta, 1932.
STP	Manulāl Miśra. *Sahaja Tattva Prakāśa.* Calcutta: Author, 1309 B.S. (1902).

SONGS OF ECSTASY

Translator's Note

"The Secret Mastery of Difference"

The translator is the secret master of the difference of languages, a difference he is not out to abolish, but rather, he puts to use as he brings violent or subtle changes to bear on his own language, thus reawakening within it the presence of that which is at origin different in the original. (Maurice Blanchot)

This book is a companion volume to another book, *The Economics of Ecstasy: Tantra, Secrecy, and Power in Colonial Bengal,* also published by Oxford University Press. Whereas *The Economics of Ecstasy* engages the theoretical issues of secrecy and concealment, as it played in one particular Tantric sect known as the Kartābhajās, the *Songs of Ecstasy* is a body of translations meant to accompany the first text. Together, I would hope, these two volumes open up a surprising and revealing new window, both onto the world of colonial India and onto the larger issues of secrecy, discourse, and power in the history of religions as a whole. Those of you who have already read *The Economics of Ecstasy* may therefore wish to skip over most of chapter I (this volume), which summarizes the main arguments of the companion book.

From the outset, however, I should also admit the limitations of this book. The songs translated here are surely among the most difficult and most esoteric songs known in the Bengali language. They are, moreover, songs that are clearly rooted in a specific social and historical context: the context of colonial Calcutta at the dawn of the nineteenth century. Hence, rather ironically, a huge amount of the language and imagery of these songs no longer has much relevance to contemporary Kartābhajā practitioners, who will often either ignore or else strongly reinterpret the language drawn from a century before. A large portion of the Kartābhajā songs, for example, use the imagery of the British East India "Company" (*kompānī*), imported goods from England, and the mercantile trade in the bazaars of the colonial center—little of which has any meaning for contemporary devotees. Therefore, in my own attempts to make sense of these enigmatic songs, I have had to go back and resituate them within the context of colonial Calcutta and its environs at the dawn of the nineteenth century. And in so doing, I have often had to disagree in many fundamental ways—though always respectfully—with the interpretations of contemporary Kartābhajā devotees, for whom much of this early colonial language is no longer relevant and is often ignored or covered over. To read these songs historically, therefore, often means to read them against the grain of the ways in which they are read and used by disciples today.[1]

As such, the Songs of Ecstasy raise, in the most acute way, all the critical debates in contemporary translation theory and in the problem of crosscultural understanding as a whole. First, and most basically, they raise the question of whether we ever really *can* translate a body of esoteric texts—that is, texts deliberately concealed within highly enigmatic and encrypted language. As Arthur Schopenhauer put it, "Poems cannot be translated, they can only be rewritten, which is always quite an ambiguous undertaking"—and this undertaking is perhaps only infinitely more ambiguous and complex in the case of specifically esoteric poems.[2] Originally designed to be transmitted in narrowly controlled channels between masters and disciples, the Songs of Ecstasy are intended to generate an intense experience of gnosis and spiritual ecstasy, something that cannot be communicated in ordinary exoteric language. Some scholars, such as Edward Conze, have therefore concluded that the esoteric discourse of Tantra simply cannot—and ethically, *should* not—be translated or understood by anyone other than initiated insiders: "There is something both indecent and ridiculous about the public discussion of the esoteric in words that can be generally understood."[3]

Second, these songs also raise the larger ethical issue of translation in a postcolonial—and some would say, *neo*colonial—world order: namely, *should we even try* to penetrate, uncover, and translate the esoteric teachings of a formerly colonized people, recasting them and thereby assimilating them into the now globally hegemonic discourse of American English? What right does yet another American scholar have to come and tell Indians what their religious and cultural traditions "*really* mean?" In his work *Kālī's Child,* for example, Jeffrey Kripal attempted to delve into the secrets of the great Bengali mystic, Śrī Rāmakṛṣṇa, by retranslating the original Bengali texts and unveiling some of the saint's deep sexual conflicts and homoerotic impulses. This same book, which won a major award from the American Academy of Religions, faced intense controversy, scandal, opposition, and finally censorship among the Indian community itself, many of whom felt that it was yet another example of Western cultural imperialism and exploitation.[4]

Yet, as Jacques Derrida aptly observes, *every* original text, no matter what its historical or cultural origin, not only can be but, in a certain sense, *demands* to be translated. For every text is to some degree incomplete, lacking, divided, and torn within itself. No text is entirely self-transparent or self-sufficient but, rather, requires a supplement, another text, to comment on and interpret it, however incompletely and inadequately. "The translation will truly be a moment in the growth of the original which will complete itself in enlarging itself . . . And if the original calls for a complement, it is because at the origin it was not there without fault, full, complete, total, identical to itself."[5] Perhaps nowhere is this more true than in the case of the Songs of Ecstasy, which are, in themselves, some of the most confusing and mystifying texts in the history of Bengali literature, whose meaning is uncertain and fiercely contested, not only by outsider scholars, but also by members of the Kartābhajā community itself. Hence, not only can these songs be translated, but they also in a sense insist on some sort of rendering into an alternative discourse—even while always remaining at some fundamental level untranslatable and inscrutable.

In a similar way, of course, the translation cannot claim to be a total, complete, and transparent mirror of the translated text but must also be recognized as divided and plural within itself. Its aim is not to cover over or correct but, rather, to *reveal and explore* the cracks, conflicts, and fault-lines within the foreign text:

> A translation is never quite faithful, always somewhat free, it never establishes an identity, always a lack and a supplement, and it can never be a transparent representation, only an interpretive transformation that exposes multiple and divided meanings in the foreign text and displaces it with another set of meanings, equally multiple and divided.[6]

Nowhere is this more true than in the case of the songs translated here. Not only are these songs clearly the work of many authors over a long period of time, and not only do these songs contain many apparent contradictions and seeming absurdities within themselves, but there have also clearly been many profound disagreements among the Kartābhajās themselves as to precisely what these songs mean. In the course of my research in West Bengal and Bangladesh, I encountered a tremendous variety of interpretations of even the same song or the same verse, reflecting the many different factions and schisms within the community over the last 200 years. Hence, my translations are not intended to smooth over these conflicts, schisms, and contested interpretations but, rather, to *expose and highlight* them through my own often conflicted and confused encounter with this tradition.

As Blanchot points out, a truly good translations is one that recognizes the ultimate difference and otherness of the foreign text. As the "secret master of difference," a good translator not only acknowledges but celebrates that difference, using it in order to view his or her own language in a new light, to stretch, to challenge, and at times to shatter the conceptual structures that comprise his or her own world. A similar point was made by Walter Benjamin in his famous essay, the "Task of the Translator," where he quotes Rudolf Pannwitz:

> Our translations, even the best, proceed from a false premise. They want to germanize Hindi, Greek, English, instead of hindi-izing, grecizing, anglicizing German. They have a much greater respect for the little ways of their own language than for the spirit of the foreign work. The fundamental error of the translator is that he maintains the accidental state of his own language instead of *letting it suffer the shock of the foreign language*. . . . He must *widen and deepen his language through the foreign one.*[7]

The Songs of Ecstasy, I hope, will force us to reimagine some of our own most basic categories—the categories of secrecy and esoteric discourse, the status of the subaltern within a situation of political rule, and the relation between religion and economics, spiritual ideals and the secular marketplace.

I

The Spirituality of the Subaltern

The Historical Context and Literary Significance of the Songs of Ecstasy

See all the subjects dwelling under the Emperor and the Minister;
in this world, everyone's filled with bliss!
They appear to be high or low class men
but this is only an illusion—they're all equal;
whether Hindu or non-Hindu, they all worship God.
. . . Look: united in Love, all these animals, birds, men, and living beings,
are overwhelmed with the Ecstasy of Love! (BG 93; II.61)

As the title *Bhāver Gīta* implies, the songs translated in this volume are a genre of deeply mystical, esoteric songs (*gīta*), composed in the Bengali language, and centered around the experience of religious ecstasy (*bhāva*).[1] The theme of intense spiritual emotion or ecstatic outpouring through song has a long, rich history in Bengal, dating back to the oldest known texts written in Bengali and continuing to the present day in folk traditions such as the songs of the wandering "madmen," the Bāuls. Yet in the case of the *Bhāver Gīta*, this tradition has undergone a series of profound transformations in a changing sociohistorical context. First, these songs are the most sacred text of one of Bengal's most enigmatic sects—the Kartābhajās, or Worshipers of the Master.[2] As such, the songs of the *Bhāver Gīta* are clothed in the Kartābhajās' unique form of esoteric language, drawn in large part from the older traditions of Indian Tantra. Second, composed at the dawn of the nineteenth century in the area around Calcutta, these songs are also clearly the product of the British colonial era, incorporating a vast amount of imagery drawn from the marketplaces of the imperial city. In the songs of the *Bhāver Gīta*, the experience of ecstasy is by no means a purely disembodied, otherworldly state; rather, it is a profoundly *embodied* kind of ecstasy, rooted in the most immediate experiences of the human body, society, politics, and economics.

Amid the long, rich history of literature in Bengal, few traditions remains so poorly understood or so sadly neglected by contemporary scholarship as the Kartābhajās and their songs. Founded by a semilegendary holy madman named Āulcāṅd, who is said to have been Śrī Caitanya in the disguise of a Muslim fakir, the Kartābhajās represent the most important later branch of the Sahajiyā tradition which survived in colonial Bengal. In many ways the Kartābhajās are a tradition much like the Bāuls—that eclectic tradition of folk singers who had long been denigrated until they were rediscovered by Rabindranath Tagore in the early twentieth century.[3] Indeed, at the height of their power in the nineteenth century, the Kartābhajās were more numerous and more powerful than the Sahajiyās, the Bāuls, or any other of Bengal's "obscure religious cults." A variety of authors have commented on the importance of the Kartābhajā songs, which represent both a unique form of Bengali song and a highly influential body of religious thought. No less an authority than Sukumār Sen even compared them with the songs of the great poet and national hero, Rabindranath himself:

> Among the songs there is some philosophy, but its value is not as great as their unusual simplicity and the originality in their composition. . . . There is no influence from the high-class *sādhubhāṣā*. The unrestricted emotion of Sahaja is expressed with the simple language of the spoken word. . . . Within these songs flows the life blood of Bengali literature which one cannot see anywhere prior to Rabindranath.[4]

Yet despite their acknowledged importance, the songs of the *Bhāver Gīta* have never been studied in any critical way by modern scholars; indeed, some have suggested that a careful study of the *Bhāver Gīta* remains one of the most needed projects in the study of Bengali literature.[5]

One of the primary reasons for the neglect of the Kartābhajās is the long history of scandal, slander, and controversy that has surrounded the sect from its inception. Above all, the Kartābhajās have been attacked because of their alleged associations with the practices of Tantra—a highly esoteric tradition, notorious for its antinomian practices, which came under intense criticism during the colonial era.[6] As a suspected "Tantric" movement, the Kartābhajās were fiercely attacked for their violation of caste laws, mingling of social classes, and use of sexual rituals. In the face of the changing moral norms of British rule and the reform movements of the Bengal Renaissance, the Kartābhajās were identified as one of the worst examples of all the polytheism and licentiousness believed to have corrupted Hinduism in modern times. By the end of the nineteenth century, they were reduced to a sad laughing stock and object of ridicule. In response to this criticism and controversy, therefore, the Kartābhajās tended to conceal their teachings in profoundly esoteric forms, composing some of the most obscure, deeply encoded, and difficult songs in all of Bengali literature. As another respected historian, D. C. Sen, put it, the songs of the *Bhāver Gīta* are like the songs of birds—mysteriously beautiful, yet generally unintelligible to the uninitiated.[7]

Perhaps most striking is that not only do these songs employ a wide range of esoteric mystical imagery, drawn from the Sahajiyā and other Tantric traditions of medieval Bengal, but they also clothe this Tantric imagery in a huge amount of idiosyncratic economic discourse, the mercantile terminology drawn from the teeming marketplaces of colonial Calcutta. Throughout these songs, the metaphor of the marketplace (*bājār*) is the dominant trope and recurring motif. And even more audaciously, the Kartābhajās also appropriate the image of the British East India Company itself. Hailing themselves as the "new Company" or the "poor

Company" (*gorib kompānī*), they promise to bring a host of spiritual goods for the lowly and downtrodden of society.[8]

Based on my own research among the Kartābhajās of Bengal and Bangladesh, I believe I have been able to unravel at least a few of the secrets of the *Bhāver Gīta*. The Kartābhajā songs, I argue here, emerged at a key geographic locus and a critical historical moment—the area around the imperial city of Calcutta at the turn of the nineteenth century, the high point of European capitalist penetration into the subcontinent. As such, they offer a number of striking insights into this crucial period in the history of Bengal.[9]

In my analysis of the Kartābhajā songs, I adapt, but also criticize, certain insights of Ranajit Guha, Partha Chatterjee, and other members of the Subaltern Studies collective. I am in many ways sympathetic to their attempt to give new attention to the creative agency of lower-class, dominated peoples under colonial rule.[10] At the same time, however, I remain critical of their work in the following two respects. First, with their emphasis on the most radical and violent forms of subaltern resistance, such as peasant revolt, the subaltern scholars have typically overlooked the more quotidian, less violent, yet no less significant forms of resistance.[11] Second and more important, with their heavily Marxist and reductionist orientation, they have also failed to deal adequately with the specifically *religious* dimension of subaltern consciousness. As I argue in the case of the Kartābhajās, it may be true that colonized peoples often use religious symbols to express underlying material or economic interests, but it is no less true that they can *also* manipulate economic imagery to express profoundly religious concerns and spiritual ideals. Ultimately, they may also use such symbols to express alternative visions of community, new ideals of human society, distinct from both traditional hierarchies and modern capitalist forms.

After a brief introduction to the Kartābhajās and their historical context, I argue that the importance of the *Bhāver Gīta* is fourfold. First, stylistically, these songs represent a fusion of two different song forms of nineteenth-century Bengal: the folk styles of village Bengal and the parlor styles of colonial Calcutta. Second, in their mystical symbolism, these songs represent an important moment in the history of Bengali religious song, combining the secular imagery of urban life in Calcutta with profound spiritual imagery such as the haunting figure the Man of the Heart, which would later become famous in the songs of the Bāuls. Third, with their extensive use of mercantile terminology, these songs open a fascinating window on the lives of Bengal's lower orders—the poor men and women laboring in the underworld of the imperial city at the dawn of the colonial era. And, finally, the Kartābhajā songs are also a clear example of the deeply ambivalent status of Tantra during the colonial era. Although filled with references to Tantric sexual practices, these songs conceal Tantric elements behind an elaborate veil of coded discourse. Above all, they employ the complex vocabulary of mercantile trade, masking their esoteric rites with the imagery of the British East India Company itself.

A Simple Path for the Poor: The Rise of the Kartābhajās in Colonial Bengal

The Kartābhajā sect has recently emerged—now hear some funny things about them!
. . . They see no distinctions between boys, old men, youths or women; thus they go along,
. . . Brothers, if any of you wish to go to the Kartābhajā festival,
you'll have to go where thirty-six castes go—and caste will have to be left behind.
(Dāśarathī Rāy, "Kartābhajā," a satirical poem ridiculing the Kartābhajās)

Throughout the world of Bengal, the Kartābhajās have a long and controversial reputation—a reputation due in large part to their alleged engagement in secret, scandalous, and immoral activities. The dangerous practices of the group were discussed fairly widely throughout nineteenth-century Bengali literature; the great Calcutta saint Rāmakṛṣṇa, for example, had close personal contact with the sect, which he described as a powerful but frightening group comprised largely of "bitches," whose path could only be described as a sort of "latrine door"—a quick and expedient, but also rather "filthy," way of approaching God.[12] Still more scathing attacks came from the orthodox Hindu and Muslim reformers of the colonial era. "The class of Fakirs called Kartābhajās," as Muhammad Riāzuddin Āhmad wrote, "is a group of necrophagous goblins who have spread their terrible poison throughout our community. . . . They are the refuse of our society."[13] And even in recent popular literature, the dangerous power and lurid attraction of the Kartābhajās survives in Bengali imagination; as the widely read novelist, Kālakūṭa describes them, "At the very utterance of this word 'Kartābhajā' my family and neighbors would make mocking and disgusted remarks . . . "Oh! such a disgraceful thing has never before occurred in this world!"[14]

The teachings of the Kartābhajās are largely rooted in the older Vaiṣṇava-Sahajiyā and other Tantric schools, which had proliferated in Bengal since at least the sixteenth century.[15] Like the Vaiṣṇava-Sahajiyās, the Kartābhajās identify the Supreme Reality and Divine Essence as *Sahaja*—the "in-born, spontaneous or innate"[16] condition of all things in their true nature, unobscured by the veils of ignorance and the illusion of the phenomenal world. *Sahaja* is present within every human being, dwelling in the form of the Man of the Heart (*maner mānuṣa*), the inner core of the Self and the divine spark of the Infinite within us all. When asked "to which caste does *Sahaja* belong?" the Kartābhajās respond, "*Sahaja* is of the Human caste . . . Its arising lies within the Body itself. . . . It is without refuge in any religious views. . . . Hear this law: Man is supreme" (BG 48). As such, the means to attaining *Sahaja* does not lie in rigid rituals or orthodox religion; rather, the means lie within the individual human body, to be realized through techniques of yoga and meditation, and, in some cases, through rituals of sexual intercourse between male and female practitioners.[17]

All things and all events lie within the microcosm of the human body;
Whatever is or will be lies within the Self-Nature.
There is no difference between human beings . . .
The infinite forms in every land, all the activities of every human being,
all things rest in *Sahaja.* (BG 32)

The Kartābhajās, however, represent a fascinating transformation of the older Sahajiyā tradition under the new conditions of British colonial rule. Indeed, this sect emerged at a critical historical moment and geographical location—the area in and around Calcutta, the "Imperial City," at the turn of the nineteenth century, the high point of early capitalist development in the subcontinent. The majority of its following was drawn from those classes who had been most negatively affected by the rapidly changing economic context under colonial rule. In the village areas, they came primarily form the poor peasantry of rural Bengal, who faced increasing hardships under the new land revenue policies of the British East India Company: "Members were low caste, poor, illiterate people engaged in agricultural operations," as Geoffrey Oddie comments, "Change was in the air. . . . Because of chronic rural indebtedness, landlord oppression and famine . . . thousands of the poor low caste people were seeking something better."[18]

In the colonial center of Calcutta, the sect attracted the poor laboring classes who had recently migrated to the city from the villages and now filled the slums of the Black Town. As the nineteenth-century paper, *Somaprakāśa,* reported, "This religion holds sway particularly among the lower classes. According to Hindu scriptures . . . they do not have any freedom . . . but in the Kartābhajā sect they enjoy great freedom."[19] We might say that the Kartābhajās represented the *underworld of the imperial city*, the lower strata inhabiting the slums of Calcutta's Black Town, who posed an embarrassing eyesore to the wealthy, Western-educated upper classes. "One sect that raised a lot of controversy in those days was the Kartābhajā group," Sumanta Banerjee comments; "The stress on equality of all people irrespective of caste . . . drew the lower orders in large numbers."[20]

According to the Kartābhajā's mythohistorical narrative, the Vaiṣṇava movement led by Caitanya in the sixteenth century had been progressively corrupted and perverted by the later Vaiṣṇava lineage; although initially opposed to caste hierarchies and Brahminical power, it had gradually reintroduced social divisions, strict orthodoxy, and rituals while progressively marginalizing the poor lower classes. Therefore, the story goes, Caitanya decided to become reincarnate in the form of the poor wandering madman, Āulcāṅd, in order to found a new religion as a simple, easy (*sahaja*) faith, a religion of humanity (*Mānuṣer Dharma*) for the poor, simple people. "At present," Caitanya thought, "there is no simple method of worship for the poor, lowly, powerless people; that's why I've revealed the easy [*sahaja*] path, so they can worship the truth within themselves, the worship of Humanity."[21] According to one of the most telling Kartābhajā metaphors, the "old marketplace" (i.e., Vaiṣṇava community) had become corrupt and full of thieves; thus it was necessary for Caitanya to come in a secret (*gupta*) form, to found "the Secret Marketplace" (*gupta hāṭ*) or "Secret Vṛndāvana," which is none other than the Kartābhajā path.[22]

Between the Parlor and the Streets: The Style and Structure of the *Bhāver Gīta*

One Kartābhajā sang some of their songs for me . . . I couldn't understand a word of it! The words were indeed Bengali, but the meaning could not possibly be understood! (Nabīncandra Sen, "Ghoṣpāṛār Melā")

Like the wandering mad minstrels of the Bāul tradition—with whom they share many close ties—the Kartābhajās convey their mystical teachings through the medium of music and song. Composed sometime in the first half of the nineteenth century, the songs of the Kartābhajās emerged during what has often been characterized as the most uncreative era in the history of Bengali literature—what S. K. De calls "the barren and uninteresting period" from the mid-eighteenth to mid-nineteenth centuries, which was torn by "moral depravity," economic chaos, a "decline of religious life," and an "absolute dissolution of social solidarity."[23] Thus, a close look at the Kartābhajā songs might help us to reevaluate this often neglected period in the history of Bengali literature.

More than 600 cryptic songs have been gathered in the corpus of the *Bhāver Gīta*, which is traditionally ascribed to the second and most famous Kartā, Dulālcāṅd (1793–1833). Dulālcāṅd is said to have assumed the name Lālśaśī ("redmoon") and recited the songs orally to four disciples, the foremost among whom was one Rāmcaraṇ Caṭṭopādhyāy, a man who, according to tradition, had been a Tantric Aghorī before taking initiation at Ghoshpara.[24]

Based on my own close reading of this text, however, I have come to the conclusion that this highly diverse, eclectic, and rather chaotic corpus of songs is quite probably not the product of any single author. Even Romeścandra Ghoṣe, who compiled the first complete edition of the *Bhāver Gīta* from a variety of handwritten manuscripts, commented on the difficulty of these songs and the uncertainty of their authorship. Rather, the *Bhāver Gīta* is more likely the cumulative result of a long process of composition, alteration, and transformation at the hands of many authors, which took place in the decades between the first known manuscript of 1826 (which I recently discovered in the Bāṅgīya Sāhitya Pariṣat collection) and the first printed editions of 1870 and 1882.[25] As a whole, the songs are an unusual, diverse, and often maddeningly confusing collection, drawing on a wide range of poetic styles and varying tremendously in readability and intelligibility. The end result is not a unified, coherent treatise, reflecting a single point of view, but a messy hodge-podge, embodying many competing, sometimes contradictory, voices and interests.

In its structure, language, and style, the *Bhāver Gīta* is arguably among the most enigmatic and difficult texts in the history of Bengali literature. As one nineteenth century author, Nabīncandra Sen, described his own frustration in trying to make sense of these cryptic songs, "There is a secret key to understanding them. Revealing the key to anyone who is not a Kartābhajā is the supreme 'heresy.' This is their version of 'Free Masonry'!"[26] Stylistically, as Sudhīr Cakravartī points out, these songs are an odd fusion of rural and urban forms, wedding the simple language of folk songs such as those of the Bāuls with the more complicated styles of the *vaiṭhakī* or "parlor" songs of nineteenth-century Calcutta: "Lālśaśī's *Bhāver Gīta* is half urban and half rural in its language. That's why it found an audience in both contemporary and later generations."[27] Typically performed on the more urban, parlor-style instruments of nineteenth-century Calcutta, such as the harmonium, the Kartābhajā songs also make use of the colloquial, rustic language of the outlying villages.

Let us take the following example, the first song of the *Kartābhajā Gīta* manuscript (KG 1; BG 54).[28] Songs of this sort usually consist of three stanzas: the first is of medium length (typically 6–7 lines, each line consisting of anywhere between 9 and 15 syllables), the second is shorter (5–6 lines of similar length); and the third is the longest (8–9 lines).

BG 54; KG 1	***Translation***
Balbo ek majār kathā rājār samācār tār sahare rāstār dhāre sāri sāri dokandār sadare mājhāre se bājār rājdhānī niśānī ār khās bikikiṇī āmdānī raptānī baro mās ār āṛate kaṛtāte ojon alpa ki bistār tār	Let me tell you a funny story about a king: In his city, all along the road are rows and rows of merchants. In the city-center there's a bazaar, [with] the seal of the Royal House. Twelve months a year there's buying and selling, importing and exporting, Whether the weight of the tares in the warehouse is little or great.
āmi dekhe elām he ṭhāi ṭhāi bahut mate teman kabhu dekhi nāi ei jagate yato tār mat bistārit lay to mane hay to katak kahite pāri ār sojāsoji bojho yadi bhavanadī kalpa pār	I came here and saw— Everywhere there were so many things! I had never seen such things in this world! So much was spread out everywhere; I'm thinking, how can I speak of it? And if you understand this straight-away, [you can] cross the river of the world and this cosmic age.

dān tolā māśul kāru se lay nāko kakhan	[The king] never takes gifts, tax or tariffs.
se kāraṇ yato mahājan	That's why the merchants all revere him.
tārā kare ārādhan	He waives all the taxes on the waterways.
ei māl sāyerer jamā yā kṣamā korece	Everyone pays him the capital of respect.
khātir jamāy hāmesā sakale āche	So listen to what I say:
śune śune bali he āro	No one has [need for] brokerage, commissions or such tactics!
dālālī dasturi jārijuri nāi kāro	The Moon is the assistant and Kalki the Avatār.
ār śaśadhar sahakār	
ār kalki avatār	

The rhyme scheme in this song, as in virtually all the songs of the *Bhāver Gīta,* is fairly simple and generally consistent: The rhyme of the first line reappears throughout the song in the final line of each verse. Thus the typical patterns is: AAABBA/ CCDDA/ EEEFFGGAA. Despite their apparent uniformity of rhyme, however, the songs of the KG and BG are highly erratic in their meter: Lines range anywhere from eight to eighteen syllables, with little effort to follow any standard metrical formula such as the traditional forms of classical Bengali verse. Thus, if we apply a standard system of scansion, such as the classical *akṣaravṛtta* or *payār* system,[29] we find only a loose metrical structure even within a single song, with no apparent logic.

The second most common form, which does not appear at all in the KG manuscript, differs markedly in style and content from the main body of the *Bhāver Gīta.* In Miśra's edition, these are included under the headings *Prem-Bājārer Sāṭ* and *Sahajer Sāṭ.* These songs are characterized first by their much shorter rhythmic pattern (usually only six or seven syllables per line) and second by their far more obscure and difficult style. Case endings and other grammatical markers are frequently omitted, leaving the interpretation of the syntax largely up to the reader, and even ordinary words are used in unconventional ways. Moreover, although these songs do refer to the mysterious figure Lālśaśī, they do not use the common formula, "Lālśaśī says"; instead, they employ more obscure references, such as "with the passage of the moon, the heart of darkness is destroyed" (BG 41). Consider, for example, the following cryptic song, part of which I cited earlier:

BG 48	***Translation***
sahaja jāti mānuṣe	*Sahaja* is of the human caste.
basti sahaja deśe	It dwells in the *Sahaja* land.
ki mati prakṛti bujho ābhāse	Know, in a hint, what its nature is:
yaś asambhab	Public exposure is impossible,
rasanā sambhab	[but] a taste [of it] possible:
udbhab deha biśeṣe	its arising is in the body [in the bodily type].

hita bihita abārita yāy abagata rīta habe ki kathāy binā matāśray śune ki tā hay niścay louha parśe	[It is]unrestricted by good or bad; what use will known laws be? It is without refuge in religious views. Hearing this, what happens? Surely, it is [like] iron [transformed by] the touchstone!
śakti puruṣa ati rati upaje kāje kāje dekho to bujhe satīr pati sahaje sādhya sādhak saṅger saṅgī abhed he ardha aṅger aṅgī śuno he bidhān mānuṣ pradhān sandhān śaśī svarase	Intense sexual love arises [between] a man and a woman; so look and understand— In Sahaja, he is the husband of the chaste wife The accomplished *sādhaka* and his consort in practice are united without division, like a limb to a body. Hear this law: "Man is supreme." And the quest lies within Śaśī's own *rasa*.

The overall structure of this song is similar to that of the preceding ones, using the same three-verse format, with the same rhyme scheme; yet, the meter of each line is very different, being much shorter and concise, while the language is far more obscure and often incomprehensible.

A third distinct group of songs, mostly compiled in the last portion of the printed text, consist of more devotional Vaiṣṇava songs in praise of Kṛṣṇa, Rādhā, and the love-sport of Vṛndāvana. Although the structure and rhyme scheme of these songs is outwardly similar to that of the others, the language, imagery, and style are notably different. Unlike either the large body of mercantile songs or the deeply coded Sahaja songs, these are composed in a far less ambiguous style, with little use of the cryptic language of *sandhābhāṣā*. Instead, they often take the form of lovers' dialogues between Kṛṣṇa and Rādhā, or a devotee's lament about the wiles and cunning of the illicit lover, Lord Kṛṣṇa.[30] As such, Debendranāth De speculates that these may well be later additions to the text and part of an attempt to cover over the more objectionable elements of the Kartābhajā tradition with a more acceptable Vaiṣṇava veneer.[31]

At the beginning and end of the present edition of the BG, there a few miscellaneous songs composed in very different and uncharacteristic styles. These range from highly devotional, sentimental praises of the Kartābhajā Great Mother, Satī Mā (the wife of Rāmśaraṇ Pāl and the mother of Dulālcāṅd), to extremely cryptic, esoteric, and almost unreadably difficult Sahajiyā songs. These, too, have a late, rather artificial appearance, and were probably added in the early twentieth century by Manulāl Miśra or one of his descendants.

In addition to the songs of the *Bhāver Gīta*, there is also a large number of scattered songs found in various sources, which I have collected and translated in chapter IV (in this volume). The majority of these songs reflect a more rural, folk-Bengali style, often indistinguishable in form and content from the songs of Bāuls. Perhaps the most important of these are the songs of the Sāhebdhanī sect—the "Wealthy Gentlemen"—a sort of sister sect or closely related branch of the Kartābhajās which emerged at roughly the same time in the rural areas of Nadia district. In fact, the songs of the Sāhebdhanī poets Kubir and Jādubindu continue to be sung by many Bāuls of West Bengal today. Perhaps most striking is the fact that these songs of the Wealthy Sāhebs make extensive use of imagery drawn from colonial Bengal, such as the railway system, the growing urban center of Calcutta, and the new economy of Indigo trade (IV.25–27).[32]

Not surprisingly, given their eclectic and enigmatic style, it is extremely difficult to classify the songs of the *Bhāver Gīta* among the various genres of Bengali literature. In the most general terms, they may be said to belong to the class of Bengali folk music (*lokasaṅgīta* or *deśīsaṅgīta*), which is contrasted with classical or *rāga*-based high-class music (*uccāṅgasaṅgīta*). Yet within this diverse class of folk music, the Kartābhajā songs stand out as oddly unique. They do not seem to fit the more traditional Bengali styles of Vaiṣṇava *kīrtan* (songs in praise of Kṛṣṇa, Rādhā and the Caitanya), the Śākta songs to the Dark Mother (such as Rāmprasād Sen's hymns to Kālī),[33] *kheur* (love songs), *kathakathā* (mythological stories), or *yatra* (folk theatre).[34] Nor do they even seem to have close similarities to new styles emerging in the growing metropolis nineteenth-century Calcutta, such as the *pāñcālī* (songs based on mythological themes, interspersed with contemporary social commentary and satire, made so famous by Dāśarathī Rāy) or the *ākhṛāi* ("clubroom" music, a semiclassical form using orchestra which came into vogue in late eighteenth-century Calcutta).[35]

If we examine their metrical structure, we find that these songs also do not fit neatly into any of the classical systems commonly employed in earlier Vaiṣṇava poetry. They are by no means as orderly or consistent as the traditional *Payār* style—typically comprised of single lines of fourteen syllables proceeding one after another—or the *Tripadī* style—containing three measures to a verse, two on the first line and the third comprising the second line—which are so prominent in Bengali devotional poetry.

As Chakrabarty aptly observes, a large part of the unusual style of the Kartābhajā songs is due to their specifically *oral and spoken style*, a style quite different from the literate prose style more popular among the upper classes of nineteenth-century Bengal, and one deserving of special attention by literary historians:

> It must be noted that these songs . . . were composed in spoken Bengali. Dulālcāṅd . . . carefully avoided the literary style at a time when Bengali prose . . . was almost indistinguishable from Sanskrit, and when spoken Bengali was not the literary medium. . . . Historians of Bengali Prose have so far ignored the songs. . . . The linguistic peculiarity of the *Bhāver Gīta* deserves a special study by competent scholars.[36]

The uniquely oral style of the Songs of Ecstasy, I would suggest, is closely related to the unique nature of their *performance contexts* in living Kartābhajā practice. In general terms, we could say there are two main types of performance of Kartābhajā song—what we might call the exoteric and esoteric sides of the tradition. Originally a highly secretive tradition, the early Kartābhajā movement centered around private gatherings of masters and disciples, who met in small numbers in Calcutta homes, usually on Friday evenings.[37] Here the songs were intended to transmit esoteric knowledge from master (*mahāśay*) to disciple (*barātī*), through the medium of dense symbolic imagery and obscure symbolism. "Brother, understand through hints and symbols!" the *Bhāver Gīta* frequently reminds us (BG 97; II.73).

However, as the movement grew and evolved into a more exoteric popular faith, the secretive Tantric elements were often downplayed or excised altogether as the tradition adopted a more acceptable public face.[38] Hence from the mid-nineteenth century, we also begin to see the public performance of Kartābhajā songs in large-scale gatherings, such as the various festivals in Ghosphara. The most infamous of these is the great Ghoshpara Melā that takes place each spring at the time of Holi, attracting many thousands of devotees. Here, the songs function more as popular devotional performances, which often generate intense ecstatic states and conditions of overflowing emotion or divine madness—tears and laughter, trembling with joy, writhing in ecstasy. As Akṣaykumār Datta described them in his classic account of 1870: "Their primary practice is the 'gathering of love.' By means of the repetition of mantras and the gathering of love, they progressively manifest the signs of ecstasy, such as tears, horripilations of joy, laughter, trembling, gnashing of teeth, and so on."[39]

One of the few close parallels we can find to the *Bhāver Gīta*—at least in terms of content and imagery—lies in the songs of the Bāuls, those self-styled "madmen" and enigmatic folk singers of Bengal.[40] Though there is some dispute as to their historical origins,[41] the Bāuls have had a major impact on Bengali folk music since at least the late nineteenth century, above all through the songs of the great singer Lālan Śāh, whose poems were made famous by Rabindranath in the early twentieth century. The songs of the Bāuls and Kartābhajās share many common themes: the rejection of orthodox religious institutions and social hierarchies, emphasis on the immediate, inborn presence of the Divine within the human body, and, perhaps most notably, the beautiful image of the elusive "Man of the Heart." As we see later, there is some evidence that Lālan may have drawn inspiration from the songs of the *Bhāver Gīta*. Yet unlike the more rural songs of the Bāuls, which are rooted in the folk traditions of the Bengali countryside, the songs of the Kartābhajās are far more urban, rooted in the newly emerging styles of early colonial Calcutta.[42]

Hence, in their style and format, the Kartābhajā songs are perhaps closer to the new hybrid song forms of the imperial city—and perhaps, above all, the songs of the Kobiwallas, or the poetic contests sung back and forth between rival poets, which were so popular in the streets of Calcutta in the nineteenth century.[43] Like those of the Kartābhajās, the Kobi songs often used a question-and-answer (*sayāl-jabāb*) format, with a question sung first and a response to follow. The Kobis, too, employ a conversational and spontaneous, rather than formal and literary, style, and they shared the Kartābhajā's lack of concern for all standard systems of poetic meter. Hence, much like the song of the *Bhāver Gīta*, the Kobi songs have long been ignored by modern scholars, who have dismissed them as an inferior, low-class form of literature. As S. K. De remarks, the Kobis were largely "pretenders," not true artists, whose works were primarily "popular amusements" performed before a motley assembly and characterized by "vulgar and abusive verbiage," mingled with "coarseness, scurrility and colloquialism, unredeemed by any sense of artistic expression."[44]

But most important, the Kobis share a similar concern with contemporary social life in colonial Calcutta, with the real lives of common lower-class men and women, as well as a similar delight in ridiculing and satirizing the foppish babus and pretentious upper classes.[45] Long disparaged by modern scholars as vulgar, low-brow, ribald and offensive lower-class literature, the Kobi songs were particularly popular among the common masses and uneducated *itar lok* of nineteenth-century Calcutta. Most of the Kobiwallas, as the great nineteenth-century scholar of Bengali literature, Īśvara Gupta observed, came from the lower castes of the city—"from the cobblers, weavers, and lower classes."[46] As Banjeree has argued, the Kobis forged a new song form, combining rural and urban styles, which appealed to the poor working classes who had been drawn from the villages to the new urban environment of Calcutta: "The Kobis, many among whom came from the city's lower orders, played an important role in the experimentations which transformed the traditional rural folk style . . . into the distinctly urban popular *kobi gān*." At the same time, the Kobi songs also opened up a new freedom for the lower orders to poke fun at and satirize the social world around them, particularly the world of the wealthy elites and Western-educated middle classes: "As most of these kobis had no stake in the formal societal structure, they were . . . free to offer their view from the bottom of society with unabashed satire. . . . They became the mouthpiece of the masses. . . . The license they enjoyed . . . was in continuance of the tradition . . . where court jesters were allowed to laugh at the expense of kings."[47]

With their mixture of rural and urban styles, the Kartābhajā songs were to have a similar appeal for the displaced rural classes who had migrated to the bustling world of Calcutta. The songs of the *Bhāver Gīta*, as we see in the following sections, adapt much of the satirical style and urban imagery of the Kobis; yet they mingle these with older Tantric connotations, employing them in ingenious new ways to express profound religious ideals.

In Search of the Man of the Heart: Mystical Imagery and Social Ideals in the *Bhāver Gīta*

He who knows all places within the threefold universe
is Himself the Man of the Heart;
yet even when you see Him, you can't recognize Him, can you?
If you could gaze upon Him with half-closed eyes, seated upon your throne,
in a single moment, He would be united with you! (BG 242)

O say, who can understand them? Everyone's got a religious disease!
Leaving their husbands at home,
[the women], with various presents—milk, curd and sweets—go there each Friday.
. . . There's no consideration of caste; ritual is empty; thirty-six classes come
together in one place.
Washermen, oilmen, tanners, low classes and untouchables, Brāhmaṇs and Kāyasthas,
police chiefs
and those who burn the dead, all together eat the same food!
(Dāśarathī Rāy, "Kartābhajā")

Beyond their stylistic originality, however, the songs of the *Bhāver Gīta* also contain a unique form of religious discourse—an idiosyncratic discourse which combines the most profound spiritual insights with the most secular and urban metaphors. In essence, the Kartābhajās' philosophy is rooted in the older Sahajiyā and other Tantric schools of medieval Bengal. But while employing the older Tantric language of *Sahaja* and the divinity of the human body, the Kartābhajā songs clothe these traditional ideals in the symbolism of a new historical context: the context of colonial Bengal and the shifting life of the imperial center of Calcutta.

One of the most beautiful images of the *Bhāver Gīta* is the elusive figure of the Man of the Heart (*Maner Mānuṣa*), an image that embodies both the mystical faith and the social ideals of the Kartābhajā tradition.[48] This mysterious figure is our innermost self, our constant companion, and our identity with the absolute reality; yet it is also the most elusive of figures, the "uncatchable" person always just eluding the grasp of the foolish mind. Today, this image of the Man of the Heart has become widely known to both Bengali and Western scholarship through the songs of the folk bard, Lālan Śāh, whose works were made famous by Tagore in the early twentieth century.[49] And it is generally assumed that this is a fairly ancient concept, dating back to the Sahajiyā authors of medieval Bengal. Historically, however, this seems to be a rather recent creation. Although some earlier Sahajiyā texts had employed terms such as the *Sahaja Mānuṣa* or the in-born, spontaneous Self,[50] the concept of the *Maner Mānuṣa,* which would later become famous in the songs of Lālan, does not seem to be any earlier than the latter half of the nineteenth century.

A few have even argued that Lālan's famous image of the *Maner Mānuṣa* was itself borrowed from the Kartābhajās.[51] It seems that there are some popular legends that Lālan used to go to the Kartābhajā festival, as well as a number of songs attributed to Lālan which praise Āulcāṅd and the wonders of Ghoshpara. For example: "At the Ghoshpara Melā there's no consideration of caste; I can find the Man of the Heart in Ghoshpara, the secret Vṛndāvana!"[52] Although there is no way of knowing just where Lālan derived his inspiration for this image of the Man of the Heart, it would seem that the 1870 edition of the *Kartābhajā Gitāvalī* is probably the oldest known text in which the *Maner Mānuṣa* makes his mysterious appearance.[53]

As we can see in the following selections from the Bāul and Kartābhajā songs, both Lālan and Lālśaśī share the same kind of poignant sadness in their search for this ever-elusive Man of the Heart. They lament how difficult it is to find or even speak of this mysterious "person" who is at once the most intimate companion and the most estranged "other" to oneself;

When will I be united with the Man of my Heart?
Day and night, like a rain bird, I long for the Dark Moon,
hoping to become his maidservant.
But this is not my fate.
I caught a glimpse of my Dark Lord in a dream,
and then he was gone, like a flash of lightning,
vanishing into the cloud it came from, leaving no trace.
Meditating on his image, I lose all fear of disgrace.
Poor Lālan says, He who always loves, knows.[54]

What use is there in trying to bring that Man of the Heart outside?
Always eternally happy, united with the Self, he remains seated within the heart.
So why now would he come out?
. . . O My mind, who knows what sort are the habits of the Man of the Heart?
And if one could know them, could he express their form?
The mind cannot know that sweet beauty!
As long as life remains in my body, I fear to speak of it—
I saw it in a dream, and my heart was rent! (BG 243; see BG 241; II.78)

It is the quest for this most elusive, most hidden, and yet most intimate Man of the Heart that drives both the mystic practice and the social ideals of the Kartābhajās.

In the context of Bengal at the dawn of the nineteenth century, amidst the rapidly changing social order and the new reform movements of colonial Calcutta, the songs of the Kartābhajās represented a fairly radical and controversial social ideal. With the concepts of the Man of the Heart and a "Religion of Humanity," the Kartābhajās offered a spiritual path open to men and women of all religions, castes, and social strata. Notorious for their free mingling of social classes, allowing Brahmins to eat side by side with harlots and leather workers, the Kartābhajā gatherings were frequently commented on in nineteenth-century literature. In both their small esoteric meetings and their large annual festivals, the Kartābhajās opened a kind of alternative social field, a free space for interaction, beyond the strictures of caste, labor, and wealth—as Partha Chatterjee puts, it "a congregational space defined outside the boundaries of the dominant religious life, outside caste society or the injunctions of the *shari'ah*."[55]

According to the Kartābhajā songs, all human beings possess this inner divine self, the *Maner Mānuṣa*; for all human beings are, in their innermost nature, identical with the absolute reality—the "in-born," natural, spontaneous reality of *Sahaja*. In *Sahaja*, there is no caste, no good or evil, no distinction between any of the forms or events of the phenomenal world:

There is no division between human beings.
So brother, why is there sorrow in this land?
Look and understand: In *Sahaja*, in their own Self nature,
the infinite forms in every land,
all the activities of human beings,
the expanse of all events—all things dwell [in this very *Sahaja*].
. . . Every human heart is rich.
It is not possible in separate forms
for it is eternally conceived within every man and woman. (BG 32, II.57)

As one ardent Kartābhajā spokesman, Gopal Krishna Pal, explained to the *Bengal District Gazetteer* in 1910, the Kartābhajā tradition is thus the true "Religion of Man," for it honors all human beings equally and offers new status to the downtrodden and oppressed: "All members stand on the same footing and distinctions based on caste, wealth, etc. are not recognized. . . . Degraded humanity finds a cordial welcome and ready recognition."[56]

The radical social ideals of the Kartābhajās quickly became the subject of intense debate—both positive and negative—among the elite classes of Calcutta. On the one hand, the more conservative Brahmins such as Dāśarathī Rāy were generally quite horrified and scandalized by the free mixing of castes, sexes, and religious groups at the annual Kartābhajā festival in Ghoshpara: "There's no consideration of caste; ritual is empty; thirty-six classes come together in one place. Washermen, oilmen, tanners, Bāgdis and Hāṛīs, Brāhmaṇs and Kāyasthas, Ḍoms and Koṭāls all together eat the same food!" (see chapter IV, this volume). Yet on the other hand, the more liberal reformers often praised the Kartābhajās' seemingly egalitarian and humanistic vision. "We were amazed," the Calcutta paper, *Saṃvāda Prabhākara*, reported in 1848, "For Brahmans, Śūdras and non-Hindu classes make no distinctions regarding their own food, and eat and drink here together; nowhere before had I seen or heard such a thing!" Not only did some of the most prominent reformers of Calcutta, such as Śaśīpad Bābu, Nabīncandra Sen, and Vijaykṛṣṇa Gosvāmī, take an active interest in the Kartābhajā faith, but, as Nabīncandra suggested, the Kartābhajās were among the first in Bengal to preach the brotherhood of mankind. According to Sen, the first Kartā, Rāmśaraṇ Pāl, was "the first to feel the harmony of scriptures or unity of religions. He taught that all religions have one foundation and was the first to spread the idea in this land, which is torn by sectarian divisions."[57] In any case, as Sudhir Cakravartī points out, the frequent debate over the Kartābhajās among Calcutta's upper classes is clear testimony of just how controversial a social movement they represented in nineteenth-century Bengal, and perhaps even "an unstoppable revolution in the caste-based social order."[58]

In fact, a few more ambitious scholars have even tried to find connections between the ideals of the Kartābhajā songs and the new social reforms of Bengali movements like that of Rāmmohun Roy and the Brāhmo Samāj. Founded in 1828—at precisely the same time that the Kartābhajā songs were first being circulated—the Brāhmo Samāj also preached a universalistic and humanistic faith, hoping to reform caste and improve the status of women.[59] Hence one rather ambitious scholar even claims that the Rāmmohun both knew of and even drew his inspiration from the Kartābhajās, who should therefore be recognized as the "popular foundation for the Brāhmo religion of Rāmmohun."[60]

What seems far more likely, I would argue, is that lower-class movements such as the Kartābhajās and upper-class elite movements such as the Brāhmo Samāj represent two parallel, but clearly different, responses to the same social and political situation of early colonial Bengal. For the most part, lower-class sects such as the Kartābhajās neither knew nor cared much for the new moral and educational standards of the Brāhmos, the rationalism and scientific advances of modern Europe, or the ideal of a golden age of a pure, monotheistic Hinduism embodied in the Vedas. As most scholars agree, "The vast majority of the population of Calcutta was entirely unaffected by them."[61] Instead, the Kartābhajās drew their inspiration from the rag-clad madman Āulcāṅd, intense devotional practices, and the ecstatic devotional songs of the *Bhāver Gīta*.[62]

Hence, we might more accurately think of the Kartābhajās not as a folk foundation for the so-called Bengal Renaissance but, rather, as a sort of "counter-renaissance"—a popular undercurrent of mysticism, magic and ecstasy, which ran against the grain of the rational reforms of the elites.[63] Like the Brāhmos, they offered a universal, nonsectarian, caste-free religion of man, embodying more liberal attitudes toward women and lower classes. Yet the Kartābhajās also popularized and democratized these ideals, transferring them to the level of the lower classes and taking them to more radical extremes: "Running parallel to the *bhadralok* community's attempts to reform society, this underworld of plebeian religion often went far beyond these reforms," Banerjee comments, "Brahmans, Shudras, and Yavanas sat together at the Kartābhajā festivals and ate the same food—a practice which even the bhadralok reformers did not follow publicly."[64] As it so happens, in fact, the counter-renaissance of the Kartābhajās would later come to be severely criticized by the leaders of the Bengal Renaissance in Calcutta's upper-class Westernized *bhadralok* society. In sharpest contrast to Rāmmohun's rational reforms, the Kartābhajās were singled out as a lower-class cult of superstition, immorality, and ignorance—what Dāśarathī called a band of thieves, necrophagous ghouls, prostitutes, and "ugly old sluts in a place full of rubbish and dung."[65]

The Marketplace of Ecstasy: Mercantile Discourse and Economic Imagery in the Kartābhajā Songs

Ten, twenty, thirty Poor men gather together and become a Company.
There's an account book, in which so many things are recorded—
so many imported and exported goods!
Examining all the permission slips and seals, item by item,
the shopkeepers engage in business. (BG 218; II.1)

Perhaps the most unusual feature of the Kartābhajā songs is their extensive use of mercantile imagery and the economic discourse of colonial Calcutta. These songs are saturated with the language of commerce, market exchange and even the striking use of terminology borrowed from the British East India Company itself. Indeed, the Kartābhajās even coined their own form of esoteric code language or "intentional language" (*sandhābhāṣā*): the "language of the mint" (*ṭyāṅkśālī bol*), which I have translated in chapter III (this volume). A language of strange metaphors, riddles, and bizarre and at times quite shocking imagery, the Language of the Mint is for the most part in continuity with the older tradition of coded discourse in the Sahajiyā tradition.[66] Yet, as Debendranāth De points out, what *is* unique about the Kartābhajā songs is precisely their unusual choice of metaphors—specifically, metaphors drawn form the realm of the marketplace. "In their effort to conceal their meanings in riddles there is widespread use of the metaphors of business, trade, buyers, shopkeepers, the Company, import and export, profit, etc."[67]

This use of imagery drawn from the world of the marketplace is surely nothing new in Bengali literature. As early as the fifteenth-century *Caṇḍīmaṅgal* and continuing through Rāmprasād's hymns to Kālī in the eighteenth century, and even the teachings of Śrī Rāmakṛṣṇa, the *hāṭ* or *bājār* has been a persistent trope throughout Bengali poetry. Indeed, as Sudipta Sen has argued in his work on eighteenth-century Bengali literature, the marketplace could well be said to be the "worldly metaphor" par excellence—the supreme metaphor for all the transactions and exchanges, wheelings and dealings of this mortal life in *saṃsāra*.[68] But what *is* unique about the Kartābhajā songs is, first, the sheer quantity of mercantile discourse they employ—comprising some 70 percent of the songs, by Chakrabarty's count.[69] Second, these are also among the first religious songs in Bengal to make explicit use of imagery drawn from the British East India Company and the capitalist discourse of the European merchants. Not only do they make extensive and sophisticated use of the language of contracts (*koṇṭrakṭ*), invoices (*inbhāis*), and permits (*parmit*), but they also employ the image of the Company (*kompānī*) as a key metaphor for the Kartābhajā tradition itself.

To understand the central role of the market metaphor in the Kartābhajā songs, we also need to understand something of the larger role of the marketplace in Bengali society as a whole. The *hāṭ* or *bājār*, as Sen has argued, was a critical knot in the complex flow of power and the exchange of social and economic resources during the rapidly shifting era of eighteenth-century Bengal. The Rājā or Zamindār depended for his political power on intimate relations with and authority over the market, which represented a nexus of commercial trade, finance, social life, and religious worship alike. As such, the market appears throughout Bengali literature as a key metaphor for worldly power, political dominance, and official authority. During the colonial era, Sen argues, the marketplace became a critical nexus of power and authority, as the British East India Company sought to undertake a progressive "conquest of marketplaces"—a systematic effort to regulate, control and effectively administer these key economic and political foci.[70]

Yet, at the same time, if the marketplace could serve as a key metaphor of ruling power and political control, it could also serve as a key locus of subversion and critique of the dominant order. As Mikhail Bakhtin has argued, the marketplace is a zone of social interaction which transcends most ordinary class barriers, bringing together men and women of all strata in a common sphere of exchange and allowing an unusual freedom to speak critically. It is thus a key locus of dissident and disruptive language, a place where the "unofficial" and "extraterritorial" discourse of the lower classes can circulate "in a world of official order and ideology; it always remained 'with the people.'"[71] Similarly, as Guha has argued in his study of peasant resistance in colonial Bengal, the marketplace was a special site of social critique, a realm where the lower classes could criticize the dominant order and the wealthy upper classes. As a place where people gather for trade and popular entertainment, the market was always a potential threat to the ruling powers, "identified in colonialist thinking with the dissemination of subversive discourse among the lower classes."[72]

Nowhere is this ambivalent status of the marketplace, as both a center of power and a potential cite of contestation and critique, more apparent than in the realm of religious discourse. A key metaphor for political rule, the marketplace was also often deployed as a metaphor for religious power and spiritual authority. One of the most striking uses of this market metaphor in a religious text is the *Hāṭ Pattan* or "Foundation of the Marketplace," attributed (probably falsely) to the famous Vaiṣṇava poet, Narottam Dās. In Dās's narrative, Caitanya himself is transformed into a kind of holy businessman who founds the spiritual Marketplace in order to distribute the goods of love and prayer throughout the world. Caitanya's chief disciples are then appointed as the various agents and brokers of this market—Nityānanda becomes the ruler, Mukunda a clerk (*mutasaddī*), Advaita a scribe (*munśī*), Gadādhar a treasurer (*bhāṇḍārī*), while Narahari Dās is transformed into a flirting courtesan. The host of devotees flocking to the holy bazaar become the merchants and traders, selling their goods of Songs (*kīrtan*) in praise of Kṛṣṇa.[73]

However, if the marketplace could be used as the key symbol for the spiritual life embodied in the mainstream Gauḍīya tradition, it could also be turned into a subversive symbol for the critique of that same dominant tradition. For the Kartābhajās and other "deviant orders" such as the Bāuls and Sāhebdhanīs, the marketplace becomes one of the most important symbols for all the greed, corruption, and futility of mortal life in this world of *saṃsāra*. "In contrast to the appropriation of the market as a lordly domain," Sen observes, "in the songs of other sects—particularly ones that subvert kingly rule or prescribed religious leadership—the marketplace appears as a classic metaphor for material illusion in mortal life."[74] As the Kartābhajās sing,

I've quit this business, brother.
There was no profit in it—I had to give up my earnings too easily!
Is one more merchant any use in this land?
I labor in some city; I go to the marketplace and toil, breaking my back,
and as the days pass, do I get even a piece of bread in this kingdom?
  I conducted business in this land eight million times—
but see, brother, my troubles haven't left me!
Seeing and hearing all this, I've gone mad! (BG 214; II.27)

In this respect, the Songs of Ecstasy have much in common with the songs of the Kobis and other popular genres of colonial Calcutta. Like the Kobis, they take a merciless delight in satirizing the various characters competing in the bazaar—the petty shopkeepers, the cheating moneylenders, and the poor overworked porters. In the following song, the author pokes fun at a poor merchant whose business has failed and who now labors as a porter under the company:

O, how wonderfully funny you are!
You've quit your business, and now, I see, you're paying homage to the Porters
in the marketplace and at the wharf!
I see no shortage in the jurisdiction of the Company.
. . . So freely, I know, you had abandoned all your wealth,
wandering and searching throughout the entire Company—
that's why you break your back working here!
Your name is written in the account books of the Company Warehouse.
  . . . You had come to work as a merchant in this land;
but when that business failed, you found a lot of work in this market and bazaar.
And now the Porters, both petty and great, all control you!
. . . You've labored for the Company for so long a time—
And Śaśī Lāl laughs and says, "oh, see how manly you are!" (BG 215; II.31)

As Śaktināth Jhā suggests, the Bāul singers also often use the imagery of the bazaar to describe the sad fate of those who seek happiness in the world of material wealth: Just as so many petty shopkeepers were reduced to tremendous debt and abject poverty as the British capitalists and wealthy moneylenders progressively took control of the marketplace, so, too, the mortal human soul wanders in the endless debt and poverty of this realm of *saṃsāra:* "The East India Company monopolized control over business, and many small merchants had to take loans from Money-lenders, then lost their wealth and fell into poverty. . . . The Fakir religion is their last refuge."[75]

In the Kartābhajā songs, however, even more scathing observations are directed toward the rich and the greedy men of the marketplace, those who profit most and inflict the most suffering on others—above all, the moneylenders (*mahājan*), brokers, and middlemen (*dālāl*). As Banerjee has shown, the poor classes of Calcutta often used poetry and song to complain of the sorrows of their laboring existence, as well as to mimic, parody, and ridicule the wealthy elite culture of the day. Throughout their popular ballads, we hear about the greedy and pretentious middle-class babus who have risen to new status by riding on the coattails of the company: "The earliest specimens of urban folk culture can be found in the humorous doggerels and proverbs, jokes and rhymes about society. . . . The rat race among English traders and Bengali banians to make fortunes . . . was a target of raillery on the part of the lower orders."[76] As the Kartābhajās sing:

Why else would we honor these men as "Brokers"?
For so many Princes and Nobles
are always paying them respect!
Without any power of their own, they quietly increase their wages.
Brother, that's why the Brokers have now attained such great status!
The wise Broker can attain anything, finite or infinite;
they devise the means for whatever comes and goes.
And that's why, without any power of their own, they come and sit as if they
were Princes! (BG 268; II.35)

Whenever someone wants to buy something, they ask, "how[good] is it?"
The Brokers say, "it's genuine," but give them the fakes!
. . . The wretched Brokers have become a terrible nuisance! (BG 267; II.38)

In contrast to the incessant greed and thievery of this marketplace of the world, the Kartābhajās sing of a wondrous new marketplace—the bazaar of love (*prema bājār*), ruled by the just merchants, the Kartā, and his Mahāśays. Whereas the old marketplace of the Gauḍīya Vaiṣṇava tradition has become corrupt and overrun with cheating moneylenders and rapacious brokers, the Kartābhajās have founded a new marketplace—the "secret marketplace" (*gupta hāṭ*)—where the true spiritual goods of love and devotion can be exchanged:

Those who engage in business within the Bazaar of the *rasa* of Love
take the Government Merchandise to the warehouse owners again and again.
Some put the goods into boxes and determine the weight,
and some go to the market and joyfully engage in business!
Twelve months a year they deal in imported and exported goods.
. . . The Bazaar is filled with so many kinds of things!
If there were any lack in this land,
[Kṛṣṇa] would return once again.
He's everyone full of delight and free of poverty! (BG 247; II.56)

But perhaps the most remarkable aspect of the Kartābhajās' economic imagery is their frequent and elaborate use of the English term "company"—a term that occurs close to 100 times and in several long interconnected series of songs (BG 218–220, 152–161, 65–66, 116–119). Many of the songs contain long and extremely detailed accounts of the arrival of the company ships, with vivid descriptions of all the wondrous foreign merchandise which they unload at the docks. "'The Company's ship is coming!' the *Bhāver Gīta* eagerly narrates, 'I just now heard about it in the bazaar; in each and every shop there's whispering!'" (BG 65; II.16).

Hey look—the ships of the Company are coming, with all their sails erect:
in the middle of the bay, what a spectacle is seen!
    And so many still remain in the water;
They came and shouted the news at the top of their voices—
They'll come and unload in the city! (BG 65; II.17).

The authors then go on to recount—in elaborate detail—all the incredible merchandise carried by these ships from overseas—their trinkets and mirrors; their pistols and foodstuffs; their goods from China; their candy, fruit, and other foodstuffs (BG 66; II.18).

The good Merchant has returned from England;
so when I bring the news, land, sea and city all rejoice!
. . . From beginning to end, the merchandise in Calcutta is being accounted;
The Clerks have begun to calculate and record the value.
. . . How can I describe them? I've never seen such things produced in India!
If I wish to count the imports and exports,
at the very sight of such things, all my vanity is destroyed!
The merchants search for these goods on every shore of this world.
    Seeing all these imported goods of the Merchants,
with all their labels, I'm struck with amazement!
Thousands and thousands of ships sail upon the wide Ganges;
so many mirrors, pictures, and goods with Arabian labels!
Seeing all this, the honorable, good-mannered Company does what is impossible!
. . . Lālśaśī says, "as they come, an era passes away!" (BG 376; II.20)

Now, the key to interpreting this complex imagery of the company is provided for us in other songs scattered throughout the BG. In another long series of songs, the author makes it clear that the company is here a metaphor for the birth and spread of the Gauḍīya Vaiṣṇava tradition itself. In fact, these songs deliberately play off the double meaning of Caitanya's epithet, *gour* or *gorā*, which carries the sense of both "fair-skinned" and "an Englishman." Hence the movement founded by Caitanya now becomes the *gorā kompānī*—the "fair skinned Company." And the coming of the company ships refers to the coming of the Vaiṣṇava community, following in the wake of Caitanya, which has brought a wealth of new "spiritual goods" to Bengal and displaced the many small traders of the other religious sects (BG [1882] 127).

Govinda, his mind filled with bliss, assumed the name of eternal joy: Gour Nitāi.
When He became Caitanya in the form of Gour [fair-skinned], a delightful thing occurred!
. . . Look—a Fair-skinned Man has become overwhelmed with love—he's utterly maddened!
The Fair-skinned One has been destroyed, hewn down, and falls to the ground!
And the Company has shown the proof of it throughout the streets!
Those Three who came together as one and drowned this land [in *rasa*]—
are the Fair-skinned Company [*gorā kompānī*]; but what do I know of them? (BG 415)

Unfortunately, the Kartābhajās tell us, the original company founded by Caitanya eventually became corrupt and filled with thieves. In place of Caitanya's original teaching of love, they asserted new kinds of power hierarchies: wealth and greed. "Once the Company [Gauḍīya Vaiṣṇavism] was very rich. But its porters were extremely poor. They starved and begged but the kings and emperors, who controlled the Company, were worthless men, given to robbery."[77] It was therefore necessary for Caitanya to return to this world in a new form—in the concealed form of the poor mad fakir, Āulcāṅd. The "secret Caitanya," Āulcāṅd, thus becomes the "fourth madman" who "completes the Company" and fulfills the revelation begun by Caitanya, Nityānanda, and Advaita. Thus, "Out of the ruins of the company a new Company was made."[78]

This is the story of the Three [namely, Caitanya, Nityānanda and Advaita],
. . . The Good Mannered Company was comprised of the three worlds.
Even if they went to travel to different lands,
and found the three Men [Caitanya, Nityānanda and Advaita],
why would they return here and cease to wander?
For only when the four Madmen [the three plus Āulcāṅd] join together and cross over is [their search] completed. (BG 189; II.9)

A 100-petalled lotus floats upon the immeasurable waters
and upon it is a poor wretched Madman [Āulcāṅd].
. . . That Heavy-bearded One made everything complete.
. . . At the gesture of the Bearded One, their wandering has ended.
The four [Madmen, namely Caitanya, Nityānanda, Advaita and now Āulcāṅd] have joined together in one community and have crossed over. (BG 190; II.10)

The new company founded by Āulcāṅd is thus very different; unlike the old company of the Gauḍīya Vaiṣṇavas, which had become corrupt and overrun with greed, this new religion of the Kartābhajās is not a company of the rich and powerful but a poor company (*gorib kompānī*) or a "platoon of the poor" (*kāṅgāler palṭan*). Unlike the wealthy Vaiṣṇava Company, this new company opens its doors to the poor and lowly, placing beggars above kings, and praising the starved and crippled as the holiest of sages:

Look, the wonders of my Poor Company are something truly delightful!
The Emperor gives no commands; the king punishes no one.
If someone, out of need for money, commits a theft,
the Company gives him infinite wealth;
his poverty disappears, and he no longer covets anything.
Lālśaśī says, thus the thief Ratnakār became the sage Vālmīki! (BG 220; II.3)

One who sits with a broken begging bowl in his lap,
everyone calls the [true] "Ruler" of the land!
Those whose bodies are emaciated by famine,
we consider the Princes and Ministers!
Look—they all have a means of escape:
they cannot really be called "Poor!" (BG 218; II.1)

In a still more striking juxtaposition of metaphors, this poor company is also proclaimed as the mad company (*pāgal kompānī*), or the company of the land of madness. The leader of this company is Caitanya himself, who has now "come in the form of the Madman," Āulcāṅd. In his kingdom, "Madness is the rule" (BG 149, 152), for this great madman has intoxicated the members of the old company, driving them insane with devotional ecstasy and love of God:

When that Company of your country becomes [full of] madmen,
they'll be able to taste that fruit.
When they taste it, they'll feel the ecstasy of madness.
Having become connoisseurs in that taste, they'll engage in a wondrous play
. . . Look—one madman, two madmen, three madmen, a festival of madmen!
I can't understand all this play of madness—the uproar of all this madness!
People say, they're making a terrible commotion;
O how wonderful! no one can understand their condition! (BG 154; II.86)

But what are we to make of this strange use of mercantile imagery and the language of the "company?" Is it simply a jealous mimicry of the wealth of the British masters, or a kind of magical fetishization of the newly arriving commodities from abroad? As I suggest, this elaborate imagery of the company represents something more than a simple passive assimilation of British capitalist discourse. Rather, following the lead of authors such as Marshall Sahlins and Jean Comaroff, I would argue that this represents a far more active sort of appropriation and transformation. Commodities, as Sahlins has persuasively shown, are never simply dead, lifeless signs without social significance. Instead, they are always invested with symbolic meaning, embedded in social relationships and organized by a cultural logic.[79] Yet precisely because they have an implicit cultural value, commodities can also be appropriated as signs by different competing factions within a given society. The commodity is not exclusively a sign of bourgeois capitalism; it can also be appropriated or "stolen" by marginal groups and transformed into a sign of resistance. As Dick Hebdige has shown in the case of punks, mods, and other subcultures in England, such ordinary commodities as safety pins and hats can become powerful agents of subversion: "Commodities are open to a double inflection: to 'illegitimate' as well as legitimate uses. These humble objects can be magically appropriated, stolen by subordinate groups and made to carry 'secret' meanings."[80]

Perhaps nowhere is this subversive appropriation of commodities more apparent than in cases of colonial contact. As Comaroff argues in her study of the South African Zionist movement, conquered and colonized societies are never simply "made over in the European image"; rather, they very often work to "deploy, deform, and defuse imperial institutions."[81] That is, they actively appropriate, transform, and turn to their own advantage a number of key symbols drawn from European culture and Christianity—including the symbolism of money, along with selected elements of the Protestant capitalist ethic. The result is a kind of "subversive bricolage" which adapts strategic elements of colonialist discourse as "captured bearers of alien power." In a similar way, I would argue, the Kartābhajās appropriated key elements of capitalist discourse, turning them to their own advantage in an esoteric society. In so doing, they offered their low-class followers a new kind of spiritual "company," with a new kind of "capital" and social status.

The Secret Back Door of the Kartābhajā Path: The Ambivalent Status of Tantra in Colonial Bengal

The Kartābhajās are a degenerate [*bhāṇgā*] form of the Tantric religion. . . . In the Kali age, people are deluded by ignorance, therefore the desire for the five M's is the religion of this era; and for this reason the Kartābhajā teaching has secretly become very powerful in this land. (Rāmcandra Datta, *Tattvasāra*)

The final and in many ways most interesting reason for the importance of the Kartābhajā songs is the unique insight they give us into the problematic status of Tantra in colonial Bengal. As it is commonly defined in modern scholarship, Tantrism refers to a specific form of Indian religion common to both the Hindu and Buddhist traditions since roughly the fourth or fifth century. Above all, Tantrism is said to be characterized by the use of practices that are normally prohibited by orthodox social and religious law—such as the infamous "five M's" or five transgressive substances: meat, fish, wine, parched grain, and sexual intercourse, often with prostitutes or untouchables.[82]

However, as André Padoux and others have shown, the concept of "Tantrism" as a unified, singular coherent "ism" is in fact a relatively recent creation, and in large part the product of European Orientalist scholars of the nineteenth century. Moreover, it has from its origins been a key part of the Orientalist construction of India and Hinduism as a whole, as the quintessential "other" of the West. Above all, Tantrism was defined in the Orientalist imagination as the very worst, most degenerate and disgusting aspect of India religion—what we might call the *extreme Orient*, the most extreme example of all the polytheism, idolatry, and licentiousness believed to have corrupted Hinduism in modern times. As the Sanskritist Sir Monier Williams described it, Tantrism is "Hinduism arrived at its last and worst stage of medieval development."[83] And the Kartābhajās were often singled out as the very worst and most dangerous of all Tantric cults—a "degenerate form of Tantra," as Rāmcandra Datta described them, and even the "foremost of the Aghorapanthīs," according to Dāśarathī Rāy. As Rāmakṛṣṇa put it, the Kartābhajā path is a kind of "secret back door path." Though a rapid and powerful way to reach liberation, it is also a dangerous and dirty one, rather like entering a house through the toilet instead of through the front door.[84]

Throughout the Songs of Ecstasy, we find numerous references to Tantric sexual practices—though always cryptic and clothed in highly enigmatic terms. Like the older Tantric Sahajiyā schools, the songs of the Kartābhajā make frequent use of the imagery of the "bee drinking the nectar" (a classic Sahajiyā references to Tantric sexual techniques) or "swimming in the ocean of impurity without getting your hair wet" (a reference to the paradoxical act of engaging in intercourse without ejaculating) (BG 413, 52; II.81–85; see also IV.8–14). Yet, emerging as they did amidst the highly sensitive new social and moral context of colonial Calcutta, surrounded by reform movements such as the Brāhmo Samāj, the Kartābhajās are also clearly deeply ambivalent about the presence of sexual practices within the tradition. Hence they often go to great new lengths either to deny and eradicate them or else to conceal them behind an ever more elaborate veil of secrecy.

Perhaps the most striking example of this ambivalence appears in a long series of songs that center around the metaphors of the company, the fruit garden and the "stinking fruit," which corrupted the company's garden. The hero of this complex narrative is the great "madman," who is clearly the holy madman Caitanya now in the form of the poor fakir, Āulcāṅd. The madman originally planted a wondrous, delicious fruit in the garden of love, a fruit which intoxicated all the men of the company with the sweet aroma of devotion. And this sweet fruit, as we are told at the end of this cycle of songs, turns out to be none other than the Tantric practice of *parakīyā* love—sexual intercourse with a partner who is not one's own wife, a practice that had become the subject of intense controversy and debate within the Vaiṣṇava and Sahajiyā communities since at least the eighteenth century. At the end of the last cosmic cycle, at the "dawn of the Fourth *Pralaya*, or the beginning of the Kali Yuga," Kṛṣṇa came to this world in the form of "The Darkness which Destroys Doubt," namely, the divine madman, Caitanya.

Previously, in this realm of the Fourth *Pralaya* [i.e., the Kali Age],
The "Darkness Which Destroys Doubt" suddenly came to this shore.
. . . He created the garden of *Parakīyā Rasa*.
There was no end to the field of night. (BG 159; II.89)

No one can reach the wondrous fruit of that land;
that's why the Madman will return and plant the fruit in heaven;
and as it bears fruit, he'll distribute it throughout the world.
Whoever receives and tastes that fruit, brother,
while tasting it, will forget everything else! (BG 153; II.85)

Soon after this fruit garden was planted, however, something appears to have gone very wrong. This once delicious fruit of *parakīyā* love became corrupted and transformed into a "foul smelling fruit," which pollutes the garden with its terrible odor. Its awful stench begins to intoxicate and madden the men of the company, even tempting them to rampant sexual license and other unspeakable acts. Therefore, this stinking fruit tree had to be uprooted by the "good-mannered" or "polite company"—the term here is *ādab*, a Perso-Arabic term referring to the qualities of good taste, refinement, and "distinction." Nonetheless, our authors cryptically remark at the end of the songs, the company still continues in a *hidden or concealed* sense, "behind the fruit garden"—a phrase which can be interpreted in several ways:

He created the garden of *Parakīyā Rasa*.
. . . But brother, a foul smell arose within it, you know.
Yet with great effort, the supreme Virtuous One preserved [the garden].
(BG 159; II.89)

When the Good-Mannered Company got wind of that smell,
they uprooted that garden, roots, flowers and all!
If the Good-Mannered Company had not gotten wind of that smell,
then everyone, the highest and the lowest, would have gone crazy—
eating menstrual blood, sleeping together!
After this happened, the garden remained empty.
But even now, behind that fruit-garden, the Company continues.
Lālśaśī says, "behind that garden, the Company continues!" (BG 159, a.2; KG 61)

The meaning of this strange cycle of songs is by no means entirely clear—not even within the Kartābhajā community itself. In fact, these songs about the "stinking fruit" and this whole idea of *parakīyā* love remain to this day one of the most conflicted aspects of the Kartābhajā tradition. From a very early date, there have been two different currents within the movement, split in large part over their attitudes toward Tantric practices and above all toward transgressive techniques such as *parakīyā* love. According to the more orthodox and conservative tradition, represented by the dominant lineage of Kartās in Ghoshpara, the Kartābhajā tradition is vehemently opposed to any sort of Tantric practice, and above all to any form of sexual techniques. As the recently deceased Kartā, Satyaśiva Pāl, argues, the "stinking fruit" of left-hand Tantric sexual practices has been utterly eradicated from the tradition, leaving only the pure, chaste practice of devotional love.[85]

On the other hand, there has from the very origin of the Kartābhajā tradition been a more esoteric and "heterodox" current which embraces the most transgressive Tantric practices. According to contemporary Kartābhajā authors such as Advaita Candra Dās, the statement that the company still continues "behind the Garden of Love" actually means that the techniques of *parakīyā* love have in fact continued—but now in a secret, hidden form, concealed *behind* the outward display of orthodox conformity. "The bestial, common person is without authority and is forbidden from this practice," Dās warns: "The method of the Kartābhajā practice remains bound in secrecy between guru and disciple; it is not known to the majority."[86]

In any case, whatever the interpretation of this rich imagery of the stinking fruit, I would argue that it is a telling illustration of the intensely ambivalent place of Tantra in the colonial era. The remarkable genius of the Kartābhajā songs is to clothe this problem not just behind the veil of well-known Sahajiyā imagery but in the wonderfully ironic terms of the "Hon'ble Company" itself.

The Legacy of the Songs of Ecstasy: Scandal, Slander, and a Decline into Obscurity

> According to a Kartābhajā saying, "the woman must become a *hijrā,* and the man must become a eunuch; then they will be Kartābhajās." But today, this has become a source of ridicule among circles of wicked men. . . . Due to ignorance and lack of self-control, they abandoned the truth and sought the pleasures of the senses; the path of religion has become the path of irreligion.
>
> (Kedārnāth Datta (Bhāṅṛ), *Sacitra Guljār Nagar*)

The later history of the Kartābhajā tradition is the rather sad and ironic story of a remarkable rise to power and wealth, followed by a steady decline in scandal, slander, corruption, and disrepute. By the mid-nineteenth century, this once largely esoteric movement, originally rooted in the Tantric traditions of the Sahajiyās, had grown into the largest and most infamous of Bengal's so-called deviant orders or obscure religious cults. Yet, strangely, by the end of the nineteenth century, they had become increasingly attacked and ridiculed, finally reduced to a sad laughing stock and the butt of many jokes among the *bhadraloks* of Calcutta.

The reasons for the later decline of the Kartābhajās and the eventual neglect of the Songs of Ecstasy are twofold. The first and most obvious reason was the intense scandal, slander, and ridicule to which they were subjected during the late nineteenth century—slander directed precisely at their alleged use of Tantric sexual rituals. Already by the 1850s, the Kartābhajās had begun to generate intense suspicion and hostility from among the wealthy, Western-educated middle and upper classes of Bengal, who were often shocked and scandalized by this seeming breakdown of traditional social, religious, and sexual barriers. "Everybody shuddered at the name Kartābhajā. The vices which they imbibed from the Tantriks became most prominent. . . . Kartābhajā became a term of ridicule."[87] As the Calcutta satirist, Dāśarathī Rāy, mercilessly described them in scathing verse,

The Kartābhajās generate much smoke and violence, like the God of Death himself—
everyone's sleep is broken by their uproar!
They have a separate Tantra; they abandon all other sacred *mantras,*
and are initiated by a human Mantra.
Religion is mixed with all irreligion;
they turn every deed into the enjoyment of sensual pleasures.
The basis of all their teachings is deception and fraud.
. . . They don't regard anyone as great or little—
they've become all mixed up together.
Brother, there's nothing they haven't done!
The murderous highwayman became a holy man;
the harlot became a woman of good family
. . . Let the people beware:
[they think that] heaven lies within one's own body!

They overturn all Hindu religion;
they don't believe in gods or Brāhmaṇs, they are the foremost of the *Aghorapanthīs*!
. . . At each full moon, there's a dance,
where they all wish to sleep together,
without consideration.
Alas, all the old whores who aren't yet dead enjoy marrital relations—
just seeing this, I died in shame![88]

As Sudhīr Cakravartī suggests, the Kartābhajās quickly became "the most debated and the most numerous of the folk sects"; but increasingly since the end of the nineteenth century, "because of ill-repute and slander surrounding their Sahajiyā practices, they have now lost much respect."[89]

The second reason for the gradual decline of the Kartābhajās, however, seems to lie in the progressive corruption and degeneration within the upper rungs of the Kartā hierarchy itself. Already by the second half of the nineteenth century, the poor company of the Kartābhajās had in fact grown to be the largest and most powerful of Bengal's many folk religions, amassing a remarkable amount of wealth and land holdings at their center in Ghoshpara. As Banerjee observes, the Kartābhajās evolved from a small highly esoteric sect into a huge, generally exoteric, devotional and progressively more institutionalized popular movement. This was due in large part to the growth of the annual Melā or festival in Ghoshpara at the time of Holi, which attracted thousands of poor devotees from nearby Calcutta and became a tremendous source of income for the Kartās.[90]

Along with this new-found wealth and capital seems to have come a fair amount of corruption among the later Kartās. From a fairly early date, in fact, the Kartābhajā movement had grown into a complex and elaborate spiritual-economic hierarchy, extending from the Kartā through a network of regional gurus (*mahāśays*) down to the common devotees (*barātīs*), and demanding a series of taxes imposed by the elder gurus upon their disciples. As many critics have observed, this hierarchy bears a suspicious similarity to the traditional zamindāri system in rural Bengal, with its hierarchy of *zamindārs* (landlords), *taluqdārs* (intermediate landholders), and *raytadārs* (peasants). "In the hierarchy of the all-powerful Kartās," Māṇik Sarkār observes, "the influence of the feudal system is much greater than democracy. . . . The economic disparity between the Kartā and the barātīs is analogous to that between the zamīndār and the tenant."[91]

The spiritual-economic principle behind this practice is the ideology of "corporeal taxation" or "bodily revenue" (*daihik khājanā*)—a regular tax imposed on the devotees, to be paid each year at the seat (*gadi*) of the Mahāśays at the Melā in Ghoshpara. According to this system, the Kartā possesses the body of each of his disciples. Just as a tenant owes a regular tax to his local Zamindār for the lease of his land, so, too, the devotee owes a tax to his guru for the privilege of occupying his body with his soul. "To be ready with a pretext for exacting money from his followers [the Kartā] declared that he was the proprietor of every human body and that he was entitled to claim rent from every human being for allowing his soul to occupy his body."[92] As one contemporary Kartābhajā, Advaita Dās, explains this practice, "Out of reverence for the Guru, the disciple surrenders his body . . . Nothing remains of his own power. . . . The living soul dwells within its house. It is for the sake of dwelling in this house that they surrender to the Guru."[93]

Rather ironically, this elaborate hierarchy and system of taxation allowed the gurus of this "poor company" to become perhaps the wealthiest sectarian leaders of nineteenth-century Bengal, with a prosperous estate in Nadia district. Hence, it would be a mistake to romanticize the Kartābhajās simply as an example of "native resistance" or a triumph of the oppressed over their colonial oppressors. Indeed, these lower-class peasants and urban workers appear to have been reinscribed into a new, in some ways equally exploitative, hierarchy in which the primary benefits were received by the Kartās and upper-level gurus. J. C. Marshman wrote, describing his visit to residence of the Kartā, Dulālcāṅd, in 1802, "Dulal's handsome house, exceeding that of many Rajas, and his garners filled with grain, all the gifts of his deluded followers, convinced us of the profitability of his trade."[94] Thus, the poor company of the Kartābhajās appears to have appropriated not only the economic terminology but also some of the lucrative business practices of the British East India Company. It is thus no accident that the greatest period of disillusionment among the poorer Kartābhajā followers occurred during the period of the greatest wealth and power among the sect's leaders. By the late 1830s, some 500 Kartābhajās would convert en masse to Christianity.[95]

Conclusions : The Spirituality of the Subaltern and Alternative Imaginings of Community

Brother, tell me, how can you say that they are "poor men?"
Those sixty men made a vow and came together to this land as the Company;
brother, they're not insignificant!
. . . All the weak, illiterate and lowly people
are [now] great holy men and rulers of the three worlds!
Don't call them "poor men"—consider them great men! (BG 219; II.2)

In sum, the songs of the Kartābhajās appear to represent something far more interesting than just an unusual form of popular song in nineteenth-century Calcutta. Indeed, they shed some fascinating new light on a pivotal moment in the history of Bengali literature, popular religion, and economics. First, with their intriguing fusion of urban and rural styles, the Kartābhajā songs stand out as an important bridge between the "parlor and the streets," that is, between the popular music of colonial Calcutta and the rustic forms of the villages. Second, with their strangely beautiful imagery of the Man of the Heart and the mysteries of the body, all clothed in the secular language of urban life and trade, these songs also hold an important place in the religious history of Bengal; they might be said to form a key link between the older Tantric schools of the Sahajiyās and the later songs of the Bāuls and other folk singers of the nineteenth and twentieth centuries.

Finally, and most important, the Kartābhajā songs also bear larger comparative implications for South Asian and subaltern studies as a whole. With their rich use of imagery drawn from the underworld of the imperial city, they provide a new window onto the lives of the subaltern classes at a key geographical locus and a critical historical moment. At the same time, I would suggest that a careful study of the Kartābhajā songs can also help us to rethink and redress some of the lingering problems in much of the current literature on subaltern and postcolonial studies. Basically, the Kartābhajās remind us that there are many ways for dominated groups to express their resistance to the dominant order, apart from open revolt or violent insurrection. As Partha Chatterjee suggests, much of the past literature on subaltern studies has concentrated almost exclusively on the openly rebellious and radical forms of resistance, often to the neglect of the more subtle, yet perhaps more pervasive, forms of nonviolent or "everyday" resistance:

> Perhaps we have . . . missed those marks . . . of an immanent process of criticism and learning, of selective appropriation, of making sense of and using on one's own terms the elements of a more powerful cultural order. We must . . .

> remind ourselves that subaltern consciousness is . . . also history, shaped and developed through a changing process of interaction between the dominant and the subordinate.[96]

With their ingenious use of the imagery of the marketplace, the songs of the Kartābhajās stand out as a striking example of this "selective appropriation," or the "using on one's own terms the elements of a more powerful cultural order." To borrow the terms of Michel de Certeau, they demonstrate the many ways in which the weak make use of the strong, the various "tactics" by which dominated classes can appropriate, transform, and turn to their own advantage the discourse of the dominant order. Rather than a form of violent insurrection, this ingenious appropriation of the Company metaphor represents something more like what de Certeau calls the "arts of making do," or the ways in which poor, disadvantaged consumers survive within a dominated social marketplace. Indeed, it represents a kind of symbolic poaching or pilfering, by which dominated subgroups can adapt and hide behind the discourse of the dominant classes themselves; it is part of "a logic whose models go as far back as the age old ruses of fishes and insects that disguise themselves in order to survive. . . . Their use of the dominant social order deflected its power, which they lacked the means to challenge. . . . Their difference lay in procedures of consumption."[97]

At the same time, the Kartābhajā songs also force us to take fuller account of the specifically *religious* element of subaltern consciousness—the spirituality of the subaltern—which has often been ignored in much of the past work in subaltern studies. "Subaltern theorizing realizes that the religious consciousness is a vital subject of study," as Gerald Larson comments, "but frankly admits that it is has not made a great deal of progress in treating it."[98] Typically, the religious dimension is reduced to either (1) a mystifying opiate, in the conventional Marxist sense, as an illusion which hinders genuine historical progress; or (2) an ideological weapon, in a Gramscian, Neo-Marxist sense, as a tool which can in certain rare circumstances be turned into a source of revolutionary violence. In his early work on peasant insurgency during the colonial era, Ranajit Guha was initially quite disparaging in his attitude toward the religious dimension of subaltern consciousness. Defined as a mask and mystification of political power, religion serves primarily to delude the subaltern into accepting his dominated status within an asymmetrical, exploitative social hierarchy: "All the force of ruling ideologies, especially that of religion, imbued the peasant with this negative consciousness and pandered to it by extolling the virtues of loyalty and devotion so that he could be induced to look upon his subservience not only as tolerable but almost covetable."[99]

In his more recent work, however, Guha appears to have revised this reductionist attitude, pointing to the more positive aspects of the subaltern's religious ideals. In his discussion of the Santal Hool of 1855, for example, he criticizes traditional Marxism for ignoring the mythic and ritual dimension of peasant insurgency, calling for a clearer recognition of the religious element in Subaltern consciousness. "The specificity of rebel consciousness eluded radical historiography as well. . . .

Since the Ideal is supposed to be 100 percent secular in character, the devotee tends to look away when confronted with the evidence of religiosity . . . or explain it away as a well-intentioned fraud perpetrated by enlightened leaders on their moronic followers.[100]

The songs of the Kartābhajās offer strong evidence that the religious element of the subaltern cannot be reduced simply to underlying economic and material forces. As the subaltern scholars have persuasively argued, it is true that social agents are capable of appropriating religious myths and rituals in order to express more concrete economic or political motives.[101] Yet at the same time, I would argue, religious actors are also capable of appropriating very "secular," economic and political discourse, while transforming it into a profound bearer of deeper religious ideals. As we see in the Kartābhajā songs, the poorer members of Calcutta's Black Town were able to appropriate the symbolism of the marketplace, mercantile trade, and even the British company itself; indeed, they were able to "pilfer" the economic discourse of the dominant classes, to steal the language of their masters, and to redeploy it as a powerful expression of religious meaning.

Perhaps most important, the Kartābhajā vision of a caste-free company of the poor offered the hope of a radical new vision of *community*[102]—a community based not on wealth or class but on the universal religion of humanity (*mānuṣer dharma*) and the recognition of the inherent divinity of all men and women. This was a communal ideal distinguished both from the traditional class-based religious hierarchy and from a secular materialist social order of the sort championed by the subaltern theorists. But it was also a highly conflicted and ambivalent vision of community, one that ultimately seems to have collapsed under the weight of its own inherent contradictions. As Saurabh Dube has argued, in order to understand subaltern groups such as this one, we need to "defy easy dualisms and recognize the mixed up nature of social life," seeing these groups neither as backward primitives bound by religious superstition nor as precursors of a new secular, socialist community, but rather as "complex fusions of the conventionally . . . opposed categories of modernity and magicality, history and myth, rationality and ritual. . . . An uncritical celebration and lyrical romanticisation of a people or community—which fails to recognize the contradictions and the underside of cultural worlds—has little place here."[103]

It is precisely this sort of complex, ambivalent vision of community that we find in the songs of the Kartābhajās—a vision defying the conventional social order around them, but at the same time constructing new asymmetries of power. Although it would ultimately fail as a result of internal corruption and external attack, this vision of a new, egalitarian, classless community of the poor continues still survives, if only in the mysterious, enigmatic songs of the *Bhāver Gīta*.

II

From the Songs of Ecstasy

Select Translations from the *Bhāver Gīta*

Because the songs of the *Bhāver Gīta*[1] are compiled from a variety of manuscripts and oral sources, with no particular order or structure of their own, I have chosen the songs I consider most significant and organized them under thematic headings. In most cases, the section titles are my own. I have numbered my translations sequentially and provided the corresponding page numbers of the BG and KG at the end of each song. Songs appearing in this volume and in *The Economics of Ecstasy* are identified by the page number of the BG, followed by a roman numeral and a number for each song in this translation; thus, "BG 218; II.1" refers to *Bhāver Gīta,* p. 218; translated here in chapter II, song 1.

Following is a thematic outline of the songs translated here.

The Inward Voyage to the Altar of the Supreme Self
The Man of the Heart

Songs of Lust and Love (97–108)
The Dalliance of the Royal Goose and His Beloved Lady Goose
The Savoring of Licit and Illicit Love
The Stinking Fruit in the Garden of Love
The Cunning Play of the Illicit Lover
Robbing the Treasury of the Illicit Connoisseur of Love

Other Songs of Faith and Worship (108–110)
Paying the Price of Sin
In Praise of Sātī Mā, the Savior of the Poor

Company Songs

The following collection of songs all center around the key metaphor of the company (Bengalicized as *kompānī* throughout the songs), which serves as a dominant symbol for the following of Caitanya generally and for the Kartābhajā tradition in particular. Given the critical historical and economic situation in which they emerged—the underworld of Calcutta at the beginning of the nineteenth century—it seems fairly clear that the Kartābhajās are deliberately appropriating and adapting the language of their colonial masters, the British East India Company itself. The wonderful irony here is that they have also more or less turned the image of the company on its head, transforming it into the poor company (II.1–7) and the mad company (II.11–14).

Śrī Caitanya thus becomes the "fair-skinned" hero who founds the company—and here the author is almost surely playing off the dual meaning of *gorā* as both "fair skinned" and an Englishman (i.e., those who run the *real* East India Company) (II.8). The Kartābhajā founder, the mysterious Āulcāṅd, then becomes the fourth madman, who "completes the company." As the fourth and final figure in the lineage of the three madmen, Caitanya, Nityānanda, and Advaitācārya, Āulcāṅd reveals the true inner teachings of the Vaiṣṇava tradition (II.9–10).

Finally, a surprisingly large body of songs contain long eulogies describing the arrival of the company ships, along with detailed inventories of all their wondrous merchandise from abroad. These songs appear to embody a mixture of genuine awe at the new European goods now pouring into Bengal—a sort of Cargo Cult phenomenon—as well as a clever adaptation of this historical event in the service of religious discourse. The arrival of the company thus becomes the arrival of the fair-skinned Caitanya, bearing his treasury of spiritual gifts and miraculous merchandise from the wondrous land beyond the ocean of this world.

The Poor Company and the Platoon of the Poor

1

Ten, twenty, thirty Poor men gather together to become a Company.
There's an account book, in which so many things are recorded—
so many imported and exported goods!
Examining all the permission slips and seals, item by item,
the shopkeepers engage in business.
Brother, though they quickly grow old, still they don't stop and reflect!
You've heard the name of the Company's warehouse;
but you don't know who or where the Company is.
Because I became a Porter under the Headman,
brother, you joked and made fun of me.
Yet you've never once cast your gaze at the Headman himself!
Look, in this kingdom, if someone's born in the house of a merchant,
and is completely infatuated with wealth,
we call that man a "Rājā," brother.
But one who sits with a broken begging bowl in his lap,
everyone calls the "Ruler" of the land!
Those whose bodies are emaciated by famine,
we consider the Princes and Ministers!
Look—they all have a means of escape: they cannot really be called "Poor."
He who has a great amount of capital in hand, which instantly grows sevenfold,
and then goes throughout the seven cities, beating his drum, brother, we call "great."
But he who at no time has had any riches,
who possesses no wealth at all—he is the Lord of the three worlds!
He who knows no *tantras, mantras,* or meditations,
I count as a holy man and sage!
Lālśaśī says, none of them has ever seen "poverty." (BG 218, a.3)

2

Brother, tell me, how is that I hear you calling them "Poor Men?"
Those sixty men made a vow and came together to this country as the Company;
brother, they are not insignificant!
If you say that sixty men join together in one Company,
how can you say they are "Poor?"
I've never heard such words with my own ears!
See how much merchandise there is in this land, in the house of the Company!

But no one can find its whereabouts in any way!
Various kinds of import is going on.
Why don't you look and see: the Company's house has been illuminated,
and I find no sign of "Poor Men" among them!
Look, the starving and poor people who wander about with begging bowls—
have you heard?—they are counted as Great Kings, Nawabs, and Ministers!
All the weak, illiterate, and low-life people
are great holy men and the rulers of the three worlds.
Don't call them "poor men"—consider them equal to great men!
They see no "poverty" in the entire threefold world.
How many great, mediocre, and lowly people there are in the world!
None of them is comparable to a poor man; so who are you calling "poor?"
What no one has ever heard or seen, brother,
can be seen and heard from you.
And from seeing and hearing there is faith.
So I'll bear the whole burden in the warehouse.
Śaśīlāl laughs and says, "I'm wondering day and night!" (BG 219, q.4)

3

Brother, I do indeed call that Company "Poor:"
for whenever and whatever comes to pass, they accept it without excuse—
even the touch of poison!
What shall I say about that Poor Company?
They do what has never in any way been done before!
All the rules of good conduct bear their signature and seal.
If the house of *your* Company presents itself as wealthy,
then many good things may come to light.
But look at those who are in *my Poor* Company:
when anyone hears this brilliant Name, they are enchanted!
Even though, brother, apart from a broken old stair,
there's nothing else to be seen in that house!
If someone commits a theft in the kingdom of *your* Company,
when the Magistrate catches him, he sends him to prison.
Even if the verbal evidence is weak,
still, he'll easily be hanged upon the scaffold!
It seems that that your Company has some respect—
for otherwise, how could the Magistrate give such a command?
But that would not be tolerated by this Hon'ble *Poor* Company![2]
Just see the fun within my Poor Company—it's rather strange!
The Emperor gives no commands; the King punishes no one.
If someone, in need of money, commits a theft in this land,
the Company freely gives him infinite wealth.
Then and there his poverty disappears,

and he no longer covets anything!
Lālśaśī says, "thus the thief Ratnākar became the sage Vālmīki!"
(BG 220, a.4; KG 56)

4

The Master of the forty worlds is the "Good-Mannered Company."[3]
So why do I hear you calling them the "Poor Company?"
Of which land is it the Proprietor?
They've become the Masters of the world;
can you really call them "poor," brother?
Look and consider: "poor is only something insignificant!"
Whatever remained to be heard about that Madman and that wondrous thing,[4]
you told me, and you dispelled the doubts from my heart.
If some other doubt occurs again in my mind,
when you tell me, I'll consider it.
And all those things which were concealed, you yourself reveal!
Brother, amidst heaven, earth, hell and the forty worlds, where is His Office?
Now show me, brother, where they've built the Company's Fort.
Surely, there is a flag planted upon it.
How far does the moat around it stretch?
How many guns and supplies, and how many soldiers are there?
In this place, whatever happens, day or night, is auspicious!
I've heard that ten, twenty, thirty men have gathered together.
They have become the Company—tell me, brother, when did this happen?
In that land, in a certain city, the Emperor has a throne.
Together with the Company, he oversees whatever happens.
That city is the throne of the Company.
Brother, tell me precisely how far away those two places are.
There are so many imported and exported things—but whose seal is on them?
Lālśaśī says, "whose seal is on the invoices?"[5] (BG 160, q.1; KG 61)

5

That which encompasses the thirty-six castes and the four classes,
bearing rule over the sixty cities—that is the "Poor Company."
In every respect, everyone accepts his own status.
I'm evaluating everything, front and back—
Apart from [the Company's] seal, everything else is fake!
Brother, no one examines the merchandise itself; that's why there are seals upon it!
Look, thirty-three million men have united
and sit, paying honor to that Company—

the Poor Company.
When it puts its seal [on the merchandise],
it will be honored by everyone!
Brother, He whose pen causes the very world to move—
would you call Him "insignificant?"
The land of the Poor Company is very open.
Previously, the high, the low, everyone [was spread throughout] these ten directions;
But then, six cities and six kings [were appointed] in each direction.
At the command of the Poor Company, they sat upon their thrones.
In the good name of the Company, all things move.
That's why no one is ever engaged in thievery.
Even if someone is accused of theft, he's freed from sin immediately!
[Suppose there is] 100 percent foreign silver or gold:
if sixty men take and divide it up, it becomes diluted.
But when they put the seal of this "Poor Company" upon it,
then, by that very seal, it becomes 100 percent again in the form of a Sikka coin!
[In the same way] the sixty *rasas*[6] [are divided up] among thirty-six [castes] and ten [elements].
Rasa is divided up into ten parts; but by that [seal] the *rasas* become twelve.
The Supreme Virtuous One comprises the five material elements, the five devotional states,[7] and the three constituents of existence.[8]
Lālśaśī says, "the Supreme Virtuous One consists of the twelve seasons and the three constituents."[9] (BG 161, a.3; KG 62)

6

The land has been secured with a contract.[10]
There's an Emperor in this land,
and beneath him is the Good-Mannered Company.
In the twinkling of an eye, they produce and sell so many items!
They go to see the Proprietor of this land;
and with those who hold jurisdiction over this land,
the Landlord does his business.
And then the stupid, snub-nosed Rent-Collector, wearing his long loin cloth, follows along behind!
Heaven, death, the upper world, the underworld, and the fourteen worlds—
at every moment, one sees this dream of the threefold universe.
Those who wish to see the Landlord with their own eyes,
whether He reveals Himself or not, they'll attain great wealth!
They put their affairs under the care of the Custodian, and then they float upon the ocean of Love!
Let me tell you the nature of this Landlord's estate:
there are four castes—Brāhmaṇs, Kṣatriyas, Vaiśyas, and Śūdras.
He came with merchandise to join all four together.

It's said that the Emperor of this land kept the merchandise hidden.
He came and gave initiation to the Proprietors of this land;
he taught them about calculation, price, profit, and gifts.
Those ten men gathered together, received ownership and made a Contract!
For as much capital as a man had within his house,
in the twinkling on an eye, within that marketplace, one grew to twenty-one!
Some go along with them, thoroughly intoxicated [with wealth];
then with a sidelong glance, they cheat them out of whatever capital remains in their hands!
But to those who forget all else, open their hearts, and say "Everything is yours!"
I wish to offer a thousand salutations!
Lālśaśī says, "at twilight, they call upon you as a friend!" (BG 265, a.1)

7

How can one hope for any more pleasure,
if he can float in *rasa*,[11] whether in the market, at the wharf, or in the temple?
Whatever happens from country to country,
time and again throughout the three worlds,
the Company itself knows everything,
like merchants accompanied by so much merchandise.
Look—no one ever asks about anyone in any way,
or as to how the business of *rasa* takes place or doesn't take place.
I see a festival of all the *Rasikas,*[12]
staggering along behind.
Come on! what a wondrous play!
And as it begins, *rasa* grows in all directions!
Look—an Emperor sits upon a throne, and merchandise comes into his hands.
He's closely examining me, brother.
See—all the *Rasikas* are intoxicated with bliss!
Everyone mixes freely together!
Not thinking of how they'll find salvation from this world,
they are as if laid bare.
Perhaps what's happening is what will happen at that very time.
Lālśaśī says, "day and night they go along, laughing and laughing!" (BG 82; KG 23)

The Fair-Skinned Madman and His Fair-Skinned Company

8

The three Madmen[13] have become drunken in this play!
The single path and the single emotion of all three is Love.

Their meeting took place in India.
When he proclaimed the supreme Name of Hari,
—whether it was "the breast of the lady of the dawn," "Haribol" or "catfish curry"[14]—
Nityānanda, by hook or by crook, created a great commotion!
Having experienced the waves of love,
with horns, handclapping and drums,
many more got up and danced with him!
This Kali age has been blessed—
so hear of this wondrous thing, brother!
Govinda, his mind filled with bliss, assumed the Name of eternal joy: Gour Nitāi.
When He became Caitanya, in the form of Gour, the "fair-skinned" one, a delightful thing occurred!
One can never attain nonduality in the state of duality.[15]
Some feel suffering in their bodies,
and some feel suffering in the hearts—
that's why I listened and fell into Hari's embrace.
Just look—a fair-skinned man has become overwhelmed with love; he's utterly maddened!
The Fair-skinned One has been destroyed, hewn down, and falls to the ground!
And the Company has shown the proof of it throughout the streets!
Those Three who came together as one and drowned this land
are the Fair-skinned Company;[16] but what do I know of them?
What has happened in the end?
Brother, abandon the idea of duality and contemplate the eternal Caitanya!
Become non-dual and remain united with Caitanya!
Brother, Man no longer wants to wander in that game of truth and falsehood.
For now all his work is set in order! (BG 415, q.4)

The Fourth Madman, Who Completes the Company

9

I'm struck with amazement at this news![17]
Seeing this, I beat my breast with great respect.[18]
Or is there some danger in that?
Why do those who have doubts
accept this [news] simply at a few more words?
Are one's doubts dispelled simply by beating one's breast?
In Āṣāṛ month of 1233,[19]
You sat upon this seat and sang this song:
"A Poor Wretched Man came,

progressively, he completed the cycle."[20]
But why did he come to complete the cycle in this way?
This is the story of the Three [Caitanya, Nityānanda, and Advaita],[21]
The [first] song was the petition; then he sang a wondrous answer.
The Good-Mannered Company[22] was comprised of the three worlds.
Even if they went to travel to different lands,
and found the three Men [Caitanya, Nityānanda, and Advaita],
why would they return here and cease to wander?
For only when the four Madmen [the three plus Āulcāṅd] join together and cross over is [their search] completed.
I heard all these words from start to finish,
and, for the whole year [since last Āṣāṛ month], I've been wondering in my heart.
What has never before been seen or heard
I can only hear in your verses!
I ask about that, not knowing this wondrous thing,
hoping to hear it again.
Brother, that's why I ask: "where did you hear this?"
Lālśaśī says, "where did you hear this?" (BG 189, q.1)

10

This is wondrous[23] news!
If you beat your breast and show respect,
I'll tell you a little more.
On the shore of that water
lies the threefold world,
as if on all four sides there were the dominion of four kinds of joy.
A 100-petaled lotus floats upon the immeasurable waters
and upon it is a Poor Wretched Madman.
He is himself without any pretensions;
If he had any pretension, there'd be terrible trouble![24]
Once He remained gazing at this land of delusion.
That Heavy-bearded One made everything complete.
Look, brother—He wandered through heaven earth and hell,
and all that remained to complete [the universe] was the land of the Poor Wretched One.
If that were to happen, the Heavy-Bearded One would be filled with happiness.
He came in search of this;
You can see that the Poor Wretched One came to the land of falsehood.
And now one can grasp the cluster [of fruit] upon the Wretched One's tree.[25]
Because of the sweet smell of that fruit,
some have become *Rasikas* and no longer desire anything else in the three worlds

The Good-Mannered Company goes to bring that Medicine;
and when one gets it, then and there he is filled with joy.
At the gesture of the Bearded One,
their wandering has ended.
The four [Caitanya, Nityānanda, Advaita and Āulcāṅd] have joined together in one company and crossed over.
Lālśaśī says, "joined together as one, they crossed over." (BG 190, a.1)

The Rag-Clad God and the Platoon of the Poor

11

What shall I tell you about our state?
The one who founded this Platoon of the Poor[26] is the Great Poor God!
When you hear this, your mind is in turmoil!
When I remind you of this state of affairs,
then and there, brother, your eyes stream with tears!
And even as you engage in your mundane chores, your head spins!
Why don't you all revere the Creator?
This is most terrible!
First, second, third, and fourth—
in all things, there are only these four laws.
Look—the three worlds were created with four classes.
Even if you look again, still you don't see!
So where else will you go to see this?
The gods give joy and suffering to everyone;
I've explained this matter to you again and again!
And as much as each one needs—
food and clothing—everything is just.
Everyone's home is a splendid, multistoried palace,
adorned with gems and pearls and new leaves.
No one is ever deprived of happiness, brother.
And look—in his manner and behavior, God is like a great benefactor.
See the ragged clothing of our Creator;
if one desires anything, He will import it!
Brother, just look at His seal.
Within the warehouse, there's a great store of water mixed with grain.
Whether we ask for something or not, we can always get it—
—even if the room and the foundations are not to our liking.
For, apart from a poor shanty, the Creator can build nothing else!
And Śaśī Lāl laughs and says, "His bed is a date-palm leaf!" (BG 112, q.3)

The Mad Company and the Crazy King of the Land of Madness

12

Don't you know the news about the land of Madness?
You won't dislike the craziness of the Madman,[27] you know!
But never speak about that at all!
Look, He has come in the form of a Madman—
Does He who makes such mischief commit any sin?
Unless you frolic with that Madman, you can't dispel the darkness!
You can easily find deliverance from the hand of time—
For anyone who is intimately joined with this Madman,
becomes a Madman himself—and so loses himself [in Madness]!
That treasure is splendid beyond imagining!
Brother, unless you become mad yourself, then, if you suddenly see the Madman, will you be able to recognize Him?
Oh, how much Madness has arisen because of that great power!
For can one go mad without a reason?
Brother, in this world of *saṃsāra,* in this land,
there was no wealth or profit.
[But now], twelve months a year, wondrous things freely occur!
And if these fine things come into this land,
apart from a Madman, who could fathom the delight?
Brother, if one doesn't see this wondrous thing, he cannot become a Madman!
Look, in this country, there is one Company comprised of ten Madmen.
They write and write at every moment.
Brother, wherever you look, whatever you see,
as soon as you see it, you will like it!
Initially, there is darkness—
then, within the darkness, one grabs the bait.
And, having lost it again, his mind goes mad!
Lālśaśī says, I count him as equal to a Madman! (BG 149, a.1; KG 49)

13

I have no use for this news about the land of Madness!
Look—it made me burn with suffering;
Now continuing my life has become a burden!
How terrible is the business of the Madman!
For, even if He leaves sometime,
then, brother, He's met with again in some other land!
And, if I dwell with Him for even a short while, will I ever be able to leave Him again?

Having considered myself, I ask you about the Madman.
Hearing your answer, I feel pained;
I'm burning with a certain affliction.
Brother, why do you wish to afflict me twofold?
What is this excellent thing of yours?
"That very state of Madness is also my own, brother—Greetings!"
Just look—because of a Madman, I've been driven mad!
Becoming mad, you wish to see for yourself
the excellence of this land of madness!
Look—one madman, two madmen, three madmen, a Festival of Madmen![28]
I can't understand this play of madness!
The uproar of all this madness!
People say, what is this terrible commotion they're making?
Struck with wonder, no one can understand their ecstasy!
You say that many fine and wonderful things are happening in that land,
they naturally occur, twelve months a year.
It's filled with *rasa*!
Seeing these wonderful things, the people go mad!
I too have gone mad—what use is there for me in all this?
Knowing this madness, a wonderful thing has occurred!
Just look, brother, he's driven me crazy!
Lālśaśī says, "in this land, Madness is the rule!" (BG 150, q.2; KG 50)

14

I'm struck with amazement, seeing this funny thing!
The throne of this kingdom is empty—
Ten office clerks have gathered together—
and have placed a great Madman [upon the throne]!
All the people are saying, "What will happen? Alas! What will happen?"
When He sits upon the throne and acts as Magistrate for this land.
For what actions, at whose command, shall we offer obeisance?
Look—the announcement has come: a Fakir has displaced the Ministers!
I've come on pilgrimage, wandering on the road,
and I see that, for no good reason, a hoax has been played on this kingdom of stupid fools!
They took me in confidence inside the Machine Room [of the Factory]
And what I had never seen or heard before, they showed me!
When they saw that I showed such great devotion, as a "traveler" [on the spiritual path], they revealed this to me.
The Madman sits upon the throne, and then, in the twinkle of an eye, he slips aside;
making antics and leaping about, He disappears into the darkness!
When the news comes, if anyone starts grumbling,

He rises up like a great wave upon the ocean waters,
He says, "whatever happens, happens according to my will"—is that so wicked?
So why do I feel so delighted with Him?
Say—I can see clearly that all the three worlds are in agreement!
If someone marries Him and becomes the Princess,
then, with great effort, she will grasp the Jewel and sit [upon the throne] with authority.
Whenever she desires anything, He easily grants it to her,
she will keep it, and remain full of joy and bliss within the darkness.
And whenever she wishes to see the Madman just once,
in the twinkle of an eye, his vision appears before her eyes!
Lālśaśī says, "what she experiences then, no mouth can utter!" (BG 276, q.1)

15

Not understanding, they call him a "Madman."
He has abandoned the throne and sits in complete humiliation.[29]
He himself is a *Rasika,* and with a *Rasika*'s heart he created the fruit of *rasa.*
How, in what way, can anyone understand all this?
He's come to this kingdom and created so much Madness!
Whatever He wishes—let it be done! and may He live long in happiness!
For the gods and demigods, creation, subsistence and the waters of destruction
are all under the command of the Madman!
You went off wandering on pilgrimage,
and as you came into the land of delusion, the Madman was seated upon the throne!
Seeing this funny thing, the stupid person is struck with bewilderment.
Seeing this, he thinks—"what means [of salvation] is there?"
[The Madman] has come to this kingdom, and, laughing and laughing, easily engages in fraud!
From night until dawn, from morning to evening,
the Madman remains eternally in this earthly world, so that people can see Him.
For those who merely gossip and speculate,
the shadows of the tall coconut and date palm tree are long, and the fruit is far away.
But those who see the Madman but once with their own eyes
will abandon all darkness, and remain immersed in the Self-nature day and night.
What lies within the power and control of this Madman is infinite-
all that's in heaven or in the lowest hell!
That heavenly courtesan who goes to see him with delight,
will marry Him and become a Princess! Isn't this a grand affair?
He who sees the Madman but just with one eye
—this is no lie, you know!—will surely have his heart's desire fulfilled!
To those who wander through the heavens, at home and abroad,

twelve months a year, in an instant,
He's revealed, both day and night!
Lālśaśī says, "at His command, they're immersed in *rasa*!" (BG 277, a.1)

The Coming of the Company and the Arrival of the Wondrous Merchandise

16

The Company's ship is coming!
I just now heard about it in the bazaar;
in each and every shop there's whispering.
Put down your newspaper,[30]
you'll get to hear what's really happening!
He himself will tell you everything
But you'll need a little money.[31]
First go there, stand waiting and listening;
you won't have to wander around anymore, suffering the ten stages of life.
Even as I speak, I float in bliss!
When you hear those words of delight, your heart will be filled with joy!
What a wealth of honor there will be!
After asking, there will be a reply.
They've come as we'd hoped; now I'm there among them all.
If I can just get close to them I'll be saved;
Then I'll raise my hands and dance!
If anyone can act as the broker for even a single item of merchandise,
he'll become the owner of infinite wealth!
In the homes of the merchants of this city,
first we hold a secret counsel.[32]
And Śaśī, the *Rasika*, thinks there will be much buying and selling!
(BG 65, q.1; KG 17)

17

Hey look—the ships of the Company are coming, with all their sails erect:
in the middle of the bay, what a spectacle is seen!
And so many still remain in the water;
They came and shouted the news at the top of their voices—
They'll come and unload in the city!
I had come here to spend the night close to them.
When I arrived, my heart was so happy—how shall I speak of it?
But no one will tell me the whereabouts of these imported goods.
Each and every day, one should be happy with God's will, even in a state of poverty;

for that too is by the mercy of God.
Alas, brother, how wonderful, how wonderful!
Now various excellent merchandise will be displayed.
They'll go to the warehouse and take the foreign goods.
Whatever one wishes will be there!
This import from abroad is no trifling stuff,
we know, for all the goods are marked with foreign labels.
If the permit for these imported goods is genuine,
then and there I'll buy them!
And Śaśīlāl says, "Look, he floats in the ocean of *rasa*!" (BG 65, q.2; KG 17)

18

There's various merchandise in the Warehouse;
I stood up and came to see immediately.
No one could describe it—
I stood before it, amazed and perplexed.
How could I estimate its value, brother?
They have arranged it all, brother,
according to a new plan.
There are so many shopkeepers—Sikhs, Armenians and Moghuls.
The Company is calling out [the inventory] on the shelves and rows,
Opening the bags that are marked, they calculate the invoices[35] on each item.
Everyone comes and goes [in the warehouse], but no one goes out anymore on the street!
Guns, pistols, old and new fashions[33] on both sides,
knives and many fine trinkets!
Brother, what's their price?
And in a separate storeroom, there are various things from China,
pictures, hanging lanterns, and mirrors of various types,
and how much candy, sugar and fruits—
Oh! how bright and sweet-smelling they are!
And Śaśī thinks, "There will have to be a Broker for all these things!" (BG 66, q.3; KG 17)

19

Oh! all these wondrous things have come,
and as they arrive, this land is maddened with the sweet fragrance!
Who has ever seen such delightful things anywhere, brother?
The Captains[34] themselves keep watch over it.
They're selling it, item by item;
they take it to the shopkeepers;
they open their stores, selling both genuine and imitation goods!

Look and listen—these are the merchant ships of the Company:
Such wonderful imported goods have never before been seen, brother!
The wonderful scents come and go.
The people wish to estimate their value, but there are so many they can't keep track of them!
Yet out of desire for these fine things, they keep coming back again and again.
The good name of this excellent merchandise is known at home and abroad.
Whoever comes and goes—tell him about these excellent goods!
People come and go busily from street to street,
asking about these excellent goods.
When they find the whereabouts of these things,
they say, "Oh, how marvelous!" and go to see.
And brother, as they arrive,
just look—Śaśī floats in *rasa*! (BG 66, q.4; KG 17)

20

The good Merchant[35] has returned from England;
so when I bring the news, land, sea, and city all rejoice!
No one knows how much profit, debt or wealth he has;
they're constantly examining it, filled with bliss, to their heart's desire—
in the twinkle of an eye, it's delightful to see!
And as they turn it over to evaluate it, the people are all amazed!
Everyone, I think, needs to experience this feeling of joy!
The rains of Āṣāṛ month fell and the northern lands were immersed.
When they found the route, they set sail and everyone came to this city.
They raised the sail and the rudder of the dingis, and floated to the central wharf.
At every moment, the merchants haggle with one another;
those who engage in business take [the merchandise] to the platform
in order to measure its weight.
From beginning to end, the merchandise in Calcutta is being accounted;
the Clerks have begun to calculate and record the value.
How much land, sea, city and waves I can see!
How can I describe them? I've never seen such things produced in India!
If I wish to count the imports and exports,
at the very sight of such things, all my vanity is destroyed!
The merchants search for these goods on every shore of this world.
Seeing all these imported goods of the Merchants,
with all their labels, I'm struck with amazement!
Thousands and thousands of ships sail upon the wide Ganges;
so many mirrors, pictures, and goods with Arabian labels!
Seeing all this, the Honorable, Good-Mannered Company[36]
does what is impossible!
They call out to all the suffering people whom they see,

saying, "let the city, port, dry land and sea all float in *rasa*!"
Lālśaśī says, "as they come, an era passes away!" (BG 376, q.1)

The Battle of the French and British Fleets, and the Triumph of the Company

21

Who among you has seen this brothers?
You say, "there's a great splendour upon the water!"
That's why I'm inquiring—
the people are gossiping;
no one has ever seen such a strange thing!
And now I want to hear it
straight from the mouth of the one who's seen it!
I went to the city of Dhaka,[37]
and I'm returning with this news;
but I come with good common sense.
If this great happy news is true,
then I've never before heard such a thing!
This is the Company's city;
they go forth upon the water with all great accoutrements!
They've embarked upon their ships—
many merchants, both lowly and distinguished.
The canons sound in celebration!
I think they've received the good news—
That's why I returned and, having learned of this matter, go off again.
If there were any other news,
why would they go there without need?
When the Company gets the news of the fighting,
the Man-o-Wars[38] will set out;
All doubts have been dispelled from my heart!
When the Company's ships have raised their sails,
they'll set forth in all directions.
Lālśaśī says, "look, they all set sail in all directions!" (BG 116, q.1)

22

A delightful merchant is coming upon the ship,
with so many wondrous things, creating a great splendor!
He has sent the news to this office:
they want a thousand and one ships.
Everyone will guess at what the merchandise might be!

And with them, I think, a fleet of one or two thousand will go!
The English and French, with great splendor,
were all detained at the wharf from their water-route,
Look—the French, after fighting and fighting with the English,
have finally been subdued![39]
Just see—by the grace of God, a great wave has washed up over the deck!
All the danger has been dispelled;
the way has been opened,
and they're coming with all their wondrous, fine merchandise!
On each of their ships there will be a host of wealth.
We've never before seen such things, brother!
I wonder, will they all remain outside,
or will they come inside the city?
Amidst this display, I can see that they're all very distinguished gentlemen!
They've brought a ship loaded with merchandise, brother,
Look: while light still remains, they go out upon the water,
Oh, what a beautiful display of excellent merchandise they've shown us!
Oh what pomp and display is on each ship!
Now I'll go and wait there—
I wish I might stay and see this delight.
It seems as if they've built an incredible city upon the water!
Lālśaśī says, "they've built a wondrous city upon the water!" (BG 117, a.1)

23

I'm asking again about all that:
they had not come for such a long time—where were [the ships of the Company]?
When I got to hear, I laughed—
for it's as if what has never before occurred,
I have now seen and heard!
They come and go and stay again—where? to the left or to the right?
When you told me the good news,
I asked you about that:
When you gave me the news
I wanted to hear everything from the beginning.
When I've heard everything, brother, I'll have faith in your words.
Just as the Mugs[40] and the Portugese pirates used to come,
[those European men] come and stage a comic show, then go again, from country to country!
And while they're here, they take advantage of every opportunity!
They start fights and quarrels,
and finally cause terrible trouble!
When they get the chance, they suddenly swoop down like rapacious birds!

But then the English spokesman[41] rectifies the situation and dispels all the trouble!
In what land is their city?
Brother, tell me all the news, each and every word!
When I hear the name of that city and that land,
I want to consider it in my heart,
If I have the inclination, I'll go and make a purchase.
So I remain in this endeavor, looking, evaluating, understanding.
Lālśaśī says, "I continue in this endeavor." (BG 118, q.1)

24

Twenty-four hours a day, twelve months a year, they return to the city.
I can see that, to this day, they always dwell upon the water.
There's no doubt about that.
He who does business with them once,
will never again seek any other delight!
And I've never before heard from anyone such tasteful language as theirs!
Their merchandise is all invaluable jewels.
I get to see, necessarily acting like a poor man.
A thousand ships return with them—
look, on each and every ship there's an adornment of 100,000 rupees!
Why don't you go and look just once, if you wish?
O, how much wealth, property, merchandise, and, goods they have!
No one can count how much is on a single ship!
I hear that they're coming, bearing all this merchandise;
brother, we've never seen such things!
Something will happen, I think, by the power of fate.
I see it all with my own eyes, filled with praise!
Today, many great English, French, and Dutch men have met together!
Those who get to see the Buyer with their own eyes, as they desire,
then and there, will make an excuse to engage in business with him.
The Merchant on that ship has a magnificent appearance,
and as many people as are with him all engage in work.
They necessarily offer protection to the poor.
When they see him caring for the poor, [the people] acquiesce to him;
but some gossip about him and ridicule him.
Lālśaśī says, "if he's not genuine, they'll ridicule him!"(BG 119, a.2)

25

The Company is on both banks within the city.
They act as captains at the wharf.

There are import and export ships,
merchant ships and Man-o-Wars, Pākiṭ and Pāiṭ ships,
policemen, and a place for importing and exporting.[42]
The news is certain.
What more will I say? Do I know [the Boatman's][43] name?
When you asked me about the gross outward form,
I opened my heart and told you about the inner truth.
But one who is drunken [with desire] is always ignorant;
even when you [think you] understand the meaning,
you don't really understand,
[because of] idolatry, deception, bad advice and lack of faith.
Beware of this city, this bazaar and this land!
How vast is this universe, its dominions, and the great ocean—
He [the Boatman] knows the news about the high, middle and low,
directly and indirectly, on both sides,
and apart from Him, who is the receptacle of Truth?
How many great-souled men and witnesses there are—
But from whose mouth,
amidst this great difficulty,
will you know such great skill as His?
Assume the garb of a poor, lowly servant,
and search [for Him] by the light of the Moon.[44] (BG 50, a.2)

Songs of the Marketplace

A huge portion of the songs of the *Bhavār Gīta* centers around the pivotal metaphor of the marketplace, which is arguably the single most recurring theme and dominant motif throughout this tradition as a whole. The marketplace, however, is a deeply ambivalent metaphor, one that can be used in both positive and negative, in both profoundly spiritual and cynically materialistic, senses. On the one hand, the "marketplace of the world" is the most common metaphor for the greed, sin, and futility of the everyday social world, filled as it is with rapacious moneylenders and thieving brokers who deceive and exploit the poor laborers. On the other hand, the "marketplace of love" becomes the key metaphor for the spiritual life, where the true goods of devotion and ecstasy can be bought and sold.

One of the most interesting series of songs (II.47–50) also uses the mysterious image of the "Hidden City"—*ḍhākā sahar*—a double entendre playing on the dual meaning of *ḍhākā* as both "hidden or concealed" and the real city of Dhaka in East Bengal. Thus, the journey from the "Hidden City" to the bazaar of the world becomes a complex allegory for the passage of the living being from the prenatal state of the womb into this mortal realm, the marketplace of the world.

Toil and Trade in the Marketplace of the World: Porters, Brokers, Moneylenders, and Merchants in the Service of the Company

26

Brother, you've come here in the hope of doing business—
But until now, nothing good has happened; the days merely go by.
It's useless for you to say anything else.
There are so many merchants in this world,
ceaselessly engaged in trade.
As you can see, they all want to come and dwell in this land!
You've written your name in the Moneylender's account book;
and all the capital he gave you, he has now tricked you out of!
Your affairs are all in his hands—
like an earthworm, singing and dancing, crawling upon the road!
And even now I can see [the moneylender's] face, laughing at the fun!
Look—so many businessmen are coming and going in this land;
a few have found their own means of earning wealth, and remain silent.
Look—in this business, some control the weights and scales.
Twelve months a year, it freely goes on;
everyone is busily engaged in greed!
You should never feel such [greed];
and if you do, your heart will only find sorrow!
I'm thinking and wondering in my heart—
you came here with so much capital and so many borrowings;
and now I see you have spent it all!
Your dreams of splendor, like the great Princes, have all gone awry!
There is no more business—that's why all your capital is failing!
If you can do no business,
then how can you find the pleasure of profit?
Lālśaśī says, "what will finally happen with all this debt and borrowing?"
(BG 213, q.1; KG 53)

27

I've quit this business, brother!
There was no profit in it—I had to give up my earnings too easily!
Is one more merchant any use in this land?
I labor in some city;
I go to the marketplace and toil, breaking my back,
and as the days pass, do I get even a piece of bread in this kingdom?
I conducted business in this land eight million times—

but see, brother, my troubles haven't left me!
Seeing and hearing all this, I've gone mad!
But now I have settled all my debts.
Look, for my own sake,
I'm returning from this city and this bazaar.
Just see how many great and small items are in the warehouse and in the shops;
but without the goods bearing the label of the "Company," I won't break my back!
See how many imported goods are in the Company's warehouse—
The Company labels and markets them.
But [on the labels] the weight, whether great or little, is not recorded.
For if it were, the [weight] would be known, whether little or great,
and then the porters and laborers and everyone else would know its true value.
All the troubles I had have been paid off.
I'll no longer engage in all this haggling—I have had enough of it!
Now the porters and policemen of the Company
no longer deceive me about the weight [of the merchandise].
My debts have all been nullified,
and I'm filled with joy!
And by his good fortune, Śaśī Lāl has no more work! (BG 214, a.1; KG 53)

28

All this buying and selling in which you engage—is it all fraud?
You'll only get mixed up and confused; finally it will all be swindling!
Can there be any happiness in this sort of thing?
How can you hope for pleasure with these foreign men?[45]
Despite your words and devices, you'll only slip and fall;
you won't get even a little!
First of all, you should know about the homeland of these men:
losing their way, they eventually came here,
and they easily found much pleasure!
Enchanted, they came and floated in *rasa!*
[Just like] a little bird leaving its tree and rising up at dawn.
You don't know why they came here to this land—
so why do you serve them?
Brother, what's your intention?
They treat all your affectionate show of respect with contempt!
And you're soon filled once again with sorrow and sin!
Not seeing any happy faces,
but seeing only suffering, you shed tears,
as if both shores were only so much flint upon cold ash. (BG 79, a.1)

29

They've been sailing upon the waters, ever since that day
when they first mingled with the Poor folk; and now they've returned once again.
From country to country, they engage in commerce.
Look, let us tell you about their great wealth!
They say, "no one is poor, and all are our equals!"
For only when pride has been overturned
does one experience the state of [true] "Poverty!"
The sea-going Merchants have come to this land;
there's a great splendor upon the waters!
Brother, if you want to question their authority,
say nothing more—just sit and remain silent.
On this great day, the bonds of the ocean of this world have suddenly been opened!
The Merchants of this city have prepared their merchant ship.
And oh, how many foodstuffs go with them!
They display the list of rates—
for something of one value, they give the people a hundred times that—
giving out such merchandise for such a price.
They distribute it to the Poor People of this land;
and in the ecstasy of this Festival of the Poor,[46] they themselves have attained such a state [of poverty]!
Their uniforms are [seen] in the bazaar, and their ships sail in all directions.
If anyone desires anything, just see
what delight there is!
When someone wants something,
whether he asks for it or not, he'll get it right away!
Some are crying out for their own needs—
Then and there, brother, they are given respect without hesitation.
Brother, the Poor have taught them the true nature of Poverty.
Lālśaśī says, "the Poor have taught them the true nature of Poverty!"
(BG 123, a.4)

The Shameful State of Bengal under Foreign Rule

30

Brother, no one can understand all these funny things!
They've been deluded, they've abandoned the milk and cream, and wander about,
chewing husks of grain.
The Rājā of Bengal himself admits it,

angrily tugging at his beard!
The Nawab dismisses and appoints his Ministers;
I could say such things too—if I smoked enough dope![47]
The laborer can understand nothing apart from his work;
for he never knows the taste of anything else.
From beginning to end I understood everything—
you people of this land are all eternally deluded!
Brother, how can you display the manliness of another [i.e., the British], if you yourself have been castrated?[48]
He who knows the whereabouts
of the One for whose sake you have come to this world of *samsāra,*
to him I say, "Bravo!"
Brother, for whose sake does all the traffic in this land take place?
Now no one remembers any other life!
Those events have been forgotten,
due to deceitful slander,
like tiny fish floundering in a handful of water.
Just seeing their affairs, I feel ashamed!
If someone comes along sometime and shows them fear,
they let out an arrogant laugh!
He's left sitting with his hand on his cheek in astonishment;
and if someone comes and tells this story in confidence,
they thrash him, with a fine display of manliness!
For whose mouth waters when he sees mere sun-dried rice?[49]
When he sits chopping up worthless vegetables,
whose chest swells with pride?
Brother, in this story and in the magic of this song, what a wonderful straight path there is!
Lālśaśī says, "in this story, what a wonderful, straight path there is for the world!"
(BG 182, q.3; KG 73)

The Sad Plight of the Laborer in the Company Warehouse

31

O, how wonderfully funny you are!
You've quit your business, and now, I see, you're paying homage to the Porters,
in the marketplace and at the wharf!
I see no shortage in the jurisdiction of the Company.
And who else will associate with you now?
Now, finally, this good Name [of the Company] is spread throughout this land!
You've abandoned your business—you've done well!
All your worries of what will happen now are gone.

At one time there was buying and selling;
now there is no more accounting, in the morning or afternoon.
For the Light of the World has come to the land of India!
  So freely, I know, you had abandoned all your wealth,
wandering and searching throughout the entire Company—
that's why you break your back working here!
Your name is written in the account books of the Company Warehouse—
so why don't you sign on the top of the account book?
O, how many imported goods the Company has!
Surely you know that the weight is little, and not great—
But suddenly that cheating Porter says that what's little is great!
  You had come to work as a merchant in this land;
but when that business failed, you found a lot of work
in this market and bazaar.
And now the Porters, both petty and great, all control you!
Now no day is without joy!
Their pleasure grows by the hour!
You've labored for the Company for so long a time—
And Śaśī Lāl laughs and says, "oh, see how manly you are!" (BG 215, q.2; KG 18)

32

  I won't practice business anymore, brother!
There's nothing but debt in my old business; so I'm keeping my inheritance
and leaving this country!
Oh, how much debt and credit!
Let the debts be—I won't get them back.
I return without shedding tears; I opened this shop, but now I get no more profit!
  Brother, among the highest and the lowest men in all ten directions,
I made purchases; I suffered to my very limit,
so that there might be some profit.
For there were so many Porters procuring everything,
but no one was overseeing what they were doing!
  Oh, how much wealth and capital there once was!
But as I came and went doing business, the profits were all exhausted.
My own house is straw and brick,
and when they saw it, everyone said, "he's very rich!"
But now all that's been mortgaged;
I've grown thin and sold everything away.
By my own choice, I engaged in this work and now I am receiving my
  punishment!
  When I had capital in hand,
so many scoundrels used to come to me[50]
But now no one has as many enemies as I!

When I think about it, I can only say, "what a terrible mess!'
To what can I be compared?
A worthless, watery rice-paste painting!
Lālśaśī says, "there's nothing but greed in all this buying and selling!"
(BG 377, a.1)

33

I want no more of the wage-book, brother!
When the night turns to dawn, I break my back in the Bazaar,
doing what the Lord can do easily.
I husk and sift out the rice-powder again and again.
I'll go no more to win pride or a name;
for suddenly, my dream is broken, and I go along, nodding in drowsiness.
Brothers, have you returned to engage in business?
When you become a shopkeeper, there's no end of bliss!
Since everyone desires profit and loss,
business goes on with great pomp and splendor.
With this very desire I wander from street to street, searching and searching!
Hoping for profit, I'll engage in business.
I'll make some purchases in that land;
then I'll return to this land, I'll sell it!
When they see that it's cheap, they'll regret the price in the bazaar.
Who will offer me the capital of respect[51] and make me sell it?
Alas, brother, previously I knew no profit or loss—
I couldn't engage in business.
But now, hoping for happiness, I chase after the Head Porter!
If the price of the purchase is neither too little nor too great,
I'll be happy.
Brother, I sit in the shop—
If I see no deception about the weight,
I'll trust in that business, brother.
I've come to this land with many various goods.
I see many things, brother, both little and great.
But Lālśaśī says, "I don't care to engage in all this business!"
(BG 216, a.2; KG 54)

34

Will the Porters' Headman protect you,
when the Moneylender's men come to arrest you for your debts?
Then you'll suffer everything!
What's overdue is recorded in the Money-lender's account book—
Do you think you can deceive them, using the name of the "Company?"

You think you might cancel your debts by means of such a deception—
but who is capable of such a thing?
We've all written our names in the Moneylender's account book—
We became merchants and returned with all our assets—
the wealth of the money lender, together with the profits.
But even in the winning of earnings, there will be utter poverty—
I see that you've lost your profits and suffered everything!
You once had so much capital, which always filled your stomach!
But brother, now the business is over and the Porters have angrily returned.
And now, brother, you're conducting business with what little is left!
Brother, a Porter has no need of assets.
And now the whole sum [of your earnings] is but a few cowry shells!
All you possess are a few dowries and ten old women.[52]
That's why you can get a few coins—
there's more than a little humor in all this, I think!
Now you're working as a Porter with the other Porters;
and now you've fallen into the hands of the Policeman in the Company Warehouse!
I never knew how funny you were!
You break your back for the sake of all this!
You think you'll get the Company Officer to speak [on your behalf];
but you exaggerate your own manliness!
Lālśaśī says, "Your Highness has now discovered the burden of a laborer!"
(BG 217, q.3; KG 55)

The Wiles and Wickedness of the Thieving Brokers

35

Why else would we honor these men as "Brokers"?
For so many Princes and Nobles
are always paying them respect!
Without any power of their own, they quietly increase their wages.
Brother, that's why the Brokers have now attained such great status!
The wise Broker can attain anything, finite or infinite;
they devise the means for whatever comes and goes.
And that's why, without any power of their own, they come and sit as if they were Princes!
In the seven cities of the would-be Merchants, wharf trade goes on.
So the brokers gather together there and make everything corrupt!
Originally, the Brokers did business in this land,
and now, that very business makes the world go round![53]
And everyone is ceaselessly engaged in business, from beginning to end.

When the human-house[54] is covered with four kinds of thatch, what happens in the end?
With fibrous root fastened on his head—his matted hair—he calls it a "roof."
Even if the roof is covered, there is always a way for water to get through the thatch.
The Broker easily comes to such a land and does business.
If the roof is broken, then he comes and promises to save the house,
so that it may be recovered and last perhaps another twelve years.
But now look—that home no longer remains—
and now the beggar gets no alms!
Just as the merchant ships travel on rivers and streams for their business,
and one remains behind—the Owner of the merchandise, who sets everything in order—
so too, many [ships] wander back and forth between the seven cities.
Otherwise, why would even one ever set out upon the water?
The ships continue to come and go and stay;
I see, they stop and go again and again in this way.
Lālśaśī says, "all this goes along flawlessly!" (BG 268, q.2)

36

There's a great deal of thievery going on among these Brokers!
They bring so much of the farmers' goods, I see,
constantly saying, "Oh! Oh!," they go from street to street—
and so many merchants and customers do business!
The Broker comes among them and sets up his flag,
and then he hides away the fine new merchandise and makes an amicable settlement for himself!
Those who were previously respected as "brokers,"
people with common sense now disregard!
And among all those who hang out and gossip within the marketplace,
who slanders or reviles anyone, in the central city or in the bazaar?
But when they get hold of a fool, they turn mean and try to swindle him!
See how much sugar candy and imported things there are!
You see it and are filled with desire—Oh, how much I can tell you!
No one but the Broker knows where these goods are!
Just as, brother, many waves arise at one moment in a single measure of water,
and just as an elephant sees his driver and the driver sees him,
So too, in this land, [the Broker] brings things together.
And then, the driver mounts his elephant, slaps his side and travels down the road.[55]
How many children has a certain merchant in a certain shop of the bazaar?
In which store, where?—the Broker knows all this.
There are some Sea-going Brokers who engage in market brokering.

With a packet from England in their hands, they return here in this Kali
Yuga.
Those who, before, had paid homage to those Brokers,
now follow along in imitation of them, saying "that's Me!"
And Lālśaśī says, "Why must they bring this packet and hand it over to them?"[56]
(BG 269, a.2)

37

Now all at once, throughout the land, city and marketplace,
so many merchant ships,
and as many imported goods are coming!
So great a fleet is coming to the central wharf that it looks as if it's being struck
by a great wave!
And all that I've been wondering and conjecturing about, it seems, is happening
right here and now!
There's no way of counting how many merchants there are in the city;
what they do and how it happens—that's always a mystery!
And then, all at once, all the wretched Brokers get up and go to the market!
When he gets a little money, even the son of a whore become powerful.
To see this is a delight surpassing the feet of Brahma himself!
Some acquire a little wealth and, becoming intoxicated with it, continue to act
miserly;
but that party is interrupted in its journey.
In order to understand all these matters, the Company sat down in a
Committee.[57]
When the harvest is weighed the farmers sell it,
and the businessmen examine and buy it.
Those who hold the scales make their purchases.
They evaluate [the merchandise] and correct the price, saying "okay, that's a good
price."
Look—so much profit on a single item falls into their hands at a single
moment!
The merchants can do whatever they want;
and joyfully, to their hearts desire, they take it from the farmers!
Those who travel to the seven cities doing business
find the wholesale trader and happily take [the merchandise] from his
hands.
The Broker runs along behind, hoping to buy or sell something!
Even if he's not called he comes up behind,
for he knows that he was needed yesterday.
The Merchant and the Buyer both set the price;
and, knowing the price, neither takes anything from the other.
And Lālśaśī says, "let me see! I'm running up to see!" (BG 266, q.1)

38

Everything was overwhelmed with the madness of the Brokers,
and everything became corrupt!
Whenever someone wants to buy something, he asks, "how [good] is it?"[58]
The Brokers say, "it's genuine," but give them the fakes!
I hear that wherever I go, this sort of business goes on.
And while I watched and considered all this, the time passed.
The wretched Brokers have become a terrible nuisance;
and throughout the seven cities, the Shopkeepers sit and consider their fate!
All the merchants engage in business in the Bazaar of this World.
Those who toil in accordance with the law don't have even an ounce [of wealth],
while those who engage in business, holding the surplus of trade,
happily take their profits and make some more purchases.
And when a break [in the trade] occurs, they give the beggar a handful!
Those who hold the scales in the bazaar now weigh [the merchandise].
We can see whether the weight is great or little, in ounces and pounds.
What holds the measures of grain is called the balance;
and there's a long pointed instrument which rests in the hand.
There are two pans on either side, where it's weighed.
The merchant sits evaluating it;
and then the wretched Broker sends it off for shipment.
There's a Merchant sitting, engaged in business in the bazaar.
Buying his shares, his Wholesale Trader travels from country to country;
and all the common folk and the people of the hinterlands are laboring.
The fruit which they yield
the Wholesale Trader carries and presents to [the Merchant], by his command.
And if he doesn't work by the clock, he gets no daily wages.
He receives something, and then he has to run back and take something else.
And Lālśaśī says, "by his misfortune, he now plays the part of a mere farm hand!"
(BG 267, a.1)[59]

The Wondrous Marketplace of the Benevolent King

39

Let me tell you a funny story about a King!
In his city, all along the road are rows and rows of merchants.
In the city-center there's a bazaar,
with the special seal of the Royal House.
Twelve months a year there's buying and selling, importing and exporting,
whether the weight of the tares in the warehouse is little or great.
I came and saw—everywhere there were so many things!

I had never seen such things in this world!
So much was spread out everywhere;
I'm thinking, how can I speak of it?
And if you understand this straightaway,
you can cross the river of the world and this cosmic age![60]
[The king] never takes gifts, taxes or tariffs.
That's why there are so many merchants;
they all revere him.
He waives all the taxes on the waterways;
and everyone constantly pays him the capital of honor.
So listen, listen to what I say:
no one has need for brokerage, commissions or such tactics![61]
The Moon is the assistant;
and Kalki is the Avatār. (BG 54, q.1; KG 1)

40

Will there be any more profit in such a kingdom?
The one who, from time to time, engages in worthless expenditures has so many needs;
he understands nothing, and his work is futile—Oh how funny!
Wherever there is export and import,
how can there be any buying and selling without some bribe?
And for whose sake are the tares in the warehouse being weighed?
In a certain kingdom, a King sat upon a throne.
The people freely engage in business—
there are horripilations of joy at the beautiful sight!
All the people engage in thousands of transactions,
and the business in that realm goes along easily.
If there's exemption from gifts, taxes and tariffs,
how were they prevented?
Say—that indeed was [by means of] Love!
The tax upon the waterways was waived;
so I'll go and dwell in that land!
There is no brokerage or commission;
for all that ostentatious show is false!
Look: Śaśī appears amidst the company of merchants![62] (BG 54; KG 1)

The Primal Void and the Creation of the Marketplace of the World

41

The primal Void has suddenly been filled—[63]
The customers gather together, hearing the names of so many new things.

Everyone, great or small, engages in cash business.
There's a confusion of vehicles on so many streets!
Everyone—young and old, men and women—goes to the warehouse;
and look, brother, upon this warehouse, the flag pole has been erected.
The boat was drowned in the flood,
while the flood remained imprisoned within the Void.
The fruit of *rasa* was born within the heavens,
and *rasa* became violently agitated with waves of that *rasa.*
Upon the crest of the waters rest a pair of Warehouses.
The people engage in business within those warehouses.
Listen to what I say [about that merchandise], item by item—
there are six kinds of carriages,
six kinds of animals and beasts,
five kinds of birds,
two kinds of mirrors and spectacles,
and five kinds of fruit,
brother, some five kinds of sweet fragrance,
and five kinds of invaluable diamonds.
Shall I tell you the nature of those precious stones?
And there are five kinds each of mechanical devices, toys, cooking implements, and medicines.
First, a label is placed on all these things;
then they match them up, suit by suit, with the names of the warehouse owners.
All the merchants go the warehouse clerk;
haggling over the price, they spend their time in business.
Then the Broker grabs his wholesale dealer,
and the buyers[64] engage in business.
Lālśaśī says, "they follow along, bearing so many goods!" (BG 127; KG 81)

The Secret Caitanya and the Simple Path for the Poor

42

In the form of Caitanya he awakened the world![65]
Having placed His image in the home of every devotee, where did He then go and hide himself?
How could He remain in secrecy?
Was it not for good reason that He awakened the three worlds?
So why would He now engage in deception?
Now we know that His actions are always difficult to comprehend!
Look—we're all listening with constant attention
to hear of the amazing lives of Advaita, Caitanya and Nityānanda,
together with their devotees and companions.
Filled with nectar, He made them all taste the *rasa* of devotion;

and, with Hari's name, He caused the feeling of devotion to arise in all the living beings of this world.

Look—one Lord, two Lords, three Lords speak to the world, together with innumerable devotees.

The author [Kṛṣṇadāsa Kavirāja] wrote the story and maddened everyone with the ecstasy of the Lord!

It became the book, the *Caitanya Caritāmṛta,* whose events bring forth the dawn of ecstasy.[66]

But now that Man remains hidden in this lifetime.
Will we get to see him,
if all we simply remain waiting, stony-hearted?

Without distinguishing between little and great,
brother, He distributed the Name of Hari to the whole world.
There were so many wicked people throughout the three worlds;
but now, with the great *mantra*, the Name of Hari, he gave them peace.
Look—the ocean of the love of Caitanya surges up.
A wave washes over everything, whether dry land or sea!
Oh, did he come and engage in his business simply to create a deception?
Lālśaśī says, "filled with hope, I wonder day and night." (BG 420, q.l; KG 58)

43

If one is not "fortunate"[67] he can't get to see [the Lord].
But then, what means is there for the poor and lowly people to be saved?
Who will show the poor the way?
Whoever says "Hari Bol" is of one and the same kind.
So how can one distinguish between good and bad?
Brother, if one [makes such distinctions], who could call him compassionate to the people of the three worlds?

Say, from beginning to end, Gour Rāy engages in that play.
"Only some fortunate men get to see him"—
for a long time, I've heard such things being said.
But if that's the case, then it's very difficult to understand:
how can anyone who cries out "Hey Gour!" for his very life believe such things?

But so many of those "fortunate" men forgot all these things!
So in the forms of Gour, Natāi and Advaita, they mingled with the poor.
They didn't give refuge to those "fortunate" men.
Instead, upon seeing all the poor and lowly men, they revealed themselves to them.
Look—their companions are Jagāi and Mādhāi;
Gour and Nitāi revealed themselves to them
Assuming the very life of these poor men, Gour and Nitāi came to this earth!

Look—to me, you are equal to a "fortunate" man.
No one ever goes to someone
who has little knowledge of the supreme truth.

Gour, Nitāi and Advaita are the three compassionate lords.
With the embrace of love, they rescued the lowly and poor
Gour and Nitāi are the saviors of the poor.
So, having seen the poor and wretched folk, will they remain hidden now?
Brother, you'll cause all men to dwell in peace, upon hearing your words.
Lālśaśī says, "at your words, you'll make them all dwell in peace!"
(BG 421, q.2; KG 58)

The Hidden City and the Bazaar of the World

44

I went alone to the Hidden City [the city of Dhaka], brother.
The Magistrate saw me, and gave the command, "Go to the Bazaar of the World!"
I've come here at his command.
There were two men who went with me,[68]
they waited and then returned after an appointed time,
and informed him of what they had seen and heard.
Brother, I had to travel far from the place where I had been before.
Gradually I became very thin,
and as the days passed, my state fell into ruin.
And the two who had come with me returned again and lifted me up into the Void.[69]
Now I have returned here, and what funny things I see!
Look—a King sits upon a throne in this kingdom, and makes the path straight.
This king is a very formidable, powerful Magistrate.
He's made the pathways into roads, widely dispersed.[70]
And if, as you go along the road, you stop and wait,
no one asks you, "brother where have you come from?"
Brother, why don't you look and write down whatever happens, whether on dry land or sea?
Whatever I carefully observed on both sides of the road,
brother, I came with pen in hand to the Bazaar of the World [to record].
Gradually I saw with my own eyes,
people were dwelling, in 8 million forms,
countless people on all sides—
and that can't be described with any pen!
And Śaśī says, "what splendor there is upon the waters!" (BG 130, q.1; KG 35)

45

No one can remain in the Hidden City.
As soon as one goes there, the Magistrate gives the command, "go to the Bazaar

of the World!"
Then and there one must return.
But now I've made up my to stay there.
I keep accounts of so many people, coming and going and staying.
But now I will make a petition against that command.
Brother, just as there's pulp inside a fruit,
and within the pulp there's a stone;
and inside of that there's a seed,
so too, there's a seed within this world.
Look, brother, the City remains hidden within it;
and there, each and every thing is arranged in due order.
Look—he raises his hand and sends everyone to that place;
The punishment is written upon this defendant's forehead[71]
Seeing this, my heart bursts!
Oh, once I was there for six months.[72]
I asked about this place and got a hint of it.
I had heard that just as it is there,
so too, it was considered to be here.
But now I can see that one has to touch it in order to speak about it.
He who comes [to this world] to repay his father's or his own debts,
never becomes entangled in difficulties;
he lives effortlessly.
Look—he who can resolve his debts
has no expenses at all, brother.
But if one doesn't grasp the essential truth and goes to engage in business,
he'll drown endlessly in debt and costs.
And Śaśī says, "pay close attention to this song!" (BG 131, q.2; KG 36)

46

Indeed, no one can remain in the Hidden City—
so tell me, how is it that you were there?
Brother, explain this to me.
There are so many people in this land.
Here, all coming and going is regulated;
and everyone is talking about this in the marketplace!
I brought a fruit and split it open, and there I saw
that there was proof of what you said, brother.
The Bazaar of the World is a very funny place!
Everyone dwells within it—
though some are in the Hidden City, some on the dry land, and some in the deep waters.
With your pen in hand, brother, you remain observing
the people with their dwelling places in the Bazaar of the World.

Brother, in eight million forms,
throughout the city, the people engage in business.
Brother, no one can remain there.
You say, "I was there for six months."
But how can one believe such words?
For so much accounting goes on in just a few hours!
Brother you dwelt in that land for six months.
So why have you now come to India?
That's why I'm asking you, brother.
Brother, the people of this land are forbidden to dwell there;
so tell me, how could you remain there?
You're very powerful, aren't you?
Therefore, brother, we'll all offer obeisance to you!
And Śaśī says, "now that you've returned, what do have to you say about it?"
(BG 132, a.2; KG 37)

47

That's why I remained within the Hidden City—
I saw the Magistrate [*Hākim*] and haggled with his clerks!
For otherwise, no one can remain there.
He let me dwell within a wonderful palace,
which the people of this land call Heaven!
And in this land, a precious stone sparkles!
Look—when I first went there,
The Magistrate looked me over from head to foot.
The Lord became thoughtful;
In Chitragupta's[73] account book there was no trace of my name.
Then, brother, he looked at my face for some time.
Just look at the highest, lowest and middlemost beings in all three worlds—
Seeing the fruits of their deeds upon the field of action,
Chitragupta writes them all down, brother.
Brother, for the best [he gives] the best; and the for the worst, the worst—
all this is written down.
Yet two people beyond all accounting.
But no one can call upon them, whether in the Hidden City, or on land or sea.
Look: to the Most Supreme Souls, the feet of Brahma are insignificant because of their infinite greatness
who can find their limit?
They have ceased all wandering and desire
They are devoted to the nectar of Hari's name.
In ceaseless Kīrtan,
they float in the *rasa* of love with a blissful heart!
and no one can ever impede them.

Who knows the essence of the Most Vile of the Vile?[74]
You can't find it in the Śāstras or the lawbooks
or in the holy Koran.
Just look—I'm so very crazy and contemptible!
For I pay homage to the Most Vile of the Vile!
Look and consider this, all of you, brothers!
The Most Vile of the Vile is a wretched scoundrel!
For six months, that thorn had left me—
but now that trouble sticks me again!
He haggles with the Magistrate himself!
He has come here with me,
having entangled me as if within a spider's web.
See how long I've been wrapped up within it!
And Śaśī says, "He lies within the lotus of the Heart itself!" (BG 133, q.3; KG 38)

48

Brother, I see the Bazaar of the World is a very funny place!
Again and again, everyone comes and goes because of his own selfish interest.
There's nothing like these people!
Even when they feel terrible suffering,
they forget that suffering and feel happy.
And yet I too wish to come very often to this land!
People come and go from here to there, again and again.
Have they come, like me, to engage in worldly affairs?
One must remember that he'll have to return again.
But everyone is drowned in bliss,
for day and night, the Lord is contemplated.
Just see all their various activities, from beginning to end, again and again!
[In past ages], people used to come to this world for 10,000 years;
but now, at most, 120 years have been appointed as law.[75]
And brother, this law can never be violated.
Everyone sees these trifling pleasures and misfortunes;
yet the people are engaged in auspicious deeds,
and everyone's trying to secure a good life in the afterworld!
As I watch these funny things, I'm amazed!
Some have come to be Emperors;
some have come with a begging bowl in hand;
some, while begging, attain the Emperor's throne;
and some abandon the Emperor's life altogether and become fakirs!
This is the will of the infinite God—
whenever and whatever He does: I consent to that.
And Lālśaśī says, "I'm writing down everything that's happening!"
(BG 134, a.3; KG 39)

49

Brother, see what splendor lies within the Hidden City!
You say that in that place there lies a radiant Jewel[76]—
what is that Jewel? Tell me exactly!
There are many gems within the earth;
but I've never seen such a Jewel, brother!
As soon as the people hear about this they'll all gossip, whether in the City or in the hinterlands!
Brother, I want to hear your explanation;
so I'm constantly asking about this matter.
Brother, you tell such tales!
It's like a dream—so I want to hear it again!
Make it known in detail throughout this land!
Where was that resplendent Jewel created?
On what estate was it produced?
Or was it revealed in the heavens?
Brother, how far away did it appear?
Just like the movement of the sun and moon,
is its coming and going infinite,
or does it have some limit within that very estate?
Brother, was its origin on land or sea?
Tell me what kind of Jewel it is and how much it weighs,
and how many qualities are present in that gem.
Brother, I wish to hear now!
Look, there are four colors: white, red, blue, yellow;
Tell me brother, among these four, what is its color?
Is it subtle or gross in appearance?
Tell me everything brother, clearly and directly.
And Lālśaśī laughs and says, "if you ask, I'll have to tell you in another song!"
(BG 138, q.6; KG 39)

50

Brother, the splendor of that Gem does not lie in its color.[77]
The color arising from that Gem is itself its own manifest radiance.
What more can I tell you about it, brother?
Within it lies the Hidden City.
Apart from the debtors, nobody grumbles in that land!
And the sun and moon, in both form and essence, dawn throughout the three worlds.
Brother, the fruit is the manifestation of the seed—and so it is with this Gem.
(I spoke of this before in the previous song).
The City lies within the Jewel—

that's why the splendor in that land is unending!
And these three worlds constantly manifest its outward brilliance!
Brother, how can I explain just what is the color of this gem,
or what lies within its luster?
Try to grasp what I tell you.
Look—the Jeweler is the Origin of the three worlds, together with all the oceans.
And oh, how many qualities he has created with the brilliance of this Gem!
The people dwelling in the ten directions
examine its form and nature, one by one.
Brother, how can I say whether it is subtle or gross?—it's wholly flawless!
Brother, it's plain to the eye that there are four classes:
Brāhmaṇ Kṣatriya, Vaiśya and Śūdra.
Brother, look and consider—
so many beings exist in heaven, earth and hell!
And form, taste, smell, sound, and touch are all bound up in all that.
Brother, look and consider—
all things are separated into these four classes;
and, multiplied by the nine kinds of castes, there are thus thirty-six classes in this world.
Its weight is neither little nor great.
It is easily obtained; for what one experiences, with intense emotion, together with his lover,[78]
is itself the weight of this Gem!
Together with the buyer, they determine whether it's imitation [or genuine];
and from its diameter, its price is decided.
That Jewel pervades all ten directions,
both the inner and the outer, both conventional worldly life and the Hidden City.
"At His command, the land floats in *rasa*!"
says Śaśī Lāl, laughing! (BG 139, a.6; KG 40)

The Bazaar of Love and the Factory of Bliss

51

In the business of the Bazaar of Love,
one becomes entangled and falls, struck by the arrows of Kāma![79]
The God of Love[80] returns sluggishly to the port;
he sells the imitation goods and returns the genuine ones!
Alas, is everything false?
What is, is not; and what isn't is!
Oh, how can one endure this life?
But hope, authority and faith finally emerged.
For, if one could feel the touch of the *rasa* of Love,

the glory of the three worlds would be filled with the sweet aroma,
maddened by the experience of ecstasy!
Did that incomparable pure *rasa* remain far off?
The command was to move progressively through that Illusion.[81]
In this life, no one can penetrate the secret which is his own end.[82]
If one does not know how to give, how can he possibly receive?
By what qualities, by whom, can that treasure by attained?
Only by one who possesses the vessel of divine emotion.
Apart from divine emotion, how can one overpower him [Kāma]?
The nature of that *rasa* is attained by holy men,
[just as] the heart of darkness is destroyed by the passage of the Moon.
(BG 41, q.1)

52

There's a factory in the Bazaar of Love.
Is there any fear in that? There's no need for a rice-paste decoration on the floor.[83]
One can know that a seed is genuine,
for Truth only arises from what is true.
Sexual union[84] is of one kind, without division;
but some lovers are lustful and some are free of lust.
Wherever desire manifests a trace of Love,
therein lies the fullness of hope and the essence of faith.
Is there any lack in its glory or sweet aroma?
This ecstasy is both possible and true.
This ecstasy is an unfathomable ocean; and Kandarpa is but a tiny particle of it.
The Immutable Destroyer of Doubt [Kṛṣṇa-Caitanya-Āulcāṅd] consists of Love.
His chief characteristic is sexual union, which is the pleasure of living beings.
That [union] is itself the cause of birth, labor and action, in succession.
Its essence is itself the Dharma—there is no error in that.
For both [male and female], there is the *rasa* of devotional love.
It is the vessel of faith.
In even a small trace of *rasa*, one can recognize the very essence of *rasa*,
[just as], dwelling in the heavens, the Moonlight appears each month.
(BG 41, a.1)

53

What is the essence of Love?
What is its true name, and where is its dwelling place? That's what I'm asking.

What is its tendency, appearance, nature, and path?
Such a request is always denied!
Is it only a word or a feeling? There is no enmity within it; its only aim is joy!
I'm always wondering in this way—
what's the nature of Love, *rasa,* and the *Rasika*?
Brother, you are experienced in that ecstasy;
that's why I'm asking you.
I will achieve the quest; I have come to learn that knowledge.
I don't know its flavor—perhaps it's like fruit?
It is without body—so what are its qualities? Brother, where is its likeness?
I'm unfamiliar with these teachings;
but you always know in detail.
Oh holy man, open your heart and teach me:
In what flower does that nectar lie?
Calling to your Moon-face, "speak! so that I may understand,"
with such sorrow! The passage of the Moon is found in the night.
(BG 43, q.3)

54

The essence of Love consists of nectar.
The supreme nectar is the body which is free of lust.
Surely, this law is the true refuge.
The triple world is the gross physical means;
and [Love] is everything, all fruit and roots.
Its state is naturally fulfilled
when one is devoted in spiritual practice.
There is Love, *rasa,* and the *Rasika.*
The willing disciple knows that arousal [of divine emotion]
to which he is always devoted.
He is devoid of perversions.
The supreme meaning of the word becomes manifest.
A trace of the news of *rasa* is always known.
The extract is the vessel of *rasa.*
In the taste of that lies peace.
He who hopes to touch it will see it, brother.
The eternal body—who and where is it?
One can see but a shadow of it.
O holy man, with the experience of ecstasy,
that nectar flows within the lotus of the heart.
With the movement of the Seed,[85]
one's desires are eternally fulfilled.
With the dawn of the moon, the body becomes like an ocean of *rasa.*
(BG 43, a.3)

55

Will that *Rasika*[86] return again to this land?
He created thousands and thousands of cities, rivers, seas and dry land;
and, in the twinkle of an eye, he drowns them all in the *rasa* of Love!
When they said "He's coming!" we all remained seated.
Now everyone's saying, "He'll come, He'll come again!"
But brother, I can't say just when He'll come or what He'll say.
Look—all the Shopkeepers in the Bazaar of *rasa* wait in the hope of this!
There are seven oceans surrounding this earth with its seven islands;
and amidst these seven oceans, a Gallant Lover[87] appeared upon a lotus.
Then and there, His every whim was easily realized!
Once He came to dwell for some time in the Kingdom of Gour.[88]
Laughing and laughing, with his golden Moon-Face, He made us all cry for the joy in our hearts!
Look, there are so many gods—Indra, Candra, Vāyu, Varuṇa, etc.,
and so many living beings within this world!
But when one sees [Kṛṣṇa's] form, he's driven mad!
The woman of good family goes to the ocean of lust, filled with desire.
She feels lust as many times as there are clumps of lotuses;
and, as a result of lust, she goes from birth to birth.
A thousand petalled lotus floats upon the immeasurable waters.
But only if one becomes a person of the *Sahaja bhāva*[89] can he grasp a hint of it!
Brother, when that *Rasika* opens up the Red Merchant Ship,
I'll return and make my dwelling in this land.
That's why He went there at that time, they say,
when merchant trade flourished in this land.
All the people went there by the demand of His authority.
Oh, how many Emperors, Councilors, Nobles, and Princes there are!
Saying, "His ship will come!" they all went to the shore of this ocean.
Brother, I'm listening to the news, but I don't know what will finally happen!
Lālśaśī says, "I'm listening to the news, but I don't know what will happen!"
(BG 246)

56

Say, brother, will He come again to drown us all?
The empty watercourse is filled with the juices of Love; it's no longer empty.
In the name of this *Rasika*, all things are given to this land!
Once He came to this land and saw the sufferings of the people
How shall I speak of it? He immersed and drowned this land in the juices of Love!
Within this ocean, some swim and some drown, gasping for breath!
Once this *Rasika* came to the red city of Gour.

He made the people weep and freely revealed the face of the Moon.
Brother, at that, the people of this land were in no way offended.
Look—the desires of all men's hearts have been fulfilled.
So many Poor Men have become rich!
And to this day, I still hear about this.

Those who engage in business within the Bazaar of the *rasa* of Love
take the Government Merchandise to the warehouse owners again and again.
Some put the goods into boxes and determine the weight,
and some go to the market and joyfully engage in business!
Twelve months a year they deal in imported and exported goods,
but no one wants to bother with those who don't have any goods.
And whatever they get, they always keep carefully inside their houses.

The Bazaar is filled with so many kinds of things!
If there were any lack in this land,
He would return once again.
He's made everyone full of delight and free of poverty!
Brother, our path is no different from that.
It's not easy to describe His coming and going or his debts and profits.
Who knows Him, whose nature is beyond desire?
I've seen and heard everything and become peaceful; I've ceased this mania of
desire.
Lālśaśī, says, "I'm at peace, having ceased all this mania of desire." (BG 247, a.1)

Songs of Mystical Faith and Esoteric Practice

The following collection of songs deals with the more practical side of the Kartābhajā path: its attitude toward caste, gender, and social hierarchy, as well as the more intimate details of yogic practice and bodily techniques. Like the earlier Sahajiyā schools, the Kartābhajās reject caste distinctions and Brahminical orthodoxy, praising instead the central role of the human body as supreme vehicle to religious ecstasy or spiritual liberation. As a "Religion of Man," the Kartābhajā path is said to be beyond all the sacred texts of the Vedas, Upaniṣads, and Śāstras, and is open to all human beings, regardless of class or sect. It is the *Sahaja* path—the simple, spontaneous, natural path to realizing the mysterious figure of the *Sahaja* Man—the indwelling divinity or true self concealed within every heart. Some of the most beautiful of these songs also employ the haunting image of the "Man of the Heart," a figure later made famous in songs of the Bāuls, to refer to that most elusive but also most intimate presence of the divinity that lies hidden within every human body (II.77–80).

A small body of songs also deal with more concrete Tantric practices, such as Kuṇḍalinī yoga and semen retention (II.74–76). However, these bodily techniques tend to be recast in the unique imagery of the Kartābhajās—such as mercantile trade and sailing merchant ships over the rivers of the human body, to reach the hidden dwelling place of the *Sahaja* Man within the heart. Journeying through the body to find the secret place of the heart thus becomes the treacherous voyage of the merchant ships in search of the secret place of the "Great Wealthy Man," who lies seated on the inner throne of the heart.

The Religion of Man: The Rejection of Caste and the Divinity of the Human Body

57

There is no division between human beings;
so brother, why is there sorrow in this land?
Look and understand: in *Sahaja*, in their own Self nature,
the infinite forms in every land,
all the activities of human beings,
the expanse of all events—all things dwell [in this very *Sahaja*].
Good and bad desires
are equally erroneous, and go astray from the lawful path.
Every human heart is rich.
It is not possible in separate forms;
for it is eternally conceived within every man and woman.
Be judicious with regard to your particular needs:
your kinsmen, motives, wealth and earnings.
The fruit of a compassionate and generous King,
in the past, present and future,
at all times, is manifested in faith,
known to every person.
Everyone seeks this sure refuge;
and the Cakora bird[90] seeks the nectar of the rising Moon! (BG 32, q.1)

58

It can only be attained beyond duality;
for in difference, there is always suffering.
Just look—[people are] distinguished in infinite ways:
this one is a merchant of the world;
that one is a dancing beggar.
Each one acts in a particular way, according to the customs of his land.
In this world, there is always truth and falsehood.
But the Supreme Body is seen and speaks clearly;
it is pure and filled with nectar—
otherwise, perhaps, it becomes filled with poison.
Just look—that Reality in fact lies within every man and woman!

There is need for both wealth and earnings.
Wicked men are not the vessel [of faith]; nourish your own kinsman.
The fruit of the kind and compassionate King is this:
to the good go good rewards, in due time and due measure.
Look—it is revealed in a hint,[91]
to every human being, to every eye.
The true law for Humanity is to take refuge in Truth.
The sun is manifest in the day, and the moon at night . (BG 32, a.1)

59

All things and all events
lie within the microcosm of the human body;
Whatever is or will be lies within the Self-Nature.
All your false hopes in the enjoyment of this dramatic performance [of the illusory world]
are finally broken and destroyed!
The five elements are dissolved and mingled with the earth.
[Just consider] the whole expanse of all things, all forms, all types—
which belongs to me?
and to whom do I belong?
Both these ideas are equally useless.
From beginning to end, where does [the divine Reality] arise?
Can you express it as it truly is?
Arising, cessation, existence and destruction—
how can one have faith in all these forms and paths?
At every moment there is fear in your heart, so beware!
What faith, knowledge or certainty lies in that?
The means is entirely [*supādi*].[92]
It's beyond grasping—so how can you pretend to be attached to it?
For when the night is gone, the Moon no longer continues.
(BG 33, a.2)

60

There are so many views in the Tantras and Vedānta,
and as many in the *Āgamas* and *Nigamas*—[93]
they are all delusions, and whoever abandons them will experience peace!
Without any religious practice, worship or remembrance,
how will you conquer death?
For, in the assuming of this life, there is only death.
If you would be saved from the prison of this world,
engage in pure practices and steadfast worship;
speak just words with a pious mind.

But this had never been written down.
Do not travel on the conventional path, filled with illusion.
Look—there are so many things and events in this universe;
but it's all only vast perversion and darkness!
Abandon false words and take refuge in the waters of Truth.
Premature words are never true, brother.
Seeing and hearing this was not easy;
and even when it is known and experienced, is it well understood?
But now, knowing this, let us go forth with a pure mind.
For the Moon gradually rises in the night. (BG 35, a.4)

61

Oh! what a factory of *rasa* there is in this land!
Just as there is creation and subsistence, there are two forms of love: spiritual love and secret or illicit love.[94]
O look, why don't you look and see?
What wonderful things are happening everywhere!
In this land no one is a stranger to anyone;
and look, in this land, 8 million districts are united!
See all the subjects dwelling under the Emperor and the Minister;
in this world, everyone's filled with bliss!
They appear to be high or low class men,
but this is only an illusion—they're all equal.
Whether Hindu or non-Hindu, they all worship God.
He who has good or bad reputation in the three worlds,
in this land, brother, receives no special treatment.
Look: united in Love, all these animals, birds, men, and living beings,
are overwhelmed with the Ecstasy of Love!
Speaking through hints and symbols, you sit freely with your heart filled with joy.
And day and night, at every moment, [you'll attain] your heart's desire!
Brother, why don't you consider the "fruit" of this world:
time and again, Nārāyaṇa himself comes here for this purpose.[95]
You know the story of this existing three-fold world:
from age to age, [living beings] with so many desires, suffering pleasure and pain,
are always drunken with bliss!
Just look—His Friends and Devotees are never deprived of that.
And to all men, the virtues of Man
are proclaimed in every land!
Look, brother—because of desire for the Will of God, there was great profit.
And gradually, whatever the Vaiṣṇava ascetics[96] did
everyone accepted.
But if this palace falls into suffering or crucial danger,
or whenever falsehood and bitterness occur,

—look and see—even then there is no sorrow!
The king, subjects, guests and travelers are all filled with delight!
For Śaśī, the Cakora and the Gallant Lover appear in every land! (BG 93, q.1)

62

You must understand its Essence:
no one becomes a Guru
and no one becomes a disciple.
Remain steadfast on the beautiful path of Truth.
It is not found in knowledge or ignorance.
It is the task neither of the illicit lover nor of the chaste wife;
the work of the Sahaja land is of a completely different sort.
The Essence is found neither by pure nor impure practices, neither by sense-perception nor by rational discrimination.
Brother, the name of Man's abode is the "Place of Bliss."
The kingdom free of lust lies on the shore of the incomparable ocean.
He who considers distinctions between human beings
will never complete his search for this Kingdom.
Brother, abandon [distinctions between] "you" and "I" and worship!
But who am I?—I am within all created beings!
Look—that from which all things arise is the Essence of all essences.
Just as fire arises from the flint;
so in the same way, the Avatār [arises from] God,
and so too, the son [arises from] the father.
Follow that very path which is in accord with the will of God.
The true disciple obeys His command well, while the atheist ignores it.
If you consider only the parts, you yourself are but a part, and your own *dharma* is useless.
Look—living beings, God and animals, etc, have all been born in one Body!
Just see: there are thirty-six castes and four social classes; but He accepts none of them.
Among all the castes, what caste is He? He bears the seal of Man.
By his command, one becomes free of lust and abandons selfish desire.
They become His; they perform His worship; they are devoted to Him.
Analyzing the Upaniṣads is a delusion.
The most wicked dwell in the land of the wicked,
and the lowly in the foreign lands, each according to his own nature.
At His command, creation occurred on a Friday;
on that day everyone becomes present.[97]
In whichever land they live, wherever their home may be,
from every land, all the people become present.
and then after twenty-four hours, each returns to his own proper place.

Brother, with a benediction for three hours on Friday night,
whatever one's heart desires will be fulfilled.
Everyone is bound by this law:
at the command of the Master,
multitudes and multitudes [become devoted] to God. (BG 115, q.2)

In Search of the Sahaja Man

63

Why is there joy in this land?
Just what is the reason?
Both good and bad people become the vessels [of joy].
The law is always celebrated with joy,
[by] both men and women!
Do I see that what is impossible now is possible?
By what power, or by what emotion, is everyone so happy?
The highest and the lowest, the equal and the unequal,
[have] constant zeal [for] the essential Truth.
How is one initiated into the mood of devotion?
In a twinkle of an eye, it is revealed in a hint!
Everyone's talking about it.
All creatures bearing life are blessed,
with a happy face and an enlightened mind.
What will be the result?
Tell everyone, Oh pure Śaśī-Bhūṣaṇ! (BG 47, q.1)

64

This land has been submerged in *rasa*;
the *Sahaja* Man is coming!
The highest and the lowest are overwhelmed with love—
thousands of devotees, with their minds in bliss,
as the Moon touches the water.
What an auspicious day for all living things!
In all these worlds, the people are awakened,
delighted by the Name, thrilled with love.
The Essence became an individual.[98]
There are seven oceans, rivers, and streams.
In due course—know this for your own sake—
they drown the world in *Sahaja,*
in the thick, deep nectar,

in the great, unobstructed current,
with a bottomless bottom.
It becomes a floodwater, and the pure Moon arises. (BG 47)

65

It has submerged this Kingdom—
so why do you call it *Sahaja*?
To the highest and the lowest, with one and the same emotion,
you reveal this and delight them.
What is this *Sahaja*?
How does one know and taste it?
That which is the cause of the three worlds
gives blessing and knowledge to living beings,
who are devoted to the Name,
loved by that Love.
What has been appointed for this land?
The current of seven oceans, rivers, and streams
come together and issue in a pond,
which is always manifest.
He who spreads wide his vessel,
will have a wide and deep measure of water.
The bottomless lake, and the river with a bottom
are both gathered into the Moon. (BG 47, q.2)

66

Look and understood aright—
the devotee is bound to *Sahaja*.
The highest and lowest, in succession,
the whole range of the three worlds—
we are all delighted,
appointed for one purpose.
All the living beings of the three worlds,
all sentient things, make the utmost effort, for their very lives.
In this land, in a special way,
the three worlds are united in a single community!
The seven quick streams of the rivers and streams
come together and issue in a lake.
Is there any division in that heart which is bottomless?
He who is honored for his uncommon qualities,
his actions are free of duality.
Both hearts[99] become free of division.
Thus said Śaśī the *Rasika*. (BG 47, a.2)

67

Of what caste is *Sahaja*?
In what country does it dwell?
What is its appearance?
Do you know the special characteristics of its nature or its path?
Why does it come,
and why does it go again or stay?
What wonderful good news!
Shall I tell you what form that divine emotion has,
what is its conduct,
what is its behavior,
and with whom is its love?
And in what family was it born?
Tell me, tell me, O tell me again.
what good person brought it?
To whom does it belong, or who belongs to it?
With whom is its conduct or business?
Why did the Foreign Man[100] come to this country?
Poor Śaśī is unworthy. (BG 48, q.3)

68

Sahaja is of the human caste.
It dwells in the *Sahaja* country.
Know, in a hint, what its nature is.
Public exposure is impossible, but a taste of it possible;
its origin lies within the body itself!
It is unrestricted by good or evil;
so what use will known laws be?
It is without refuge in any religious views.
When you hear this, what happens?
Surely, it is [like] iron [transformed by] the Touchstone![101]
Intense sexual love[102] arises between a man and a woman;
so look and understand—
in *Sahaja*, he is the husband of the chaste wife.
The accomplished disciple and his consort in practice[103]
are united without division, like a limb to a body.
Hear this law: "Man is supreme."
And the quest lies within Śaśī's own *rasa*. (BG 48, a.3)

69

Just look—when that *Sahaja* Man comes here,
if anyone reviles Him, He embraces them!

If anyone offends Him, He simply speaks and laughs!
Come on brother, let's go bring Him here, who wears the garb of a Poor Man,
as if He had no wealth or self interest or power in hand!
Who can forbid Him from begging for alms?
Let's go with great effort, bow to his feet, and bring Him to this land!
I can hear with my own ears these inexpressible words;
upon the shore of the Ocean of Desire, it is forbidden to feel lust.
Brother, He dwelt in this land for a few days;
and by his grace, all doubts were dispelled.
Now I can see that He dwells within the lotus of the Heart, the fountain of nectar.
He who can grasp Him in His Self-Nature will attain His ultimate state.
For He'll even rescue an enemy, filled with animosity, from the Ocean of the world!
To Him, indeed, friend and enemy, good and bad, are both the same!
Everyone respects the course of action which He follows.
If one calls Him "evil," He calls him "extremely good."
In that way, let us walk upon the path of Truth.
If one speaks truth in this land, He will reveal the path,
and in an instant, the darkness will be dispelled.
If anyone offers Him jewels, long life and such things,
when he sees it, He runs away, holding his head!
If one counts up the merits and demerits, one will find that He has so many virtues!
Whatever one desires, he attains—whoever, wherever!
Each is given what is fitting and carries it off upon his head.
He from whom the godhead, all substance and all self-interest arise,
is Himself our blissful Friend—what doubt is there about that?
Lālśaśī says, "at the arrival of this *Rasika*, you'll float in *rasa*!" (BG 272, q.1)

70

You can't know [the *Sahaja* Man] simply by sitting in the house of the mind.
Everyone has taken his seat and gathered in the assembly.
I can see Him, and what I've seen I'll reveal to you; I'll tell you His whereabouts.
You can't easily see the *Sahaja* Man, can you?
Those who remain in mere knowledge can't know the *Sahaja* Man.
Deluded by doubt, they drown in the ocean.
Some come, some stay, some get up to come and go again.
When one sees how everything [truly] is, and reflects for a moment,
then why and for whose sake would he wander from country to country?
How can those who are always joined in the bliss of devotion
consider any differences between anyone?
Why don't you gaze upon them, with a pure mind and half-closed eyes?

Look—those who fled from evil company, floating upon the waves of love,
raised their flag, became Mahārājās and lived in pleasure and luxury!
And to those who wear rags, gather in monasteries and dress as poor men,
that *Sahaja* Man is revealed upon the lotus of their hearts!
Even if one drives Him away, when one calls upon Him, He is near.
He will reveal the supreme sublimity!
Sitting and gazing upon the Sahaja-essence, you'll dispel all the sufferings of
birth!
Those who regard themselves as mere base earth,
are considered the most genuine men amidst the three worlds;
and those who, at the end of he day, reflect upon their own faults
are the most accomplished disciples, adepts, holy men, and divine beings.[104]
Those who don't analyze questions of material substance or the nature of God,
within their house lies both the expressible and the inexpressible Meaning.
Lālśaśī says, "at His command, they raise the flag of joy!" (BG 273, a.1)

71

Shall I have to repeat this crazy[105] news incessantly, again and again?
The ignorant helmsman with a broken ship can't cross [this ocean]at a leisurely
pace!
After four months,[106] you came and asked me, brother:
whoever wishes, because of some need, to cross over upon this ship,
will easily cross the ocean of this world, with great honor!
Does such a man return eagerly with his boat and make a claim to fame?
At the end of the season you asked about this—
I told you a little of what it was proper to reveal openly.
When you asked, you got an answer and heard the news.
So brother say, why do I find you asking again?
What other stories do I know?—I've only heard some folk tales.
I'll tell what I know about the Primordial Mother of all things.
Cross over and travel to that land—there you'll get to see everything.
The son of a grandfather is born as the "father."
So you ask, who am I? I myself am the Grandfather of that very Mother [of all
things]!
And the descendants of my Sons are now ruling as Emperors!
My sons, knowing this, plunged me into the ocean;[107]
and now, unfastening the bolt, I sit up and sail forth upon a strong wind!
Just see the Primordial Ocean, at the limit of the seven seas.
Beneath it, the *Sahaja* Man has come and built an Office.
He has raised the flag, inlaid with so much gold lace.
When I think of it, my mind is dumbfounded; how can I describe it?
This, brothers and friends, is the ocean of *rasa*, the City of Eternal Bliss!
At His command, he plants the sapling of the *rasa* of Love in this land.

Two thousand eyes gaze upon it; in all directions, they cry out, "Alas!"
Lālśaśī sees that one thousand mouths in all directions cry out, "Alas!"
(BG 307, a.1)

72

No one can know that *Sahaja* Man!
But if one passes beyond this world, in the twinkle of an eye, he'll reach the *Sahaja* land.
One can easily see the business going on there,
and what one sees, he now desires.
The *Sahaja* Man has gone and built his Office[108] in this Land,
with all forms, millions upon millions.
Having arrived there and seen a trace of it, no one would return without good reason.
You heard the news of a Rich Man from someone or other;
that's why now, at every moment, your heart longs to see Him.
That *Sahaja* Man easily comes to this *Sahaja* land and engages in business;
and it's your wish to dwell in this very land of *Sahaja*.
So I'll ferry you across and tell you its whereabouts.
Since the time when God came and fashioned creation, subsistence and destruction,
until now, God the creator is also the mover of the ocean of the world,
which consists of heaven, earth, hell and the fourteen worlds.
That's why, when you plant a seed, you'll get to see the fruit ripen in time.
Those who engage in agriculture till the soil with confidence
that it will surely bear fruit in due time; that's why they remember their God.
And that's why, within this world, the *Sahaja* Man engages in debt and profit.
Great clouds are forming and the sky is becoming gloomy;
I see that there will be many great drops of water.
The people made an effort [to pray to God]; there was rain, and their doubts were dispelled.
The wave of Love reached the shore and rose to the very peak of the World-egg.
It's the foundation supplying so many heavenly waters, with and without bottom.
At the command of that Man the three worlds easily float in *rasa*.
Supplied with *rasa*, that Man has come to this land and engages in debt and profit.
Lālśaśī says, "that Man has come and engages in debt and profit!" (BG 309, a.2)

73

Go on brother—come to the land of the *Sahaja* Man!
He who comes in the state of *Sahaja* will arrive in the twinkling of an eye!

Brother, I've lived with that desire,
through infinite births, again and again,
and at last my wandering was successful.
Now look—He stands upon the great *sātuyā* path.[109]

Straightway, that [*Sahaja*] Man who is compassionate to the poor,
dispels all dangers with the gift of fearlessness.
The pleasures and sufferings of *karma* are destroyed.
The difficult path has become easily accessible to the lowly folk.
And look—everyone is filled with joy at the touch of that Great Man!

Brother, abandon all your wealth and stand waiting upon the path;
for at the Festival of the Poor, all troubles are dispelled!
So stand up straightway;
at the sight of these Poor Men, raise your two hands,
immersed in bliss, crying "Alas, Poor Men!"
The essence of Poverty is devotion to Love.
Saying, "That Poor Man is mine, and I am his!"
And if the sinners and penitents find that [*Sahaja*] Man, He Himself will save them!

He has no equal in any of the three worlds of this physical universe—
if you find Him, keep him in your lap;
brother, raise Him to your breast.
And if someone asks you the reason
why you make such an effort for the sake of suffering men,
saying, "we can't allay the sorrows of suffering men,"
then how can we call upon Him who is the end of all our troubles?
And the Moon rises in the dead of night—brother, understand through hints and symbols! (BG 97, q.3)

The Seed of Creation and the Jewel of Man

74

Say, can just anyone understand that *rasa*?
Spoken words are simply words—they have no use here!
One must sit within the unenterable room[110] and keep this knowledge hidden far away.
Thus, so many people carefully search for this Essence.

When you asked about the great *Sahaja Rasa*,
I told you; for I myself am floating upon the ocean in the palace of *rasa*.
Look—this world floats upon two streams;[111] but, when I speak of this, who listens?
When I show them, they don't see, as if their eyes were blinded!

Brother, how can I say any more of this thing, since I'm constantly floating in delight?
Look—from His Forehead, the seed fell from his skin into the bottomless waters.[112]
Then a Fisherman came and bound it within the net of Māyā.
Brother, know for certain that within that net lie both birth and death.
Hear and understand this well; if you can, you must keep it in the corner of your eye.
For no one can know this Essence and remain calm for long!
By the power of mere words, people think they can express and carry out the *Dharma*.
Brother, within that Seed, upon that ocean, lies Life;
and I have abandoned all my friends to search for that thing!
Look, so many things are created in a single instant by this rasa!
Falling into troubles, turning in the wrong direction, living beings wander ceaselessly.
But upon [that ocean] lies a Great Jewel of a Man.
That jewel is an invaluable treasure, like the seed within a seed!
But no one can grasp it without true companions.[113]
If there are good companions, then when you grasp this delight, it will not be lost.
Keep it with great control, gazing upon this ray of light within the Inner Chambers.
Lālśaśī says, "Gaze upon this ray of light within the Inner Chambers." (BG 414, q.3)

The Inward Voyage to the Altar of the Supreme Self

75

What's the use of delaying—Go now, set sail upon your ship![114]
I remained on the banks of the Ganges, waiting for our companions;
we can't leave until they come.
Return to this shore when night turns to dawn.
You've brought the ferry-boat to this river in order to rescue people.
Each and every day you get the news of this land from the peoples' mouths.
If we meet again, it will be revealed; at dawn I'll introduce myself to you.
You've come here to bring the boat and ferry people across;
and whoever comes with you will easily cross over.
When someone shows any need, he'll come [and cross over] whether you call upon him or not;
but for the one who does have some need, you'll call him to come and be rescued.
With this same purpose, you've raised the sail and are calling us to your boat

[Bearing] my salt and sugar-cane, I gradually crossed over the seven primordial rivers.
Sitting in good Company, with fun and good humor,
I came like a flickering flame into this mortal world.
I was a flame within that [world of death];
but there was a terrible wave upon the seven primordial oceans.
No one, not even the helmsman, brother, could quickly cross over it!
But there was a Mighty Bird[115] [from] the fifth peak;
riding upon his back, we all rose up and crossed over the seven waves.
Now finally, brother, I'll tell you what remains of this story.

At the bottom of the bottomless ocean, amidst a single stream, lies Rasātola;[116]
and within this ocean, I see with my own eyes, there lies a jeweled altar!
Above, below, within, on all sides,
Vāsuki, with 3000 eyes, guards it from all directions.
Seeing him, I said, "I've come"—but then he sent me back here.
But did my companions get to remain there, enjoying the fun?
They wandered from land to land and arrived there;
in an instant, they were filled with delight!
Lālśaśī says, "they arrived there, and in an instant, were filled with delight!"
(BG 298, q.3)

76

No one can cross [the river] without this ferry, which has been given to us.
I can't leave you behind and cross over today with all these people upon this ferry.
So long as my life remains, I'll never be able to do it.
Brother, if I go today without rescuing you,
everyone will speak slander about me.
As long as life remains, no one will come to cross over on this boat.

You're [like] a flame which has come to cross over the primordial ocean.
If you're impeded from crossing this river, what hope is there of finding your companions?
You say, "if those companions return, we'll all cross over together!
If not, then saying, 'come back, my lords!' I'll go in search of them all.
For whoever comes with me will never return again!"

So many people came, with all their friends, frolicking and joking.
The mighty Bird loaded them upon his back and crossed over the waves.
Rasātola, the bottom of the bottomless depths, lies within the single stream
Brother, whatever is or is not, we'll see for ourselves.
Those who, while traveling this path with their friends, run off in another direction
will wander and wander, and never get to join them.
Why, having found his companions and lost them again, and having seen this humorous performance, would one cease to travel [the path]?

He who is the great Wealthy Man,[117] the Author of the primordial book of all that is, finite or infinite,
lies within the ocean, upon this jeweled altar.
He is without form—above, below, or in the middle.
He bestows deliverance; but He's very difficult to grasp; He is the vessel of delight.
Say, He is the mighty Bird, with command over the river.
He's seated with the heart,[118] filling it to excess!
One who wishes to cross over need grasp onto nothing else.
Lālśaśī thinks, "he who would cross over need grasp onto nothing else!"
(BG 299, a.3)

The Man of the Heart

77

O my mind, you couldn't recognize the Man of the Heart,[119] could you?
He who has adorned you,
has also given you the charge of the Kingdom;
yet you've never searched for Him anywhere!
Even when you gazed upon that Man with your own eyes, you couldn't see Him!
When He gave you the kingdom and made you King, you thought differently of Him;
but once you've received the kingdom, and accepted it, now what do you do all day?
You've never yet laid eyes on Him who has made your own essence![120]
If you become a knower of God and abandon everything,
there would no longer be all this constant false tumult and uproar.
But you undid all your work; you became the King and still you couldn't understand!
The eternal seven islands, the ocean and the earth are constantly coming and going;
you come and go from place to place, and yet you haven't found His whereabouts!
You're searching through heaven and hell and the fourteen worlds;
coming and going throughout the worlds in rebirth, as a result of the fruits of action,
progressively coming and going.
It's a false journey!
There is no forgiveness!
What do you get, what do you give to anyone?
Say—what did you do? Brother, I can see.

Just look at the hands of the lenders, borrowers and laborers—
why do they feel so arrogant, as long as life remains in their bodies?
If you had never known or heard this before, why didn't you say so?
Sitting upon this very throne, you can see so much in the twinkle of an eye!
At every moment, you're pursuing your heart's desires.
You've traveled far and returned again, and yet you cannot grasp it!
So now, when you call you will get no answer.
You don't desire what He desires, Oh my foolish heart!
You'll fall into error, you'll become wicked, and you'll lose the invaluable jewel!
Alas, you've seen this wondrous thing,
and yet you didn't relinquish your desire for the throne!
Lālśaśī says, "you didn't listen to Him or to what He said!" (BG 240, q.1)

78

But brother, I couldn't find the Man of the Heart.
I returned and sat upon my throne; now I'm examining everything here.
That's why I'm wondering in my dreams, what will happen?
I myself am by no means a wise man.
Of what I cannot see directly with my own eyes, I can say only this—
I can only count the wings of as many as birds as I can see in the skies.
Look, until now, God has created this world;
He delighted in the infinite fount of qualities;
He created the beginning and end, and reveals it through the Tantras and Mantras.
At first, I could not see; but when my strength returns, I'll go and try to see—
for here, I can see thoroughly all that lies in the destiny of my heart.
One day, having searched for this Man at home and abroad,
I got to see a humorous spectacle upon the ocean of life!
All the ships were loaded with great gems, pearls, and jewels.
But where had their Master gone?
Apart from all this merchandise, there was nothing else.
That man had come upon the ship to engage in business;
whatever sort of thing you desire, he'll give you.
In the twinkle of an eye, he'll give you so many precious things!
Once I went alone to see the great festival at Agradvīpa;
there were so many monks, men and women that one could not count them all!
I had gone once to see for myself, but had forgotten.
So, having forgotten, how can I now speak of it? Today I look and realize it's impossible.[121]
I know that from beginning to end, my mind is always judicious;
but that Virtuous Man himself has summoned me!
So now, what I had lost, I get to see within the mirror!
Lālśaśī says, "finally, I got see what I had lost within the mirror!" (BG 241, a.1)

79

If you would meet your Man of the Heart, then listen to what I say:
With desire for devotion for the Guru, remain sitting upon your throne;
call upon Him, grasping onto the Name, Oh erring Mind!
Why do you go searching for Him again and again?
Just sitting upon your throne, you can easily attain Him!
Trying to find him by wandering from land to land is useless and vain!
Say, now your business will be prosperous,
for there are many, many borders in His jurisdiction!
He who knows the whereabouts of all places within the three worlds,
that man is the Man of the Heart—yet even when you see Him, you can't recognize Him, can you?
If you could look at Him with one eye, seated upon your throne,
in a single moment, He would be united with you!
Ah! He distributes the treasures of infinite and finite qualities—Oh, what wealth!
There's wealth and sweetness in this Kingdom.
Open your eyes and you can see everywhere!
I'm revealing this to you!
Those who, because of their own selfish interest, can't bear this splendor,
can't understand the necessity of Sahaja and so can't realize the need for this Kingdom.
For in this Kingdom, there is need of Him who has given us the burden [of rule].
Oh my heart, you call out to your heart, yet you can't argue with Him.
But because of His whims, we must search for Him in all directions.
Some sit upon the throne and rule in this land;
and some, with merchandise in hand, come and go upon the road;
some, filled with happiness, find the means of escape;
some, gasping their last breath, lose their lives in the twinkle of an eye amidst this ocean of life;
and some float upon the waters, and when they call upon that Man, they're rescued!
If you live, and if you call upon Him at any time, you must get an answer.
If you call upon Him filled with sorrow, even so, He will come.
Lālśaśī thinks, "If you call upon Him in a natural way, He will come!"
(BG 242, q.2)

80

What use is there in trying to bring that Man of the Heart outside?
Always eternally happy, united with the Self,
He remains seated within the heart.
So why now would he come out?

His heart is in accord with whatever He desires.
Engage in spiritual practice, and you'll attain Him; then, with love for Him, hold onto to the treasure that you find!
Oh my mind, who knows of what sort are the habits of the Man of the Heart?
And if one could know them, could he express their form?
The mind cannot know Him; for [only] the beauty of His outward form is known.
As long as life remains in my body, I fear to speak of Him—
I saw Him in a dream, and my heart was rent!
At the limit of the seven oceans lie the seven continents of the Earth.
There are seven heavens and seven upper heavens—and in this, we get a sign.
There is one primordial ocean among these infinite oceans;
and in this [metaphor] there is a natural example of the Man of the Heart.
Just as the primordial ocean is infinite, and unfathomable to the human intellect,
so too, the Supreme Virtuous One is like night pollen within the Lotus,
but even if one worships Him, no one can see Him with his own eyes.
Once upon a time, He came, floating upon a Banian Leaf,
and fashioned creation, in the twinkle of an eye.
A Spider came and cast his net within it,
and now so all living beings and the entire world constantly wander within it.
Everyone's wandering around within it, and no one can find the way out.
If one tries by some contrivance, he won't be shown the way out;
but he who realizes himself in his own true state will dwell free of false pretense.
Lālśaśī thinks, "you must realize your Self, and remain free of pretense."
(BG 243, a.2)

Songs of Lust and Love

Like most earlier Vaiṣṇava Sahajiyā literature, the songs of the *Bhāvar Gīta* revolve in large part around the theme of love—in both its spiritual and sensual forms. Lord Kṛṣṇa appears here as the supreme object of desire, the Gallant or Illicit Lover, while the soul plays the part of the milkmaid or bride of the divine Beloved.

Finally, a smaller body of songs also refer—in very cryptic and enigmatic form—to the presence of Tantric sexual rituals in Kartābhajā practice. The most controversial of these refer to the Tantric practice of *Parakīyā* love, or intercourse with a woman other than one's own wife, which was a matter of intense debate within the Vaiṣṇava community during the eighteenth and nineteenth centuries. The manner in which these songs are expressed, however, is so vague and murky that it has left them open to radically different interpretations within the Kartābhajā community. Among the more esoteric disciples, these songs have been read in an explicitly left-handed Tantric sense, referring to explicit acts of sexual intercourse, whereas among the more orthodox majority, they tend to be read in a far more conservative, non-Tantric symbolic sense, referring to the symbolic relationship of the human soul with Lord Kṛṣṇa.

The most important of the songs dealing with the *Parakīyā* debate center around the metaphor of the "stinking fruit in the garden of love," which is a complex allegory for the introduction of sexual practices into the tradition and all the scandal that they elicited from their many critics (II.84–89). The songs conclude with the cryptic remark that the tree of *Parakīyā* had to be uprooted from the Garden—yet it remains unclear whether these practices were eradicated altogether, or whether they were in fact simply continued but in a more esoteric form within the "secret marketplace" of the Kartābhajā tradition.[122]

The Dalliance of the Royal Goose and His Beloved Lady Goose

81

Look—your eyes filled with joy, immersed in this enchanting lake of water;
the proof and the glory [of this wondrous thing] come floating upon the slow moving Malayan breeze!
You've become overjoyed amidst the waves of this water, I see, and you wish to drown within it!
The splendor of Śiva's own realm lies at the wharf.
Then a deep sound is uttered—
like Brāhmaṇs chanting "*boba bom*!"
I think that this is perhaps the city of Kailāspurī;
and I'll go on hearing this great sound, "*bobom*!"
Look—schools and schools of Sapharī, Phalui, Rui and Ponā fish,
male and female Icla fish, Bholā and Mourlā fish,
Celā and Ḍānkonā fish,
Cāṅdā, Pābdā, Bhedā and Cāṅdkuṛo fish,
male and female Trout and Catfish—
Catch them all and gather them together in a net!
And then, swimming side by side, everyone plays together![123]
Now I see that, as a wondrous Royal Goose, He has plunged into the waters and floats upon them.
Swinging and swaying, He dallies in union with his beloved Lady Goose;[124]
and I see the dawn of both the wondrous full Moon and Sun together!
From time to time He appears upon Her Lotus, in order to adorn her in splendor.
With joyful hearts, the bees make their buzzing sound,
and as they come floating, all the flowers burst into bloom upon the Āśoka tree.
At that, the King of Bees appears!
The bees drink the nectar;

Lālśaśī says, "within the Lotus of the Heart, the bees all drink the nectar!" (BG 413, q. 2)

The Savoring of Licit and Illicit Love: Rasa, the Rasika, Parakīyā, and Svakīyā Prema

82

Who can charm that *Rasika*?[125]
Look and consider the three worlds,
perceiving indirectly, directly and immediately, in succession:
The perfect disciple is the vessel of *rasa*.
He is never bound;
whether he is or is not,
this is his identity—
surely he is a Gopī.
Say, if that *Rasika* was charmed,
then that was *Svakīyā* love.
Parakīyā is gratifying for both persons;
though one thinks it is good, it is the opposite.[126]
Considering, becoming certain,
coming to recognize what is what.
Look—the ways of Love are endlessly devious!
Though the milkmaids are charmed, they cannot charm Him.
It is proclaimed in all lands;
you've heard the news:
at the touch of that *rasa*, there is madness!
That Gallant Lover [Kṛṣṇa] is the supreme *Rasik,*
with terrible cunning from beginning to end.
Busily engaged in *Parakīyā* love,
He charms [the Milkmaids] with a single glance.
And look, before the Moon,
the Cakora bird drowns in *rasa*. (BG 52, q.1)

83

The one who can charm that *Rasika*
is Śaśī—He has become our refuge.
With the manifestation of *rasa*, the darkness is destroyed.
And look—together with that,
fear and affliction depart.
Thus, the Cakora bird
is freely bound to the moonlight.[127]

The path of love is of this sort:
where there is Desire [the first stage of the Kartābhajā path],
there is Cessation [the final stage of the path].[128]
Both [*parakīyā* and *svakīyā*] *rasas* are necessary,[129]
and thus the *Rasika* is subdued.
When they [the male and female] become one, there is love;
they'll come and worship in *Sahaja*.
The practice of both *rasas* is the embodiment of ecstasy.
The contents consist of *rasa*;
and that *Rasika* is the vessel.
The state of Ecstasy is the All of all things.
In the Self-nature, in *Sahaja*, [the *Rasika*] is enchanted.
Words cannot be attributed to it.
This is the true law:
having attained *rasa,*
and having become its very essence,
both [male and female] become full of *rasa*. (BG 52, a.1)

The Stinking Fruit in the Garden of Love: The Paradox of Parakīyā Love

84

Brother, do I ever desire anything else,[130]
now that the clever Madman[131] has come and driven me crazy?
I think about Him day and night—
His ugly form, devoid of qualities;
But I can't stand not seeing Him!
My eyes long to see that Madman again and again!
Can you show me the greatness of that place?
The Madman can do whatever, wherever He likes.
The Madman is attached to no one else.
I constantly run after him.
But can I go to that wondrous land by my own free will, or only by your direction?
Look—that supreme Madman has driven me crazy!
And when he returns and speaks,
whatever he says is good!
When he tells me of this wondrous thing, brother,
I'll go and evaluate it carefully, lest I lose the Madman.
If the Madman gives me poison,
it becomes ambrosia as soon as it touches my tongue!
For the sweet smile on his Moon-face oozes such sweet nectar!
He said, "I'll cause a sweet fruit to blossom in the heavens."[132]

As it blossoms, I'll distribute it throughout the universe,
and so enchant everyone!
That's why I listen and tell no one about this, brother.
In this world of rebirth, I think, there will be great fun!
He has planted this wondrous, delicious thing.
The sign has been seen in the heavens;
Śāśī Lāl laughs and says, "if you have eyes, you can see it!" (BG 152, q.3; KG 51)

85

No one can reach the wondrous fruit of that land;
that's why the Madman will return and plant the fruit in heaven,
and as it bears fruit, He'll distribute it throughout the world.
Whoever receives and tastes that fruit,
while tasting it, will forget everything else!
And, just look, they will know for themselves what will happen in the end!
There's an ocean surrounding this wondrous place.
Upon it, that fruit garden was born.
But because of its foul smell,[133] the Good-Mannered Company[134]
uprooted it from the garden—this we know.
Look, your Madman went crazy
by tasting this fruit.
Look, now you're paying homage to that Madman;
you know nothing impure.
That's why I'm telling you:
we never want to smell that fruit;
but you've lost yourself in the fragrance of that fruit, brother.
Now you can't stand anything else—
but never speak of this openly to anyone![135]
He who enters this world of *saṃsāra* because of the smell of one fruit,
then eats and enjoys it—don't we call him a "madman"?
There's a wondrous place within that Fortress,
in that Fort there are cannonballs and bullets, canons and guns.
Brother, this wondrous place is what you have sought.
Out of desire for awakening, you get a whiff of it.
Lālśaśī says, "at His command, the soul becomes a Mad Bāul!"[136]
(BG 153, a.3; KG 51)

86

A great splendor is arising within this garden of sweet fruit;
and look—the men of your Company come running, maddened with the sweet smell!
To those who have eyes to see it,

the Madman will give this fruit to taste.
Having tasted it, they'll be enchanted by the Madman,
and follow behind Him like a bull led by the nose!
How clever my excellent Madman is!
Whenever He thinks something, it instantly happens!
Full of desire, He brought the foul-smelling plant,
and made a plot of good land in heaven.
And now what a beautiful display of branches, leaves and flowers there is!
When that Company of yours becomes [like] my Madman,
they'll be able to taste this fruit.
When they get it, they'll feel the Ecstasy of Madness.
Becoming connoisseurs in that taste,
they'll engage in such wondrous play!
I pay homage to that Madman,
and I'm thinking, what will happen to you?
So brother, keep looking to the heavens—
for, can you see that [fruit] down here below?
That Madman said, "I'll distribute this sweet fruit throughout the world!
I'll make a deep stream in the earth,
I'll make everyone speak one and the same language,
enchanting them with this fruit, with the greatest fun!
And now the whole universe will drown in the waves of Love!"
The Madman himself will remain plunged within [the ocean of love];
and the Company will come and float [upon the waves of love] to its heart's desire.
Lālśaśī says, "That Mad Bāul can do whatever He pleases!" (BG 154, q.4; KG 52)

87

Will anyone be able understand that Madman, brother,
when He displays His amazing, incomprehensible radiance?
And when he lifts up his head,
beware at every moment!
Brother, if one abandons everything in this world,
he'll get to see the Madman, whether near or far,
and then and there, in the blink of an eye, he'll follow the true path.
You yourself have gone mad, and yet you don't know about this Madman—
when and where He went, and in what business He's engaged?
Brother, because of the incomparable greatness of the Madman,
no one can ever be his equal.
Brother, if you look and search for such a thing, you won't find it in this universe.
I've never seen such a wondrous person as that Madman!
What is permissible, and what must be abandoned—this only the Company knows.

Brother, whatever the Honorable Company itself cannot attain,
straightway, the Madman cordially brings them.
With this Madman, one becomes rich;
the fine essence arises from the worthless husk;
and even as you look, whatever touches the Madman's hands becomes a
wondrous treasure!

When the Company uprooted this garden of fruit,
the Madman himself went to see and evaluate it.
There was some foul-smell within it;[137]
and He rebuked all those who desired [the foul smell].
The Company didn't have the strength to bear that foul smell, did it?
for, upon seeing it, one is driven Mad!
He said, "I'll rebuild that [garden] in heaven!"
Lālśaśī says, "I'll enchant the Company with the fruit of that garden!"
(BG 155, a.4; KG 52)

88

When one hears these things, he'll be delighted in an instant:
one Madman, two Madmen—because of this delicious [fruit],[138] the land's
become filled with Madmen!
And by not telling me about it, Sir, [it's as if] you want to drive me crazy!
First tell me the meaning of these three [Madmen]; and then finally explain the
two kinds of Company.[139]
Tell me about this Madman, with His delicious [fruit];
but remain concealed within the Company![140]

Of all the songs that you sang before,[141]
doesn't something still remain - don't you know?
Just as you had come here once before,
and when I asked, it was fitting for you to tell me about this matter.
If my heart is to be consoled, then I must know your grace.

Where does that Madman dwell, who has driven you mad?
Why did He come to this land—tell me now!
Brother, first tell me about His father and grandfather.
Hearing and understanding this, I'll drown in delight; otherwise, what will be my
fate?
Tell me, in what family was he born?
Is He always here in this very country, or is His dwelling place over there?
And why is it that anyone who comes and sees this delicious fruit goes mad?

Brother, previously a foul smell arose within that fruit garden.
The Company got wind of that foul smell, and uprooted it.
If it was good before, that delicious fruit became foul smelling.
So now that they've replanted the seed, why has it become sweet-smelling again?
Won't the foul smell once again overpower the sweet smell?

I see that you speak with certainty.
Now, when the Madman grows that excellent fruit and gives it to us to taste, what profit will there be?
Lālśaśī says, "when the Madman grows it, what profit will there be?" (BG 158; KG 60)

89

The original name of that Madman is "the Darkness which Destroys Doubt."[142]
His house is in the City of Bliss on the shores of the Lowest Hell, which is the treasury of the Factory.[143]
Once He dwelt for some time in this land.
But I'm afraid to identify Him,
lest whoever hears it be scared shitless![144]
Brother, whoever thinks of Him has all his desires fulfilled.
If you wish to hear about this Madman of yours and His delicious [fruit],
then I'll tell you what I know.
You've asked, so listen carefully:
never think about this again—no one, at any time.
For if you think about it once, brother, you'll think about constantly!
Previously, at the dawn of the Fourth *Pralaya* [in the Kali Yuga],
"The Darkness which Destroys Doubt" suddenly came to this shore.
I don't know how He became so beautiful!
He created the garden of *Parakīyā Rasa*.
There was no end to the field of night.
But brother, a foul smell arose within it, you know.
Yet with great effort, the supreme Virtuous One preserved [the garden].
When the Good-Mannered Company got wind of that smell,
they uprooted that garden, roots, flowers and all!
If the Good-Mannered Company had not gotten wind of that smell,
then everyone, the highest and the lowest, would have gone crazy—
eating menstrual blood, sleeping together!
After this happened, the garden remained empty.
But even now, behind that fruit-garden, the Company continues.[145]
Lālśaśī says, "behind that garden, the Company continues!" (BG 159, a.2; KG 61)

The Cunning Play of the Illicit Lover: Kṛṣṇa-Līlā

90

I see your vanity, you cunning Lover!
Time and again, you roam about, captivating the hearts of the weak women.

How can you display such cunning?
In every age you come,
and we have to suffer your mischief!
That's why everyone wants to punish you for it!
You revealed yourself to the women of good family and remain staring at them;
and when you enchanted them all, you felt no shame.
When the women of good family go down to the water,
you make the sound of your flute,
and having done so, how many women Śrī Hari enjoys!
Everyone knows about your gallantry.
You have only your flute as your possession,
and a little cleverness.
How black is your color, Oh Virtuous One!
Your posture is bent and your gaze is sidelong,
and how many wiles with the women!
What can Hari not do?
So easily, you delight the lewd women of Vraja!
For a short while you're subdued in the company of the cowherds,
and you wander about, driving a herd of cows side by side.
But these cowherds and women are all weak.
Don't they burn with passion when you call?
Who can understand your humor?
But whether or not one understands it, he's thoroughly enchanted!
That's why Lālśaśī laughs and calls you "the Crooked Player!"
(BG 457, a.1; KG 15)

91

You are the princess, the goddess of the *Rāsa* [dance]—come, beautiful Lady!
Come, young lady Rādhā, my lover and desire!
To the *Rasika*, you are the ocean of *rasa*.
Come, come, love of my life—
because of your qualities, I float in bliss.
I see you but once, Rādhikā, and now I'm thinking of you day and night!
Come, come, beautiful Rādhikā and sit at my left side.
Now I'll play my flute for you.
If it pains you to come,
your moon face is tarnished.
Just seeing you, I'm torn asunder!
Alas, I die, I die!
At every moment, beautiful Rādhikā,

I always sing of your qualities, with my flute upon my lips.
You are the holy city of Gāyā and Kāśī, you are the Ganges, my lover.
At your touch, one gains the fruit of all the holy places of pilgrimage.
You are equal to my very life;
I always praise your name,
and then your beautiful form, Rādhikā;
for I am the Crooked Player.
I'm struck with love for you;
I've become a yogi and go begging alone, from house to house.
Look, I remain beguiled by union with you, Rādhikā.
I go off leading a herd of cows, to the banks of the Yamunā.
Now what more will I say?
You are mine, and I am yours.
Śaśī says, "Because of your qualities, Rādhikā, I swoon day and night!" (BG 463, q.1)

92

I can no longer forget about that Illicit Lover [Kṛṣṇa].
O my Friend, do you know where He is? I speak to you of the pain in my heart!
Apart from you, I can tell no one else.
How can I be patient?
That fellow uses his cunning with a woman,
in order to beguile the woman of good family.
Thus the World-conqueror becomes her lover!
Just look at this naive, weak and simple woman:
how can I endure the burning state of separation?
I'm very deeply distressed!
Before, I was stony hearted,
but now my heart is terribly afflicted!
and hanging on to life seems futile!
You see the business of our friend the *Rasika*:
at every moment, He's engaged in trickery!
And when I hear he's returning,
crying and crying, my two eyes always stream with tears!
Friend, I can see that you are drowned in bliss.
What will I say? Alas, what is my fate?
Look and see, in this, there's no compassion at all.
And Śaśī says, "what will I do?
For I've become impure!" (BG 59, a.1; KG 8)

93

So be it—in the first part of the night,
I'll go rob everything in the house of the Illicit Lover [Kṛṣṇa];
it requires no real cunning;
I know this very well!
In his heart, this venomous creature is entirely wicked!
But now, I'll rob him of all his vanity!
He is our Illicit Lover—
before, I used to think He was the ocean of *rasa,*
but now I've returned and can see
that He's always engaged in cunning schemes and the robbing of hearts!
So if I can, I'll give him a more suitable heart!
When I go to rob Him,
during the first part of the night, I'll act like a virtuous person.
If the Nāgar is awake at that time,
I'll make some subtle conversation with Him.
And if I get some avengement,[146]
then I'll quietly increase my treasury sevenfold!
For this is the great desire within every human heart!
But if I get caught with the stolen goods,
I'll present everything in the court of the Police.
I'll say, "this man has robbed us of all our jewelry, and now we are taking it back!"
With subtle deceptions, we'll put the Lover in prison;
and then the Lover will see that we are like Lady Lovers!
Lālśaśī says, "when one achieves this, what else is there to fear?" (BG 228, q.1)

94

So you say you'll catch the Illicit Lover?
He keeps his chest beneath him; so even if you remain staring at him, you can't see it!
Have you gotten even a trace of him?
When at first you go to converse with him,
will there be any time left to rob [Him]?
That's why I'm asking you—so tell me what you mean.
You're concocting great schemes within your mind.
You think you'll rob the Lover of everything and lose nothing!
That Lover is the Ocean of Wisdom.
He always remains satisfied with his own priceless wealth.
Apart from us, no one can see Him with his own eyes.

If anyone else but could possess his wealth,
then would we be so delighted with our dear Friend?
His refuge is our dwelling place;
if we call upon Him, we can see Him!
If anyone feels hunger or thirst, he can find and enjoy Him!
And you've never had such a wonderful thing in your mouth!
This Illicit Lover has stolen our hearts;
and because He's stolen my heart, I call him thief!
He has taken all our wealth,
He has mixed it with His own wealth and made something new!
Look—that thing has become an invaluable treasure!
But when it lost its shame, this treasure became the Vedic teachings.[147]
But what is beyond the Vedas lies within this treasure chest!
Lālśaśī says, "that treasure has remained within this chest!" (BG 231, a.2)

Other Songs of Faith and Worship

The last songs translated here are more popular devotional prayers sung at the regular Kartābhajā gatherings on Fridays and holy days. In both their form and their content, these songs are markedly different from the rest of the Bhāvar Gīta; they are composed in a completely different style and use far less mystical esoteric language. It seems likely that these are later additions geared toward a less secretive, more devotional popular following.

The first of these, the Friday song, is especially interesting in its explicit use of economic terminology, the language of debt and moneylending, to describe the sinful soul. The second, the hymn to Satī Mā, gives a nice illustration of the more devotional side of the tradition, and is directed primarily toward the loving maternal figure who is the "savior of the poor" and the one who remits the soul of its many debts.

Paying the Price of Sin: The Friday Song

95

Pardon my sins, Lord;
there is so much delusion, from birth to death!
In your world,
it's as if I never existed.
I've become terribly weak and crippled;
how many millions are my sins!
When one starts recording my sins in the account book,
there's no limit to them.

Now, having become a poor man, I run after you without fear!
O Lord, how many have achieved salvation?
Surely I have at times committed sins—
abundantly, repeatedly, in my actions—
they are innumerable!
This great sinner cannot perform any worship.
Full of deluded ideas, [searching for] the end of suffering, in the hope of happiness;
I wander in delusion, saying, "renounce, renounce," but I do not want to renounce!
The slanderer reproaches me, seeing my behavior.
I am the Bailiff,[148] and You are the Proprietor of everything;
I say, "Yes," and You make it so.
Take and control all my wealth, my self-will, my strength.
Save me, in your record office,[149]
from the guns of the slanderers!
I am false and wicked at heart;
but I call upon you with the *Mantra* that you have given me to speak.
You are to be served by all things, to be loved by all;
You are the sublime Lover of all Love;
You are the Lord of the sun!
Because of my own selfish interest,
I abandon the milk in this land and drink the poison!
But now, abandoning the poison,
I'm drowned in the juices of love—
for that is itself God!
I'm filled with bliss;
I've plunged into the deep waters.
With a single tongue, everyone floats upon the waves of love;
drowning, we gasp to the point of death!
For endless time, I've suffered due to the fruits of *karma*.
Plunging and sinking into the water,
I wait, counting the time—
minutes, seconds and hours;
Lālśaśī says, "I wait counting the time,
minutes, seconds and hours." (BG 3, q.1)

In Praise of Satī Mā, the Savior of the Poor

96

Oh Mā, the Eternal Brahma—
having fallen into the terrible waves, I call upon you, Mother!

You are the Savior of the poor, the Mother of the World;
Mother, dawn upon the lotus of my heart!
I am terribly stupid; I know nothing of worship;
Mā, dawn upon the lotus of my heart and make me aware!
Always thinking of you, I'll attain the Wish-Fulfilling Jewel by the virtues of your Name!
O Mā, the savior of the poor,
I hear your name sung in the Purāṇas.
But the six enemies [of the passions] are relentless. Hear me, Mother!
Because of my six enemies and six evil thoughts, I'm traveling on the wicked path.
To stay always on the path of salvation is a very difficult thing!
The five elements within me stray in five different directions;
when and how [can] this afflicted creature [be saved]?
The five elements within me wander about in five directions.
None of them pays heed to the Mind, the King!
I know that my life's at its end!
Oh Mā, the days pass, one by one.
Now there are no more days remaining.
The ten senses are ruling my mind, I fear!
There used to be five senses of knowledge—
but now the five senses of action have become decrepit!
And within this body, how can they administer a just rule?
Lālśaśī says, "this is my time—
Mother, please appear within my heart!" (BG 2)

III

The Language of the Mint

Manulāl Miśra's Collection of Mint Sayings

The following collection of "Mint Sayings" was compiled in 1902 by Manulāl Miśra, the most important Kartābhajā author after Dulālcāṅd, who did the most to try to systematize this ortherwise wildly eclectic and confusing esoteric tradition.[1] As a whole, these sayings present what is surely among the most formidable obstacles to the task of translation. With their intentionally obscure, enigmatic, and deliberately confusing form, they are clearly designed to mislead and befuddle the uninitiated outsider. Having no written commentary of their own, they are also intended to be transmitted in the secret oral context of a master-disciple relation.

Miśra himself only comments on a few of these sayings, and among the various Kartābhajā gurus whom I have interviewed, there is virtually no consensus as to the meanings of specific sayings but, rather, a wildly diverse conflict of interpretations. I have therefore tried to translate these sayings as literally as possible, discussing in the footnotes the various possible interpretations and the many inscrutable enigmas in the text.

The value of these Mint Sayings, however, does not appear to lie in their "meaning" or content—indeed, they often appear quite intentionally meaningless and absurd. Rather, their value lies in their *form* and the *ways in which they are exchanged.* Miśra himself explains that they are called *Ṭyāṅkśālī* precisely because this secret discourse operates much like a physical mint: "Just as by means of the Mint—that is, the device by which coins are fashioned—gold, silver, etc., are stored up in vast amounts, so too, in this precious treasury, many valuable meanings are hidden within each word."[2] In other words, just as a mint transforms ordinary metals into legal currency, so too the Mint language transmutes ordinary words into highly valued commodities that can be exchanged in the "secret marketplace," which is the Kartābhajā sect itself.

The Mint (*Ṭyāṅkśāl*)

This law is only for the poor. This law is only for those who follow the practice of the compassionate Fakirs. This is the command of the Lord's mouth.

1. The Word is the Guru and the Word is the disciple. From Word to Word, illumination arises. He who dwells in the abode of the Word is himself both the Master and the Servant.[3]

2. Remain [in contemplation of] the form and essence of the Word, and you will know your own time of death. Constantly remember, in body and mind, the words of the sages. Recalling their meaning, dwell within your own body. When that happens doubt will be overcome; and then the Truth will be manifest, both before and behind.
3. The name of Man is "a Jest";[4] the name of his work is *Sahaja*. His appearance is variegated.[5]
4. One must remember the state when he collected cakes of cow-dung. If one does, he will no longer feel the madness of sensual desire.
5. Truth heard from a speaker of Truth is the most difficult Supreme Reality.
6. True actions and judgements are very rare.
7. If one's actions are not motivated by self-interest, there is no trickery or deception.
8. If one is not born in the house of his Mother and Father,[6] he won't be upright in his conduct.
9. Many very small fruits are produced by a great banian tree; but if one examines the many small seeds which lie within each fuit, he will also know the great banian tree.
10. If one's own words are not true, he will not have a true nature.[7]
11. If one does not see Man with the eyes of devotion (that is, passion), he cannot see true beauty.
12. Remembrance, knowledge and vision—when one attains each of these separately in succession, there is no more distinction among them.
13. Consider your own self. Sometimes the child is in the lap of the old woman, and sometimes, the old woman is in the lap of the child.
14. If one can abandon the desire for his own well-being at the hands of a Virtuous Man,[8] and if he becomes upright in his conduct, he will attain "integrated"[9] devotion.
15. When this integrated devotion becomes one's own self-nature, it becomes unified.[10] When one feels the burning pain of the workman's shoes, he'll feel true compassion.
16. From such a state comes business in cash and merchandise.
17. As soon as one pronounces the name of Hari even once, He becomes present in the voice itself.
18. Upon the waves of Love there is no intoxication.
19. In no way does the Kartā "exist."[11]
20. And in no way can [He] be grasped.
21. He moves, looking in all directions (His name is Man. He is respectful and remains aware).
22. Transmitted orally from person to person, understanding is attained; then the meaning is of one form and one kind; and from this follows action.
23. One need not taste a hot chili in another's mouth.[12]
24. In the healthy state, there is only the Poor.
25. He who would become a Cātaka bird of Vraja must remove the thorn and drink the nectar.
26. Letter, name, meaning and emotion—all of these are contained in the letter itself.

27. When true speech becomes one's very life, one becomes his own name.
28. When these letters are united, there's nothing more to be sought.
29. Everyone wishes to have a peaceful mind.
30. The pure *rasa* is everywhere. But except in manifest devotion, it cannot be expressed.
31. One always wants to have a joyful mind.
32. The caste of the *Ātābak*[13] and the voices of the *Ātābak* are devoid of any requests.
33. If one is upright in political[14] affairs, the Religion of Truth will be manifest.
34. With respect to one's motive, bathing in a scum-covered betel-grower's pond[15] is better than bathing in the Ganges.
35. It is good to love one's neighbors, because their fathers and mothers[16] are of one's own country. This is because their dharma and karma is like one's own.
36. There is no lack within the family of devotees. As soon as one becomes the Master,he must give answer.
37. The money one earns digging with a shovel will not disappear; it remains intact.
38. He whose *Rasa* lies unconcealed in his house no longer wishes to be a *Rasika.*
39. If one is not born within the house of his Mother and Father, he cannot know true compassion.
40. If one follows the commands of his father, he can gain control of his father's wealth.
41. The son of a Brahmin also becomes a Brahmin.
42. [But] the son of a Guru will not be a Guru if he does not worship in this religion.

    The commandments of this religion; What is prohibited:

    1. Speak the truth; walk in good company.
    2. Do not speak falsehood.
    3. Do not desire another's wife.
    4. Do not commit injury.
    5. Do not kill.
    6. Do not steal.
    7. Do not eat remnants of food.
    8. Eating meat is forbidden.
    9. Do not drink wine.
    10. Love your neighbors. Consider them as equal to your father and mother.

43. If one doesn't cry out and fill his belly, he won't have a full belly.[17]
44. If you can't know yourself, you cannot discern and know the qualities of Hari.
45. The color of Man is neither black nor white.
46. If one dies alive, he'll never have to die.
47. If one displays no egotism, he remains immersed in the current; and his name is the "Magical Play of the Ocean."[18]
48. If one takes sure refuge in the Door of Man,[19] there will be no doubts whatever and no concerns about anything.
49. What is said should also be done.
50. I am not, you are not—He is.

51. If one's self-contentment[20] is as a servant at the Door of Man, he must be upright in his conduct.
52. If your words are your self-fulfillment, so too are your actions.
53. He whose conduct is his own self-contentment is virtuous; all his actions and all his business are "politically correct."[21]
54. If true speech, following the command of a holy man, becomes one's very life, then his voice becomes his own self-fulfillment.
55. The work is in the hands of the servant; [but] there is need of a Master.
56. Sharing food and going with others is like stealing and appealing to God's justice.[22]
57. If one has faith in the command of a holy man, then nothing more need be sought.
58. If one abandons the wish to live in the land of deception, he can be employed in governmental work.
59. And as soon as this happens, he can be said to have a heart free of duality.
60. Always have a joyful heart and gaze with a mind full of remembrance.
61. One should eat and sleep, giving a welcome place [to others].
62. One must understand lower-class religion.[23]
63. One should desire the work of a servant.
64. If one is satisfied with suffering he will attain invaluable wealth
65. Through love (when one feels love) great wealth can be attained.
66. Without relying on endurance, one cannot be employed in any work.
67. It is not permitted to cross over with even one finger remaining.[24]
68. Everyone wants to reach the shore: but some know the steamers and some know the little dingis.
69. If you work zealously amidst the rubbish of the house, a pile of garbage can become a mass of fine essence.
70. And apart from this fine essence there is no other harvest.
71. Inside a dreadful dark house, no one but an old woman can give you water.
72. In a pure place there is need for a sprinkling pot.[25]
73. If one has faith in the command of Man, then land, time and the vessel [of this physical body][26] can be overcome.
74. It is good to dwell in a lonely place.
75. Never talk about that of which there is no need to speak.
76. One should not pass time uselessly.
77. Everyone should look where he's going.
78. One must always travel with Him.[27]
79. If one puts a slave woman upon the Emperor's thone, the slavewoman still remembers her own proper state.
80. One must not become maddened with sensual indulgence.
81. If one becomes maddened with indulgence, he cannot engage in the worship of Man.
82. If one doesn't know that the Central City and the Regional District are of one kind, then [he can't know] the Conventional and the Ultimate Truths;[28] and that man cannot be addressed as "Master."
83. If one doesn't abandon the desire for the outer vestige, he can't know the Supreme Truth.

84. The Supreme Truth doesn't lie upon the Lion's Throne.
85. I wish to become a poor man; if one attains the state of poverty, there is supreme happiness.
86. If you are freed from the divisions of worldly doubts, you can know yourself; and then you can be freed from the sins of the destoyer of faith.
87. Hearing, knowledge and vision—even if one attains these each separately, he can be satisfed, and the distinction [between the lover and Beloved] will no longer remain. And when both [the lover and the Beloved] become one body,[29] there will be both vision and direct perception.
88. You must make abundance out of lack; when you call Him you'll get an answer. One need not taste a hot chili in someone else's mouth.
89. Does a barren woman feel sympathy for the pain of childbirth?
90. An adopted son (a dependent) doesn't feel the tug of the umbilical cord.
91. If one does not love with suffering, he cannot know true happiness.
92. One should always desire to be grief-stricken.[30]
93. If there's no mouth, there's no entry.
94. One mustn't abandon the genuine and worship the imitation.
95. A measure worth a 100, 000 *ṭākās* is not to be sold in a half-*ṭākā* gunny sack—for that is not the honest price.
96. As soon as one is freed from diverse emotions, he becomes truly compassionate.
97. This world need not be renounced; only evil thoughts must be abandoned.

[no number 98; two no.99's are given].

99. All this [world] is itself *Sahaja*; thus, if one renounces it, he cannot attain *Sahaja*.
99. One should eat and sleep, giving a welcome place [to others].
100. Show devotion for all living beings; then you will understand this amusing performance [of the world]. But the signs of this performance are only for the Poor.
101. Difficult practices are made possible by grace.
102. He is grateful to the lovesick woman; therefore, at the cries of the love-sick woman, He becomes present.
103. If one does not become a love-sick woman, one cannot become truly compassionate.
104. Always remember the state of compassion; and in this very state lies remembrance, contemplation and vision.
105. Everyone is the wife of the husband, and everyone knows the name of the husband. But if one does not enjoy him sexually,[31] then the love is mere hearsay.
106. If there's no action there's no accomplishment.
107. If one finds the people of his father's and mother's country, there's nothing else lacking.
108. The spinach of this land is good; by that one can recognize [the people of his father's and mother's land].
109. Even among all the heavens, there's no equal to a poor thatched hut in which there's light.
110. One settles his debts at the feet of a Brahmin; but one never has to settle his debts at the feet of a servant.

111. If one calls, anywhere, he'll get an answer; and then he'll know the state of his own salvation.
112. Where there's a wound there's both pain and pleasure.
113. The letter, the meaning and the emotion are all together in one place. As soon as one recognizes the letter, the nature [of the word] becomes evident.
114. And in this very place, he will find the people of his own name, his own caste and his own country.
115. Wordy affairs, food, a name, religion, etc.—even if one attains all these things, he still won't find satisfaction.
116. This is because, even if one speaks great words, and even if one is a crocodile in the Ganges, a cat is still just a fat tiger in a forest of Tulsi trees.
117. Wherever there's a little white shrine to Hari set up inside a house, that very house is called a "Temple of Hari."
118. And the man who dwells in such a house will freely offer the true evening prayer to God within this little white temple.
119. Who is Man? He shows due respect and remains aware.
120. If an imitation sword remains sheathed within a ten-rupee scabbord, it seems to be invaluable; but if it does not remain inside the scabbord, it's called "unsheathed," and then its price will be fitting.
121. One who is secret is liberated; but one is who is manifest [outside the veil] is an adultress.[32]
122. Apart from the slightest iota, nothing else exists.[33]
123. These Mint Sayings are neither for the marketplace nor for wealth; they are only for the poor.[34]
124. The command of the Lord's Mouth is "the poor belong to me, and I belong to the poor."
125. I run along behind the Poor Men; apart from the Poor, there is no one else. But if one simply gives them some money, and if one simply approaches them, he still has no right to embrace them.
126. We live in truth, in falsehood we die; speak truth, walk in good company. False words must not be spoken.
127. The world does not have to be abandoned; only wicked thoughts and opinions need be abandoned.
128. He who has no possessions has all possessions.
129. Consider everything from beginning to end: All the four aeons are ultimately destroyed; but words of Truth are never destroyed.
130. Living in good manners,[35] remaining meek, and wearing the rosary—if one accepts these things, he'll find the path of worship.
131. One must not become maddened upon the waves of love.
132. He who is born a worm in excrement still dwells in excrement, even if he's seated in heaven
133. If one lives in the kitchen, what will happen? He'll have to walk around carrying the stench of the place.

[no number 134]

135. One must keep the pot from which he eats very clean.
136. All jackals make the same sound.
137. O my Guru, you are the Guru of the World.

138. If an utterance is heard by the command of a Great Man, then it makes no difference whether or not its subject matter pertains to another.[36]
139. If a pitcher of Ganges-water gets mixed up with other water, there's great harm; therefore one should be very careful with his pitcher.
140. If one's search is true, and if the words [come from] a Great Man, then he is called *Ātābak*.[37] By means of Him, one can acquire Distinction.[38] And if one doesn't don the cap of Distinction, people don't trust him.
141. If the cap of Good Manners is upon one's head, he can come and go anywhere.
142. Wherever the heart is earnestly devoted, both are known as "servants."[39]
143. In no way does the Kartā "exist."
144. In no way does one become entangled.
145. The world is enchanted by illusion.[40]
146. The illusion is God's.
147. God is enchanted by the Person of Truth.
148. The Person of Truth is enchanted by the lesser Person of Truth.
149. The lesser Person of Truth is enchanted by Humanity.
150. Humanity is enchanted by Love.[41]
151. The laws of the Religion of Truth: Truth is to be spoken—falsehood is not to be spoken.
152. One must not kill.
153. One must not steal.
154. Honor your father and mother.
155. Love your neighbor.
156. Do not commit adultery.
157. Do not eat remains of food.
158. Do not become intoxicated.
159. Do not eat meat.
160. Name, *rasa*, form, and power are the characteristics of Truth.[42]
161. In the company of holy men, cessation[43] is a threefold Union.
162. What is the true nature of the spiritual practitioner? Emotion.[44]
163. What is the true nature of emotion? Love.
164. What is the true nature of Love? Ecstasy.[45]
165. What is the true nature of Ecstasy? Śrī Rādhikā.
166. What is the true nature of Śrī Rādhikā? *Rasa*.
167. What is the true nature of *Rasa*? Amorous pleasure and play.[46]
168. What is the true nature of amorous pleasure and play? Sexual union.[47]
169. What is the true nature of sexual union? The Beloved.[48]
170. What is the true nature of the Beloved? The Lord Guru.
171. What is the true nature of the Lord Guru? The Companion.
172. What is the true nature of the Companion? Devotion to Him [God].
173. What is the true nature of devotion to Him? Being of one body.
174. What is the true nature of being of one body? Worship.
175. What is the true nature of worship? Attainment.

[no number 176 or 177]

178. If one has faith in the commands of a Holy Man, he is a conquerer of the Three Worlds, and he will know how to master space, time and the vessel [of the body].

178. [two number 178's are given]. With great effort, the refuse of a house gradually becomes the fine Essence.
180. In a pure place, one does not become pure without a sprinkling pot.[49]
181. If a deer doesn't suffer the bite of a jackal, it won't cry out.
182. If the Conventional and the Ultimate are not accepted as two Truths, then the nature of Truth cannot be realized.
183. As soon as one reaches a place of discernment he becomes upright in his conduct; but if he isn't born within the house of his Mother and Father,[50] this cannot happen.
184. The name of the land of one's [true] Mother and Father is the "Poor Company."[51]
185. The goal of the path cannot be achieved without the company of holy men.
186. What is said should also be done. I am not, you are not. He is.
187. If one's status is that of a servant at the door of Man,[52] then, through his conduct, he will realize his own true nature.
188. The limbs have a body, just as a company has members; and if this is the case, so be it.
189. When one pulls the hair, the head comes along.
190. An adopted son can become the inheritor of all the things of this world.
191. But he will never know the feeling of a natural-born child.
192. The Name is Brahman, which consists of nectar; but when it's sung out of tune, there's no cash-profit in business.

[two number 193s are given].

193. He who speaks mere opinion commits a transgression.
193. Even if one is married five times, if he has never enjoyed sexual union, it' mere hearsay; he never knows true affection.
194. [printed as 197] If one's own words aren't true, everything becomes a cause of sin.

[no number 195]

196. A house without an old woman lies in terrible darkness; and there, one can find no water to quench his thirst.
197. If one is the servant of one who eats *hālāl* food,[53] he should be upright [in his conduct].
198. If one knows this, he need know nothing else.
199. If one is united with the Unfathomable, the river of water [of this world] becomes a play of magic.[54]
200. Water of the Ganges water must be carried very carefully in a pitcher, otherwise other water will get mixed up with it.
201. That is to say, even if noble words are spoken, they can be concealed behind the sin of [false] courtesy.
202. The sword is not controlled by anyone.
203. Hair-splitting discrimination is like the clay of a potter;[55] one must be patient, act truthfully and have faith.
204. One can engage in moneylending with little wealth; but if there are debtors, the Moneylender dies. Thus, one must engage in moneylending with great discretion.

- On one side, there is the Creation of Brahmā, and on the other side there is Love, just as Balarāma deliberated, and then gave two chariots.
- The Creation of Brahmā is afflicted with Lust; but it is itself created from the seed of Love.
- On the day the Guru gives the command, one becomes a novice disciple.[56]
- The Guru is the Father; the holy man is the Husband; and [the disciple] is the son of the seed of Love.
- On which day did sexual intercourse occur? On the day that was desired.
- That very day is the seed of Love—it makes the feet of Brahmā seem insignificant—and that very day is the state of a Fakir; it is without duality, beyond discrimination, equanimious, and consists entirely of Love.
- Find a lonely deserted place and make your dwelling there.

IV

Songs from the "Secret Marketplace"

Other Kartābhajā Songs from Various Sources

In addition to the songs of the *Bhāver Gīta*, there is also a large body of other Kartābhajā songs scattered in a wide range of sources. Most of these are quite different in form and structure from the songs of the Bhavār Gīta, and many are almost indisguishable from more popular folk forms like the Bāul songs. I have gathered these together under three groups, adding my own titles: popular songs of unknown origin; songs from the works of Manulāl Miśra, the Kartābhajā theologian of the early twentieth century; and songs of other Kartābhajās and related groups. The most important of the related groups are the Sāhebdhanīs, a closely related sister movement, which spawned some of the most important folk songs of rural West Bengal.

Popular Songs of Unknown Origin

The following songs are not contained within the *Bhāver Gīta* but are often cited and sung by contemporary Kartābhajās.

The Twenty-Two Fakirs and the Founding of the Secret Marketplace

1

Listen with devotion, and hear the garland of Names—
the garland of the Names of the twenty-two Fakirs:[1]
the names of Becu Ghoṣe, of Jagadishpur village,
of Śiśurām, Kānāi, Nitāi and Nidhirām,
Choṭo Bhīma Rāy, and Baṛa Rāmanāth Dās,
Dedokṛṣṇa, Godākṛṣṇā, and Manohara Dās,
Khelārām, Bholānāṛā, Kinu and Brahmahari,
Āndirām, Nityānanda, Biśu and Pāñcikaṛi,
Haṭu Ghoṣe, Govinda, Nayana and Lakṣmīkānta.
Filled with devotional love, they attained great peace.

These twenty two, following their Founder,
came and established the Marketplace.[2]
—Bhaṭṭācārya, *Bāṅglār Bāul o Bāul Gān,* 64

The Delight of the Kartā-bhajās

2

The worship of the Master[3] is a delightful thing!
It is the True Worship.
Its whereabouts are not within the injunctions of the Vedas,
for all those are but the business of thievery!
The Master Himself came to this land
and planted the seed.
Who has the power to destroy
my worship of the very Master Himself?
I myself, in close company with both women and men,
will make everyone worship the Master!
In this worship of the Master,
I'll make them all look like fools!
They'll make the path straight and have great fun!
What delight there is, in heaven, hell or in the city!
—Advaita Candra Dās, *Ghoṣpāṛār Kartābhajā,* 47[4]

The Man of Ecstasy

3

Where has this Man of Ecstasy[5] come from?
He has no anger; he is ever satisfied.
He preaches that one should always speak the Truth.
There are twenty-two men with Him,
and all of them are of the same mind.
Chanting, "Hail to the Master," they raise their arms,
overwhelmed with the flow of Love!
—Miśra, *Sahaja Tattva Prakāśa*

Songs from Akṣayakumāra Datta's Bhāratavarṣīya Upāsaka Sampradāya

Published in 1870, Datta's work contains an important collection of very old Kartābhajā songs not contained in the *Bhāver Gīta,* which appear to be composed in a different style and meter. The sources for these songs are unknown, though there are many similarities to contemporaneous Bāul songs.

The Merchant of Love on the Seas of Desire

4

Who is this who has crossed over to dry land?
—some *Rasika*![6]
there are ten oarsmen,[7]
and six draw the ropes.
Even if one thinks he knows Him, one can't really know Him!
He travels in bliss;
and Oh, how many rows of followers go
with this *Rasika*!
There's a boat filled with treasure,
and within it dwells the Merchant of Love and His five bailiffs!
—Datta, *Bhāratavarṣīya Upāsaka Sampradāya,* 228

The Man of the Heart

5

Oh Madman!
Now you must recognize and worship your Man of the Heart.
If that Man of *Rasa* flees,
your house will remain empty!
—Datta, *Bhāratavarṣīya Upāsaka Sampradāya,* 228

The Begging Dervish

6

The Dervish comes, carrying a begging bowl.[8]
The Lord is the object of my unwavering love.
In Vraja, the name of the Lord is "the Flute Player."[9]
And in Navadvīpa, it is Gour Hari.[10]
He is the same one now acting as Fakir Āul,
spreading [his teachings] throught the land!
This Dervish is indeed compassionate—
whenever you want something, it immediately occurs!
But when false worship occurs,
look—we can recognize its form.
—Datta, *Bhāratavarṣīya Upāsaka Sampradāya,* 228-29

My Mad Lord

7

Oh Blessed Guru, my Mad Lord!
Alas, I die, I die, with nothing but wickedness in place of virtue!
I have not a trace of virtue; all my virtues are finished!
In confusion I abandon the sandal wood paste,
and smear my limbs with ashes!
How can I speak of meditation?
Wearing a loincloth and a torn cotton garment,
I came as a servant, bestowed by the Emperor;
who can express my desire?
Where does He dwell? where does He go?
He is nowhere!
—Datta, *Bhāratavarṣīya Upāsaka Sampradāya,* 229

Songs from the "Saṅgītamāla," Compiled by Advaita Candra Dās

The following songs are found in the collection "Saṅgītamāla," gathered by a contemporary guru, Advaita Candra Dās. Dās gives no sources for these songs; however, there is a strong element of Bāul influence throughout, and it seems likely that many were composed in imitation of the songs of Lālan and other Bāuls of the early twentieth century. The first song here (IV.8) is a clear reference to Tantric sexual practices—though these practices are now clothed in the rather ingenious imagery of the "merchant ship" (the male practitioner), which sails on the treacherous waters of the Triveṇī canal (the *yoni* of the female partner), always in danger of "dumping its cargo" (ejaculating). The second song (IV.9) is a fairly explicit description of Tantric Kuṇḍalinī yoga, detailing the arousal of the serpent power within the practitioner and its progressive ascent through the six *cakras* or energy centers of the human body. Finally, the last song in this series (IV.12) is one of the more explicit descriptions of *parakīyā* love, or intercourse with another man's wife, which became such a controversial issue for the Vaiṣṇava tradition and a major reason for the scandal and ill repute of the later Kartābhajā tradition.

Sailing the Merchant Ship of Desire upon the Triveṇī Canal

8

Filled with desire, I sailed my ship upon the Triveṇī canal,[11]
in the reverse direction, in the face of the ebb tide.
The rudder didn't touch the water.
Amidst the terrible shoals, there's an inlet,

and within it there's a crooked stream bearing a blue lotus.
But due to a foul wind, I could not cross it;
the boat of desire unloaded its merchandise!
Having killed myself, I can still save the other, by not jerking.[12]
Sweat falls, hanging on my beard—Alas, I die!
the cable holding the rudder is cut—
the boat sails off-kilter!
As long as I can, I bear the blows of the rudder—
Otherwise, I would jump up and flee!
Alas I die! The treasury has fallen into terrible danger![13]
Having lost the course, I wander and die;
I've lost my speed and am struck with grief!
My mind is depressed.
Now if I'm to save my life and my wealth,
I'll have to stop.
Alas I die!
The Self, the Paramahaṁsa, says,
"Oh, twilight has fallen;
he's become a prisoner and lost the path,
caught in the net of illusion!"
—*Śrī Satīmā Candrikā,* 89–90, song 12

Secrets of Kuṇḍalinī Yoga

9

The Guru dwells within the Thousand-petalled Lotus, above the six *cakras*, united with his Śakti, always filled with bliss.
Engage in the practices of deep breathing, turning the eyes inward, ritually touching various parts of the body.
Sit with a pure mind, fixed on the contemplation of Brahman.

Look within: the dalliance of the Iḍā vein lies on the left side of the body; within it moves the *prāṇa*-wind.
The Suṣūmnā vein is the true essence of the practitioner.
Grasp that stream within the lotus vessel.
Kuṇḍalinī is the furthest shore of consciousness, which pierces the *nāda-bindu.*

You must become devoid of all form and follow the pure path.
Having become estranged to the world, you'll see the house of Brahmā.
Always remain withn that chamber, maddened and bound by bliss!
But you must flee the finite world and cross over the universe.
Listen, my mind: if you are delivered, you will cross over the world.
Look from one shore to the other, engaged in practice.

Hauṛe says, "Yogeśvarī, when you awaken you'll go to the City of Bliss;
taking hold of the supreme Śiva, the [finite] self will grasp the Supreme self!"
—*Śrī Satīmā Candrikā,* 87, song 8

Sailing on the River of Nectar

10

Oh my mind—what practice do you follow?
Brahmā, Viṣṇu, and Śiva,
have drunk the great nectar of illusion.
I heard all this in sleep, devoid of consciousness.
Because of the wiles of the sweet sounds and smells,
you are bound by the chains of lust and wander here and there, in the reverse direction.
The one called the son of Śacī
was struck by the waves of the Triveṇī.[14]
He comes floating upon the wave, going from door to door;
he floats within the Triveṇī,
in the happiness of Śrīnivāsa.
He comes to the house of Nanda, driving a cow;[15]
he is restrained at the wharf of the Triveṇī;
the door is fastened tightly with three planks.
The splendor of divine emotion is bound to that,
under the cover of beauty and aesthetic pleasure.
There are so many merchants,
but without the steersman,
they'll become maddened [with lust], fall in and drown!
The river of poison lies on two sides;
the stream flows endlessly.
Between them is the river of nectar.[16]
"If you can understand it,"
says Khepā Madan Cāṅd,
"you must plunge within it;
otherwise you'll drink poison and lose your life!"
—*Śrī Satīmā Candrikā,* 85–86, song 5

The Imperceptible Sahaja Man

11

The *Sahaja* Man is imperceptible.[17]
He is manifest imperceptibly;

so where will you search for him externally?
By the strategems of Unseen Love,[18]
He can be grasped within the crooked vein.
Follow the water upsteam,
always causing it to flow [in the reverse direction].[19]
He himself moves within that vein;
but who can know that vein?
Who can know the Wish-fulfilling Jem, Lord?
In the *rasa* of Unseen Love, the Golden Man always floats.
O Madman, you've fixed your compass—
but you won't be able to go there!
You always wander about under the control of the enemies [of the passions]
How can you know the Man of the Heart?
On the day that you grasp Him, you'll lose your head!
—*Śrī Satīmā Candrikā,* 88, song 9

The Secrets of Parakīyā Love

12

Seeing Rādhikā greatly distressed, Viśākhā said to her:
"She who is so rich in heart has become terribly distressed.
Her dharma has become shameful.
If you become so distressed, you'll lose your very life;
so, Lady, I'll tell you what to do.[20]
To practice the *Parakīyā rasa* is a task requiring great skill.
"Go to the south; remain in the west; and sit facing the east.
Keep this secret love in secrecy;
Dwell in the joy of the heart.
Keep the secret love in secrecy,
and accomplish the work of the heart.
Make the frog dance in the mouth of the serpent,
then you'll be the king of *Rasikas.*
"One who is skillful can thread a needle with the peak of Mount Sumeru.
If one can bind an elephant with a spider's web,
he'll attain *rasa.*
One who possesses that love,
is rich in honor.
He never resides in any home.
The heart is within; but express it outwardly,
then dwell externally.
"Pay no attention to the Vedas or Vedānta,
and don't drink the nectar of the Vedas.

You'll still be a chaste wife; you won't be an adultress,
under the control of no one,
Even though you become unchaste and abandon your family,
worrying and worrying.
Seeing another's husband, with passion radiant like gold,
you'll still follow the injunctions of your own true husband.
"Swim in the ocean of impurity,
let down your hair,
but don't get wet and don't touch the water.
Thus, Caṇḍīdās says: 'At the command of Vāśulī,
I fall at Vāśulī's Feet.'
Be a cook, make the curry—but don't touch the pot!"
—*Śrī Satīmā Candrikā,* 92

Songs from the Works of Manulāl Miśra

Perhaps the most important Kartābhajā author after Dulālcāṅd, Miśra is the author of a large number of songs which combine Bāul, Tantric, and Sahajiyā elements with more devotional Vaiṣṇava imagery. Many of these (e.g., IV.13–14) contain fairly explicit references to Tantric sexual techniques. The art of *Sahaja* love is the highly secret art of arousing carnal lust (*kāma*) in order to purify and transform it into the "Great Desire" (*mahākāma*) of spiritual Love (*prema*); it is a transgressive and paradoxical kind of love, which demands that the male practitioner in fact "become a woman, and then engage in this practice with a woman."

Sādhanā Tattva (*The Principles of Spiritual Practice*)

13

The supreme *Sādhaka*[21] dwells within the glowing white 100-petaled lotus.
Upon the 1,000-petaled lotus, the name of the perfect conjugal love[22] is inscribed.
This love is like milk, of white blue and yellow colors.
If one can retain the seed, lust is conquered.
The seed, like milk, is mixed with lust.
But if it becomes free of lust, then I will enter the door of erotic play.
The cause of this amourous play lies within the power of lust itself.
The secret *Sahaja* love is a strange new kind of devotion!
I'll pray with a pure mind, full of devotion;
but you'll find Kṛṣṇa even within what is lowly!
Apart from the passion for Rādhā, there's no other satisfaction of desire.
She is herself the image of the deity, she is herself the Lord.

The foundational emotion[23] is the essence of the Guru, within the 100-petalled lotus.
Within the 1,000-petaled lotus, perfect sexual love is known.
Thus white and blue are the two colors of emotion.
Therein, white is mixed with blue.[24]
If you dwell in this emotion day and night,
you will attain the refuge of Man.
When desire becomes free of desire, then the Great Desire arises[25]
Engaged in this Great Desire, I'll reach the eternal realm!
—*Sahaja Tattva Prakāśa,* 127–28

The Secrets of Sahaja Love

14

Now let me speak of this secret Love of Lovers:
[through this love] Vine Rādhāṅga Rāy became Tripuriṇī;
by engaging in this love, by enjoying a woman, he became the Conqueror of Death.
And Vidyāpati too engaged in this love.
By her divine yoga, the Goddess [Bhagavatī] revealed her grace:
She said to him, "now hear of Love, my child;
know and unite with the body of Lachī Mā.
I have given you this wisdom."
The young maiden Lachī Mā was endowed with all virtues.
Vidyāpati united with her in *Sahaja* Love,
very secretly.[26]
Look—the thief deceives with false accusations;
the friend dies in pain;
I speak of that loving union—
O see and understand!
Caṇḍīdās and his Queen—
O their love was wondrous!
I heard it from the mouths of holy men.
If suddenly you reveal this to someone,
then, abandoning his own body,
he'll become filled with *rasa* and go to Vraja!
Become a woman, brother, and then engage in this practice with a woman.
Remain in secrecy and practice this love,
lest this *rasa* become worthless.
Once you attain this *rasa*, do not reveal it!

And so this ecstasy will arise.
Alas! how shall I speak of such a thing?
—Miśra, *Bhāva Lahari Gīta,* 57–58

The Worship of the Sahaja Man

15

The worship of Man is very simple:
there's no yoga or fasting in that—only faith.
Just see what fun it is!
Take refuge with good companions, abandon false company.
When you become inwardly at peace, you'll easily understand.
Look and see with divine eyes: "Man" is sometimes male and sometimes female.
The final goal of Man is attained when the woman is a Hijṛā and the man a Khojā,
Always satisfied with Man, they will dwell in the *Sahaja* Land.
When one dwells in the *Sahaja* state, [all other] pleasure disappears.
They speak one language, and move by one word.
There is never any discrimination among them.
They view all without distinction, whether king or subject.
—from *Śrī Śrī Dulālcānder Bhāver Padāvalī o Sahaja Bhajanā Saṅgīta,* A. Sāu, ed. (Calcutta: Anil Lithography Company, 1399 B.S.)

The Hidden Play of Caitanya

16

To this day, Gour Rāy continues his play.
The Lord can be seen when one looks for Him.
If you examine everything from beginning to end, you can known him in your own state.
You'll find Caitanya in the Self-Nature.
The final play of Caitanya took place in a hidden form.
No one can understand his power.
Engaged in various play, he mingled with mankind.
Some say that, finally, he mingled with them in a stony-hearted way;
but no one can understand the deeds of Caitanya;
and anyone who could understand such things would go mad!
He never joined with man in a hard-hearted way;
The *Sahaja* Man appeared in a natural way!

That Supreme Essence became established within the heart of passionate souls;
those who feel this ecstasy know and have faith in this.
—Miśra, *Sahaja Tattva Praksāśa,* 2–3

Songs of the "Wealthy Gentlemen" (*Sāhebdhanī*): Other Kartābhajās and Related Groups

Songs of Bāṅkācāṅd—The "Crooked Moon"

Crippled from birth, Bāṅkācāṅd was spiritually adopted by Satī Mā and became her most beloved disciple. Today, he is also one of the most beloved figures in the more devotional and popular side of the tradition. A number of short, relatively simple songs are attributed to him.

Behold the Essence

17

Now you yourself must worship your Self!
But keep yourself very cautious—
Oh my Mind—be very careful!
Remember what was said before:
for your own intimate Man is within you!
Look and see Him with upturned eyes, beyond the reach of Vedic injunctions.
Look and see with upturned eyes,
taking your seat within the Void.[27]
He is beyond the comprehension of the Vedic injunctions;
Mānuṣa-cāṅd is revealed very secretly.
Now the door to the entrace is no longer bolted shut
—behold the Essence!
—Sudhīr Cakravartī, *Bāṅglā Deha-tattva Gān* (Calcutta: Pustak Bipaṇi, 1990), 63

Man is the Avatār

18

Having worshiped so many different gods,
now you've assumed the human form.
You've come into this world in the guise of Man;
now you're engaged in the worship of Man!
This Kali yuga has been blessed;

in the Kali yuga, Man is the *Avatār.*
Having attained the human body,
can't you recognize this Man?
Look and consider—without Man,
there is no other path!
Cakravartī, *Bāṇglā deha-tattva Gān,* 63

A Song of Kānāi Ghoṣe

One of the foremost original disciples of Āulcāṅd, Kānāi Ghoṣe apparently did not accept Rāmśaraṇ Pāl's authority as Kartā and went off to form his own sect across the river from Ghoshpara. His following is now known as the "Satyaśrot" or "True Current," and also commonly as the "Secret Kartābhajās," who are said to have preserved the more esoteric side of the tradition, in contrast to the more popular and devotional Ghoshpara following.[28]

The Treasure of the Heart

19

O blind man, you grasp after perversity!
The treasure of your heart lies in darkness.
That primordial supreme Person
is your deepest foundation, yet you are unaware of him.
Alas, blindman—he is everything to you!
You've abandoned the Sun of the world—
how will you know the Man of the Heart?"
—"Sādhusaṅgīta," in *Saṅgītāvalī,* vol. 1, ed. Navakiśora Gupta (Calcutta, 1298 B.S. [1891]), song 85

A Song Attributed (Falsely) to Lālan Shāh

According to many folk traditions, Lālan is believed to have visited the Kartābhajā melā in Ghoshpara and even learned some songs there. At least one scholar, Tushar Chatterjee, believes that Lālan's concept of the Maner Mānuṣa itself is derived from the Kartābhajā songs.

20

Oh say, Ghoshpara is greater than Vṛndāvana!
the disciples all worship in the Name of the Kartā;
everyone is free from everything.

At the Ghoshpara festival,
there is no distinction of caste!
In Ghoshpara, the Secret Vṛndāvana,
I can find the Man of the heart!
—from Caṭṭopādhyāy, "Ghoṣpāṛā Melā, Kartābhajā Sampradāya o Lālan," 142

Songs of the Sāhebdhanīs, Kubir Gosāiṅ, and Jādubindu

Closely related to the Kartābhajā tradition is the Sāhebdhanī sect, a smaller and highly esoteric group, which spread primarily in the rural areas of West Bengal north of Ghoshpara. Meaning literally the "wealthy Gentlemen" or even (given the loaded connotations of *sāheb* in colonial Bengal) the "Rich Englishmen," the Sāhebdhanīs are said to have been founded by a mysterious, perhaps mythical Fakir not unlike Āulcāṅd. However, the first organizer was a Gopa named Mulicāṅd Pāl (also known as Dukhirām Pāl). The two most famous poets of the tradition are Kubir Gosāiṅ (1787–1879) and his disciple Jādubindu (d.1916), who composed a huge body of mystical songs, none of which has ever been printed.[29]

According to Cakravartī, the Kartābhajās and Sāhebdhanīs are "two branches of the same tree"; according to other scholars such as Tushar Chatterjee and Ratan Kumār Nandī, the Sāhebdhanīs are better seen as a subsect or offshoot of the Kartābhajās.[30] In any case, the songs of Kubir do make frequent reference to Āulcāṅd, who is identified as the "secret incarnation" of Caitanya in the "secret Vṛndāvana" of Ghoṣpāṛā. Like the Kartābhajā songs, moreover, those of the Sāhebdhanīs make frequent use of imagery drawn from contemporary social and economic events—the railroad, the bazaars of Calcutta, the sorrows of Indigo cultivation, and the debt of poor landowners at the mercy of the Company. And like the Kartābhajās, they use these seemingly "secular" images to express the most profound esoteric ideas. Thus, the sowing of Indigo and the exploitation of the poor farmer at the hands of the Moneylenders becomes a complex allegory for the sufferings of human life in this realm of *saṃsāra*. Likewise, the railway car becomes a dense metaphor for the human body, which travels the tracks through this mortal world, besieged by the "soldiers" of the passions, and in search of the precious treasure of God who lies concealed within the heart.

Ghoshpara: The Secret Vṛndāvana

21

[Kṛṣṇa] established the Truth of Man and engaged in the Human Play,
wondrous to see!

From beginning to end, this Human Play captivates one's entire mind and knowledge.
When one contemplates Brahmā, he gains the power of Brahmā;
[so too], as soon as one remembers Him, one sees the Lord, who is supremely attractive.
He became incarnate in Nadiya and engaged in the supreme Play;
then He was revealed in Ghoshpara, and stayed a few days in Jaṅgīpur[31]
He remained in secrecy, immersed in His own delight, with His devotees
Man is Truth; Man is Truth; the Guru is Truth; the Truth of all Truths is Hari, the friend of the Poor.
He revealed the Truth of Man, moving throughout the Satya, Tretā, Dvāpara and Kali yugas, saying "Truth, Truth!"
He's the Beggar of True Love!
Two branches of one tree[32]—it's not written within the injunctions of the Vedas—
the Truth of Jaṅgīpur and of Ghoshpara! Kubir says, "Truth, Truth, Truth!"
— Cakravartī, *Sāhebdhanī Sampradāya*, 202–3, song 61

The Play of Man

22

Nowhere has there ever been such a Play of Man in this Kali age!
Dulāl has mounted the chariot at the Dol festival,[33]
fulfilling everyone's desires!
East, West, North and South—
we came to see from many lands.
[He engaged in] the Play of the Lord in the blessed age [of the Satya yuga],
the play of Rāma in the Tretā yuga,
in the Play of Śrī Kṛṣṇa in the Dvāpara yuga,
and in this Kali yuga, He engaged in the Play of Śrī Caitanya Nitāi!
And now we can see that this very same Śrī Caitanya
has become incarnate in Ghoshpara!
I've heard there are ten *avatārs*—
He has become incarnate in the forms of the Fish, the Tortoise, the Boar and Dwarf;
how wondrous is Lord Gourāṅga!
That same *avatār* has come to Ghoshpara,
and fulfilled all our hopes!
Having established the great holy places of Golok, Baikuṇṭhapurī,
Ayodhyā, Godābarī,
Gayā, etc, He revealed Himself in Ghoshpara.

Such a thing has never occurred anywhere before!
Kubir says, "here lies the dawn [of the Moon] for all mankind—
I sing of the virtues of Caraṇcāṅd!"
—*Sāhebdhanī Sampradāya,* 205–6, song 66

The Railway Car of the Human Body

23

The Engine car travels upon the rails of a solid track;
passing through Haora and Hooghly districts, and as time passes,
everything moves along with the sound, "*hur, hur, hur.*"
The fare of the poor folk falls to two *paysās*;
but the fare for the Bābus increases—Alas!—they take a seat and sit looking around.
There's an excellent car and compartment,
and as it moves along, [the Conductor] says, "Hey you!" and tells them when to get off.
The rail car travels over land,
just as the steam ship sails over the waters, and sprays foam up to the skies![34]
The birds and insects fly up.
[The railway] has conquered the Bengalis, looted the land and taken away all the wealth!
It pervades Bengal, which is now rigged up by it; it brings the news.
"Alas!" all the other men are wondering, "what's happened?"
The Sanskrit schools have recognized its authority; its hand passes lightly over it, like a Doctor taking the pulse.
Upon a machine, cloth is woven by the threads, and oh, by a machine, water can be raised!
By a machine, rice paddies can be husked; by a machine, wheat is ground;
by a machine, *ṭākās, paysās,* and paper are made; by a machine, ropes and cords are fashioned!
By a machine, the land can be cultivated—rivers and streams, ponds and earth,
whether little or great—all by English learning![35]
Inside this machine, coal is planted like a flag, and rammed down the throat of the flag-ship [of the engine car].[36]
Within the fourteen *poyās*[37] of the body—look and see—the Englishmen have
built a machine, which travels the thirty-two veins.
Kubir sings the praises of the true machine [of the human body]—and there's no way out of it![38]
—*Sāhebdhanī Sampradāya,* 186–87, song 45

The Human Rail-Car

24

Oh my mind, you ask about the railway-car of the human body—within it lies a precious Jewel!
But not everyone can see the One
who sat in Haora station and fashioned this human rail-car.
For that Workman can only be seen with experienced eyes.
Beneath this rail-car are two wheel-like things;
and there's an engine, which makes it move.
The creator of the World is its root cause, and brother, He has no equal!
He created two roads by which this car can travel:
by one path, it goes to the house of King Yama; and by the other path, there's the kindling of divine emotion!
Its Authority is Queen Rādhā and its Cashier[39] is Śrī Kṛṣṇa.
The initiatory Guru is the Wish-fulfilling Tree, in the guise of the Ticket Master.[40]
Now take the ticket from him and join the circle of devotees;
join the company of holy men, brother, and board this car!
When the time comes, the door will open and you'll find the wondrous realm.
You'll arrive at the holy site, and enter Vṛndāvana, the city of *Rasa.*
Oh, He who has fashioned this Haora Station
—listen to what I say—has fashioned it carefully and well!
You'll find the Wish-fulfiling Jewel, you'll become rich; otherwise, you'll lose your life!
There's a fare for entering the car; for the door isn't open—it's moved by the winds of passion.
The Mind-Engineer has the task of controlling the ten senses and the six enemies,[41]
who wear the guise of Soldiers.
Inside the car there's a kind of machine fed by fire and water.
He remained inside the machine room, with watchful eyes.
From place to place, at each station, He waits and unloads [the passengers].
The Human Rail-Car is wondrous, for it has no need of rails!
It travels equally over water and land and through the jungles.
It has an enclosure of skin, but inside, it's filled with diamonds, pearls and red gold!
And this very car lies in the neighborhood of Calcutta—these words are by no means untrue!
The rail car travels out of Haora and Sheyaldah.[42]
The Holy men know that it was [created] at the juncture of the heavenly realm and the primordial Void.
The car has so many chains, which are the veins, and that was the clever means of its Creator.

Only the most profound *Rasika* can understand all these things!
Search with your own eyes and grasp the jewel, which lies within the red chamber
of the body.
The hinges of the car are joined in many places by machines;
they've given them screws[43] so there's no shaking or trembling;
and their workmanship is that of the excellent mechanic, Madhusudhan!
Within the car there are thieves, and they have both strength and courage;
they steal your wealth by pickpocketing and strike you with fear!
When your knowledge and intellect are stolen, you'll be been utterly defeated,
wretched and indigent.
Having gone to sit in the first-class seats,
a very few men go to their own land in complete equality.
And this is the reason for founding the religion of the Worship of Truth.
Taking their place in the second-class chamber,
in the community of holy men, their heart's desires are filled upon the waves of
love![44]
The font of grace, the Śikṣa guru himself, plants the seed.
In the third-class car, brother, there is no happiness!
When one attains the jewel and becomes accomplished, he goes to the City of
Profit.
You'll no more return, within the car, you hand yourself over to your Guru.
When it reaches Haora you'll be decrepit,[45] and all your work will turn to shit.
The marrow will turn to water, and the inner essence will become a wasted husk
so remain refreshed—remember the Guru with your very life!
It carries the living soul from Haora to Sealdah.
It takes your money and then breaks your knees!
There, the factory and the machine become powerful, while the moon willingly
declines.
So hide yourself in the car of the mind and remain quiet.
The Kartā, the virtuous one, will show His grace;
remain bound to his will, see and know the clear, pure path!
Upon the rail-line, there's a telegraph which bears the seal of God's own work.
The physician takes the pulse when the body has fever;
resting his feet on the stool, he acts like a king and gives the news, whether good
or ill.
There's a policeman posted there, frightning to see—
when he sees an offence, he grabs you by the hair and leads you away!
He keeps you as a prisoner in the jail, bound with your feet over your head.
Meanwhile, brother, inside the car a bomb begins to smoke!
The passengers all press into the rear of the car.
And who can understand it? The owner and legal represtantive of this sinful car
lets out an angry growl!
He who comes into this world and enters this car
searches for the invaluable jeweled treasure.

And to him who has no hatred or desire, wearing the garb of a dervish, all
Hindus and Muslims are equal!
Why don't you look and consider this work of God?
There's no equal to this railway car of the Englishmen!
They've built this car in so many new forms and in so many various colors!
There's no contradicting the words of Gosāiṅ Kubir—
the fourteen worlds are fashioned within this car.
But Jādubindu has become a worthless wretch and dies, entangled in sorrows!
—*Sāhebdhanī Sampradāya,* 194–95, song 56

The Inner Calcutta—The Wondrous City of the Human Body

25

Oh, how wondrous are the habits of the human body-Calcutta!
Brother, the water of the red pond[46] is very sweet, I hear—
but some say that it's vulgar and crude,[47] and the ruin of *dharma.*
For he who drinks this water becomes drunken beyond the world!
You dwell in Calcutta's Bowbazaar;
brother, you're entangled in so many desires!
Bring the sweet-meat of Hari's name, eat it and become refreshed!
For on the day that you return to Bagbazaar
simply preserving your life will be your burden!
Calcutta has fifty-two bazaars and fifty-three lanes
Binding [your] hands, twisting and breaking [your] back, they offer [you] up as a
human sacrifice.
And a pair of bridges by the names of Sonāgāchi and Māniktola appear with a
wondrous show!
On the shore of your Ganges your house trembles;
within it you, can see a tier of wondrous color.
Jādubindu, the fool, has become bewildered; brother, he's had the wool pulled
over his eyes![48]
—*Sāhebdhanī Sampradāya,* 197, song 57

The Sorrows of Indigo: The Blue Devil

26

Now Indigo has come in the guise of the Blue-Throated One [Śiva],[49] and
conquered the world!
Driven by the madness of Indigo, where will I go? Because of Indigo, those wily,
wicked men have taken away all our homesteads!

Those who deal in Indigo are like the embassadors of Death!
And whatever you get from them, they'll use to ruin and kill you, with their hands around your neck!
At first, when Indigo arrived in the guise of seeds,[50] everyone in every land was as if drunken with every kind of intoxicant!
At a weight of five pounds of Indigo for a third acre of land, they scattered the seed, and it sprouted up.
When they offered the loans for the Blue Jewel [Indigo], the Deowan took half of it;
the Land Surveyor, by cheating on the surveying, takes a little too!
Taking three acres for every acre of land, he snatches up everything from the bogs to the sand bars!
At the time of planting the Blue Jewel, they cast great clods of earth upon it; finally, they cast away all their harrows [for rice cultivation] and only grow a lot of Indigo.
And at the harvest time, they take the harrow and reap a great amount
When they take the plow to the earth, all the poor lowly people are afflicted by Indigo!
If they don't cry out to the petty farmers to take their harrow and remove the weeds, in the end, [the plants] will be choked and die.
From what once was fallow land, after the bullocks have ploughed it, the Land Surveyor and the Rent Collector take [the Indigo] and sell it.
The Deowan is the Blue Jewel's Uncle—his tips increase a bit; and his clerks, without even counting, take a few *rupees* too.
The Clerk of the Estate takes and offers it up annually to their Tutelary Deity.
But now all respect for this Blue Jewel has vanished; now there's only disrespect—tell me, these words aren't untrue, are they?
The high and the low have all become equal——everyone's devoid of good judgment in this Kali Yuga!
The Kasandār takes the Blue Jewel, collects it in large amounts and then sends it off in bundles with the export clerk.
—dividing and multiplying, *rupee* by *rupee*, in great confusion!
The king of death has become charitable; when one is overtaken by death, the subjects are punished by the office clerks, and all their wealth is destroyed.
"When the rooms of your house are destroyed," says Kubir, "think of this story."
—*Sāhebdhanī Sampradāya,* 207, song 68

A Petition to the Company

27

I'll go to make a petition at the door of the Company[51] itself;
I'll tell His Highness of all the suffering in my heart!

I have fourteen *poyās*[52] of land; the rent is a *sika* and sixteen *ānās*; and I've repaid the debt of its cost.
When the deputy Collector[53] came and surveyed the land, the price became great;
And when the Company's Officer came and surveyed the land, I think, right there on the spot, east and west,
north and south, it somehow became even greater in measure!
There are rivers and streams upon it; for my whole life it's been fallow land.
My foremost enemy is the Head-Man; the Tax Officer appeared, and there on the road,
Śraban Coudhurī, the Deowan, received the rent.
All of them together are my opponents; the Head Clerk [of the law court] has entangled me in a terrible mess!
Let me tell you about all the qualities of the Collector's Officers: just like the
Finance Ministers of Howrah, after they win the lawsuit, they'll all dance about!
And Kubir says, carefully consider all the sad events of my life!"
—*Sāhebdhanī Sampradāya,* 209–10, song 71

The Mysteries of Woman

28

What *rasikas*[54] you women are!
You have no compassion, you have no *dharma*; you eat and digest men!
Śyāmā[55] became Satī and, having taken control of her husband's heart, she made him penniless!!
Woman, in the form of the Primordial Śakti, brought forth the three deities and then became Rājeśvarī;
thus it's known that she is herself the primordial origin of Brahmā, Viṣṇu and Rudra!
With honor and glory, she became Rādhā.[56]
Hari worshiped her, grasping her feet.
Then He became Śiva,[57] with his horn and tabour;
but Rādhikā showed him no compassion—only a stony body and a hard heart!
In this world, [everything] is at the service of Woman.
How can I fathom the qualities of Woman? Woman is a Princess, the radiant light of the family, who enchants the family!
Having ruined her own husband, Woman goes off wandering with the spring tide!
There is an inner husband and an outer husband.
The son, the husband and Paśupati, the Master of the entire universe,
are all indebted to Woman!

Giving one body refuge inside another body, the father has concealed [his son, as the fetus] inside of Woman.

From the father, the progenitor, birth takes place within the womb of Woman.
then, falling into troubles at the hands of that very Woman, one must marry!
And a Woman sits as the Company's own Queen Victoria and rules the land!

Woman is indeed the Master[58] of the world;
everyone works without wages for Woman!
When she loots the country, the male retreats in fear, utterly defeated!
Lamenting, Kubir says, "what use is there in speaking of Woman?"

—*Sāhebdhanī Sampradāya,* 166, song 13

V

Kartābhajā

A Satirical Poem by Dāśarathī Rāy

The following is a humorous satirical piece from the famous Bengali poet, Dāśarathī Rāy (1805–57).[1] Dāśarathī was particularly well known as a master of the *Pāñcālī* form, which are basically songs interspersed with short hymns to various deities.[2] He is also noteworthy for his rather raw and gritty—and very funny—depictions of the lives of the lower orders of Calcutta during the colonial era. Largely conservative in his religious views, Dāśarathī singled out the Kartābhajās as the very worst example of all that was wrong with the Hindu society of his day—their sexual licentiousness, idolatry, violation of caste, overturning of traditional laws of purity, chicanery, and fraud. Hence, he provides a wonderful window onto the perception of the Kartābhajās in the eyes of the upper-class elites of the day.

The *Pāñcālī* is melodious and pleasing to hear;
so pay attention and I'll recite some poetry.
The Kartābhajā sect has recently emerged—now hear some funny things about them!
Hearing all this is great delight!
They see no distinctions between boys, old men, youths, or women—thus they go along,
they can't see the path because of the darkness.
Their origin is in Ghoshpara. The son in law of Gopāl Ghoṣe[3]
is their primary Kartā.
He had four disciples—Madan, Subāla, Golok, and Bhola—
they are greatly respected.
These four were monks; but, deceiving men and women,
they enticed them, caressing their heads with their hands.
At the bewitching sound of their pleasures, the housewives go to bed with them;
they make prostrations with oblations of sweets.
All the lovers, wanton women, and old prostitutes
forsake their own caste.
Whether low caste or gentlemen, everyone comes together!
Joining in one family, they say an oath.

The sorrows of the depraved whore are gone for a moment; but then they return again.
Her youth is lost, and she's become feeble;
Look, there's no end of them—and no teeth in their mouths!
But in this [religion], they find no salvation!

The Kartābhajā sect has newly emerged—
how funny, how very funny!
When a woman of good family abandons her kin, and raises the flag of this new sect.
They're all ruined in this human play;
they go far astray from the path of devotion to Kṛṣṇa.
What more can I say, what more can I say?
The family might be saved if only
the King would punish them!

O say, who can understand them? Everyone's got a religious disease!
Leaving their husbands at home,
[the women], with various presents—milk, curd and sweets—
go there each Friday.
In some places there is worship, in some *pūjā*; in some, they begin the Śiva festival;
Some of them gather together in one place;
maddened with love for the Kartā, they hear religious teachings;
then they go crazy and run all around!
There's no consideration of caste; ritual is empty; thirty-six classes come together in one place.
Washermen, oilmen, and tanners; low classes and untouchables; Brāhmaṇs and
Kāyasthas; police chiefs and those who burn the dead,
all together eat the same food.
Joyfully, they all come together, believing this to be the place of God;
there's no shortage of devotion!
They don't speak the Name of God; they don't walk on the path of devotional love.
Their only holy object is the dirt at the base of the Pomegranate tree!
They don't wear loin cloths, they are neither dervishes nor renunciants.
Do they believe in the Purāṇas or the Koran?
They understand nothing of them!
They are neither holy men nor atheists; they remain outside the door like hypocrites.
They are neither Hindu nor Muslim weavers;
they are neither sages nor idiots, neither boatmen nor wrestlers;
neither canoes nor rafts.
They are not demons or ghosts; no one knows what their state or condition might be!
They overturn all Hindu religion.

They don't believe in gods or Brāhmaṇs, they are the foremost of the *Aghorapanthīs.*
I can't stand to hear about all their deeds!
They put food into one another's mouth—Oh, Bravo! what good taste!
they consider this their *Mahāprasād*![4]
Then they gather up the remnants of the rice, eat it and wipe their mouths with their hands.
They care nothing for the water used to rinse the mouth.
On the fast day, the widow's indulge in a feast:[5] each Friday night,
There's a feast with whatever one desires—
meat, fish, curds, and butter—they indulge in whatever is present, at any time.
At each full moon, there's a dance, where they all wish to sleep together,
without consideration.
Alas, all the old whores who aren't yet dead enjoy marital relations—
Just seeing this, I died in shame!
The young beautiful women all cut their lovelocks, become Gopīs,
and play in the game.[6]
They smear perfume and sandalpaste, garlic and collyrium on the limbs of their leader,
and exchange garlands with the Kartā.
The Kartā steals their clothing—then how splendid it is to see!
They quickly cover themselves with their hands.
Seeing this, even the mind of a sage is deluded; so how much more so will others be deceived?
This kind of singing and dancing goes on constantly.
Some among the Kartābhajās are intimate friends, some are adolescent girls;
sometimes they act like the [Gopīs] in the arbor;
sometimes they enact the Kṛṣṇakālī; sometimes they wear garlands of wildflowers.
and sometimes they enact Kṛṣṇa's lifting of Govardhan mountain;
sometimes they lead cows in the pasture, singing sweet songs out of tune.
They're all enchanted by the bamboo flute.
In various ways they perform the Līlā—and they enact more than just the slaying of Kāliya!
Thus, [going to the] Kartā is going to the house of the God of Death.
Brothers, if any of you wish to go to the Kartābhajā festival,
you'll have to go where thirty-six castes go—and caste will have to be left behind.
You won't reach the gates of heaven by this diseased path—
you'll suffer in their company and fall into depravity!
They engage in this sort of Kṛṣṇa-Līlā, considering it to be the best.
Oh, how much more will happen in this Kali age!
The Kartābhajās generate much smoke and violence, like the God of Death himself—

everyone's sleep is broken by their uproar!
They have a separate Tantra; they abandon all other sacred *mantras,*
and are initiated by the Human Mantra.
Religion is mixed with all irreligion;
they turn every deed into the enjoyment of sensual pleasures.
The basis of all their teachings is deception and fraud.
O what praises to God! That's what everyone's engaged in.
They don't lift the tail to see whether it's a cow or a bull!
They don't regard anyone as great or little—they've become all mixed up together.
Brother, there's nothing they haven't done!
The murderous highwayman became a holy man;
the harlot became a woman of good family;
she who is supposed to be a "chaste wife" has no number of "husbands."
The son of the tanner became a mendicant; the Caṇḍāla reads the *Caṇḍī-Maṅgal;*
I hear that the weaver has studied yoga.
Now, how many new things are happening! Something strange is taking place!
The cat and the mouse are friends; rice cooked in ghee is the tiger's food.
Just seeing and hearing this, my mind is slain!
Let the people beware: [they think that] heaven lies within in one's own body,
and when they are put to death by hanging, they go to Benaras and so try to deceive the God of Death!
They eat the flesh of birds and beasts, calling themselves "Knowers of Dharma!"
Their "Supreme Holy Man"[7] is a fivefold sinner.[8]
Here, I see, a cripple dances; their *yantra*-flower is mere pond-scum.
A deaf man sits, listening to the song of a mute,
always saying, where, where? The horse lays an egg and the stone has a skin!
The heavenly world of the Kartābhajās, I see, is woven by a weaver on his loom.
Is it not impossible to embellish something with mere outward appearances?
Hearing the words of wicked people,the body resounds more than if it were struck by a thunderbolt.[9]
A crane is not honored among geese; is a chicken adorned like a peacock?
Is a sorry old horse the mythical Winged Horse? Is a parrot equal to a hawk?
Does an ass carry the burden of an elephant? Is a jackal king in the lion's forest?
Thus the Kartābhajā abandons Kṛṣṇa: I've never heard such a thing before in this world!

Hari Is the Master of the World [Jagater Kartā]

Look and consider—what I say is not impossible.
Listen and know that I have no enemies.
Can a man perform the works of God?
And if he can sustain anything, can he sustain the kingdom and the oceans?

Can Man Be the Master?

Who is given such respect as that given to Hari?
Who has such strength as that which sustains the earth?
Who holds the power that He holds?
Who has such powers as He who made the heavens?
Who has such thirst as the one who drinks the oceans?
Who has such virtue that he feels no sorrow, even after assuming a body?
Who possesses such things as would satisfy the desire of Kṛṣṇa?
Who has such pride as to escape the hands of time?
Does he have such things as the one who takes the honey from nectar?
Who has eyes that can see five miles?
Does he have the weapons which can destroy the lightning?
Who is such a hero that he can slay Haridās?
Who is so fast moving that he can he can move within the heart?
Is there such a fruit if there is no rain?
Who has such a mind that he can fathom Brahma?
Who is so powerful that he can write [one's fate] upon the forepart of the skull?
Who is such a healer that he can cause the dead to live?
Who is such a man who wishes to be the "Kartā"?

A Man Can Never Be the Kartā

Isn't this stupid idea impossible? Is the firefly equal to the moon?
Is the watersnake equal to the great serpent Vāsuki?
Is the crow equal to Garuḍa? Is the drum equal to the roar of the clouds?
Is the sheep equal to the horse?
It's like a thief compared to a holy man, or a forest pig compared to an elephant!
Is the flower of a silk-cotton plant equal to a lotus-flower?
What is the beauty of a vulture compared to a parrot?
What is the best pool of water compared to the ocean?
What beauty is there compared to the mythical petal from an elephant's head?
An unripe fruit is not equal to a diamond, nor a lowly worm of a guru to Satyapīr.
Even if such a one speaks truth it is not true.
Is poison equal to nectar? The supreme Lord is the creator of the world.
The splendour of any other Kartā is nothing compared to him.

But how is that Kartā said to be a "Kartā"? Listen, brother I'll tell you.
The [true] Kartā is within all things, without the Kartā there is nothing.
But what is [the Kartābhajā's Kartā] like?
Just as: a dog is the "Kartā" in a rice husking room, a beast is the Kartā in the forest;
a ghost is the Kartā in the graveyard, a ringleader is the Kartā among thieves;

a ghoul is the Kartā of a Muslim cemetary; one possessed by an evil spirit is the Kartā in a carrion-depot;
an ugly old slut is the Kartā in a place full of rubbish and dung;
a sorcerer is the Kartā at the base of a Seora tree;
a cowherd is the Kartā in the pasture; a midwife is the Kartā in the birthing room;
a calf is the Kartā in a pen full of rams and ewes;
and *that's* how this one can be called the "Kartā"!

Hari is the Master of the world, and who else in this world is the Kartā?
Drown within his lotus eyes and worship Kṛṣṇa.
When Death comes, He grabs him by the hair and kills him!
Apart from Kṛṣṇa, who else can conquer death?

The Greatness of Hari's Name

This is a "Kartābhajā": "the woman becomes a *hijṛā* and the man a eunuch."
Such a person has great power in this age of Kali!
"The guru is truth, the guru is Brahma,"
so they say—but this is not found in the Vedas.
[They say] "One must offer the fruits of action to the Guru"; but what will result from such fruit?
By that fruit, one could attain the four ends of life.
The unattainable yogic practice, the dharma-yoga, abandoning actions;
They call this yoga the Great Yoga.
There is a secret philosophic teaching; one cannot get any facts about that anywhere.
This teaching cannot be spoken of.
There is an essence which cannot be grasped; he whose hand can grasp the mountain
alone can grasp it.
Can ordinary people grasp Him? He is the eternal Nirañjana.
He is immutable and consists of eternal bliss,
both gross and subtle, and so beautiful, with 1,000 eyes, 1,000 faces,
His caste is all castes.
He is eternal and immutable. According to His will,
the creation of the three worlds occurs.
Lord Viṣṇu, having created the fabric of illusion, which is time,
in time, creates destruction.
He is without qualities, according to the words of the Vedas; and at other times He is with qualities.
Who can fathom Him?
The great yogis always meditate; but who can comprehend him?
One can comprehend worldly things, but the imperishable is unthinkable.

For the sake of His divine Play, he assumes various forms—the forms of the universe.
We can't even give a comparison for those forms.
He is within all things; if one looks and understands, He can be found in worldly things.
He who performs his actions is Govinda, the object of devotion,
He was born at the feet of Suradhunī.
For the sake of devotion, from age to age, that Object of devotion
crosses over [to this world], again and again, for the sake of his devotees.
Bearing a bow in the form of Rāma, He destroyed the armies of demons;
He engaged in the play of Kṛṣṇa in the Dvāpara age.
He stole the hearts of the Gopīs and tended cows in the field.
Just for fun, he raised up Mount Govardhan.
When Vraja was burning in the forest fire, He drank [the lake and put out the fire] as a jest!
He revealed the entire universe within His mouth.
Destroying the enemies of the gods and the family of the Karavas,
Hari removed the burden of the earth.
Who can fathom His death, the Beloved of Dvārakā, in Dvārakā?
He who is infinite has no end. The play of Kṛṣṇa is a limitless ocean; He is the friend of the world, the friend of the poor.
Who can know His greatness?
He who recites His Name is the conqueror of death; he triumphs over death,
by drinking the nectar, the ambrosia of Hari's Name.
Indra, Candra and Hutāśan[10] always act in accord with their own conditions:
Brahmā always experiences the Brahmā-state.[11]
Chidām and the others follow the devotional mood of friendship;
Yaśodā feels the devotional mood of parental love.
Gopīnāth feels the mood of the Gopīs; and Viśvatat feels all the devotional moods.
The great power of the state of devotion cannot be expressed in this world.
And all those devotional moods of Rādhā are simply beyond this world altogether!
Who can express all those moods?
Because of that very Rādhā state, Śrī Gourāṅga [Caitanya], the jewel of the heart,
became incarnate in Navadvīpa.
Now I'll describe the group that came with him,
Nityānanda and Śankarāraṇya.
He gave the Name of Hari to Jīva, and revealed its fruit:
By hearing that Name, Jīva was liberated.
Such is the compassionate Lord! Whenever you call upon Him,
you forget this worthless world.
Say, "Hari, Śrī Caitanya"!—all ignorance will depart!
Say, "Hari, Hari"! with a loud voice.
Keep calling upon Gour Govinda, raising the sign.

The god of death will be driven far away; call upon the compassionate Nitāi.
The day goes by in the marketplace of the world; the sun sets
The ferry boat was obstructed at the ghat; now look and see what the means [to salvation] is.
The finite body is not eternal; this body is aways uncertain.
No one goes with you; no one knows anything about anyone else.

Śiva composed the *Tantrasāra*, the greatest in all the world,
the fivefold initiation into the five paths.
Even the atheists believe in karma, and they too desire *dharma*.
But the one who knows Brahman is greater than all other knowers.
[The Kartābhajās'] belief is outlandish! they rub their noses in the dirt!
The Kartā of the World truly means Jagadīś [the Lord of the World].
But [among the Kartābhajās] that Kartā is not worshipped; they throw away the gold and accept mere glass!
They abandon the nectar and drink poison.

Kartābhajā Is Futile

They throw the jewels far away, and try vainly to fill their baskets,
with the seeds of jujubes.
The miller is honored, while the Brahmin is shoved aside; they throw away the sugar and accept molasses.
They throw away the valuable garment, and fight over cheap red-dyed cloth.
They abandon the flowered chariot and accept a potter's wheel.
They let the cockatrice loose, while a crow sits in the golden cage.
They throw away the milk and save the flavor of the spinach stalk!
They mix up their sweetmeats with god knows what; their highest caste is the leatherworker!
They feast on the fast day—that's their evening worship.
They abandon the fire and pour their ghee upon ashes.
The rare food of the gods is offered to dogs.
They abandon the great ritual of bathing in the Ganges and instead bathe in a pond.
They throw away the sugar of Benaras as if it were ashes.
They don't worship Nitāi—for they are Kartābhajās!

Just as one would throw away his own religion and become a Christian,
so too, the Kartābhajā religion is the first rite [on this degenerate path]!
He spoils the ritual food of thirty-six castes, and loses his own caste;
he engages in fraud with the Guru and acts like a cowherd!

Why Is the Worship of the Kartā Futile?

If one gives the kingdom over to a monkey, it doesn't honor the land;
An auspicious mark made of water is false, and doesn't last at all.
If one puts perfume on the body of a mole, the foul smell doesn't depart.
If one cuts a dried up bamboo stalk, he doesn't get the precious medicinal sap.
If one gives medicine to a dead body, it has no value.
In the worship of the human Kartā there is never salvation from death.

There is no comparison between a cat and a tiger.
Is there any comparison between a barren wasteland and the supreme Lord?
For the one who worships the feet of his deity, mere humanity is worthless ash.
There is no equal to the Lord in any of the three worlds.

What Is the Excellent Nature of Caitanya's Līlā?

The Savior of the three worlds is not equal to the Ganges.
Everyone knows that the words of the Vedas are salvation.
The essence of all liberation is the worship of Hari's feet.
Is there any agent who is equal to Śukadeva?
And where is there any place equal to Vṛndāvana?
The outward garments worn by Kṛṣṇa's followers are mere words.
And where is there any play equal to Caitanya's play?
All play is worthless compared to Caitanya's play.

The Supreme Essence

The greatest of all holy places is Jagannāth Kṣetra.[12]
The greatest of all religious practices is a pure mind.
The greatest of all merit is the gift of food and clothing.
The greatest of all Purāṇas is the *Hariguṇagān*.
The greatest of all actions is a desire which is free of lust.
The greatest of all laws is the law against violence.
The greatest of all birds is the great bird, Garuḍa.
The greatest of all trees is the Tulsī.
Among the family of demons, the greatest is Bibhīṣaṇ.
The greatest among monkeys is Pabanānanda.
The greatest among Asuras is Prahlād Ratan.
He who is great is the one who is devoted to Hari.
In this world, you wasted your days in worthless deeds;
you abandoned the supreme essence and, at the end of your days, you did not call upon Caitanya.
You did not take hold of that Name by which danger is destroyed and worship at Hari's feet.
So why, not seeing the wave of danger, have you plunged within it?

The Dazzling Show of the Kartābhajās

The foremost Kartā-Bābu of the community has become completely depraved;
he's fallen wholly into sin.
The people of his house have corrupted him, everything has become a fraud!
His hoax has dissolved like water, and his hands have been bound.
There's no more display of trickery—for three years he's been in the Calcutta Jail!
But now that's all been forgotten, and he's regained his good status.
Now where's the Kartā and where's the defendant? This farmer is a farmer of
men!
Because of his "enlightenment," there was so much praise!
He has been judged by the Puṇḍits of Navadvīpa.
They say, "brother, I've never heard of the Kartābhajās in any Purāṇa."
With their magical *mantra,* they delude people's minds.
Inside their house they [suppose they can] reveal Indra, Candra and Agni.
They show you something with the qualities of something else, saying that lead is
gold!
Seeing their dazzling display, the people are easily amazed and blinded.
Just as a Magician's jugglery can alter the scales,
they can show you all things, but feed you nothing![13]

The Kartā smokes a great deal of tobacco—now listen to the reason:
his hookah is not coconut, it is a bundle of palm!
The bowl is silver and a mouthpiece of gold hangs from it.
It is surely also set with a chain of gold.
On the night of the gathering, he smokes tobacco all the time.
It seems this is the Kartā's eager desire.
The hookah is not filled with water; but he fills it with oil and blows into it.
No one else knows that the hookah is filled with oil.
When the oil of the lamps is extinguished, they call out "bring oil!"
The lights are nearly extinguished.
Then the Kartā fills the lamps with the oil from the hookah,
and at the Kartā's command, the lights are lit with the hookah water.
Seeing this, the young widows think this is a miracle.
"O Mā! he has lit the lamps with water from the hookah!"
They say, "Lord, show your grace, never seize upon the sins of your servants.
Bless us with the base of your feet!"
Having disguised himself as the Kartā amidst this party of women, what wicked
fraud he performs!
I wish I could give him a good thrashing!
Seeing and hearing all this, I've lost all patience. But in the government of the
Hon'ble Company,
I have no authority, so what can I do?

The End Result

One should know that the Kartābhajā is just so much jugglery;
and if one doesn't know this, his entire family can be deluded.
In this community there was a great devotee named Khudirām Caṭṭo.
His disciple in Nārānpur was Kāśīnāth Bhaṭṭo.
This story occurred in Pāṭūli, but it became widely known.
The Kartābhajā religion became Khudirām's great sorrow!
It was forbidden for everyone to assemble together,
and because he didn't heed that [prohibition], Khudirām experienced great adversity
Now no one will eat with him or offer him tobacco.
Two men—Chidem Sarkār and Maṇḍal Bako—
were with him.
They knew some *mantras*, and they used to pass a few off and deceive people.
They too were actors in this farce.
Some people became greatly annoyed and went to inform the Rājā's house;
the Rājā gave the command to bring them.
Crying and crying, they went with the armed footman, trembling with terror,
the three came present before him.
They were punished by the Rājā and left his palace;
now they have shaven their beards and abandoned the Kartābhajā religion!

The joy of the Kartābhajās has ended.
The leading Kartās have abandoned the temple.
They've realized this is the end and cut their long beards.
Recently Khudirām was seen in the city of Pāṭuli.
In the name of God—what a disgrace!
All the people of the village have made him an outcast.
This Brāhmaṇ has fallen into terrible trouble.
Oh, no one gives him anything! Oh, what terrible suffering!
The boys and girls of the house cry out and say, "our intimate friend has forsaken us!"

Notes

Translator's Note

1. See EE ch. 4–6; Urban, "The Poor Company: Economics and Ecstasy in the Kartābhajā Sect of Colonial Bengal," *South Asia* 19, no. 2 (1996): 1–33; Urban, "The Torment of Secrecy: Ethical and Epistemological Problems in the Study of Esoteric Traditions," *History of Religions* 37, no. 3 (1998): 209–48.

2. Quoted in Rainer Schulte and John Biguenet, eds., *Theories of Translation: An Anthology of Essays from Dryden to Derrida* (Chicago: University of Chicago Press, 1992), 4. My approach to the task of translation has been most informed by theoretical literature, such as Walter Benjamin, Jacques Derrida and Maurice Blanchot; for a good overview of the approaches to translation, see Lawrence Venuti, *The Translator's Invisibility* (New York: Routledge, 1992), and Lawrence Venuti, ed., *Rethinking Translation: Discourse, Subjectivity, Identity* (New York: Routledge, 1995).

3. Edward Conze, *Buddhist Thought in India: Three Phases of Buddhist Philosophy* (Ann Arbor: University of Michigan, 1967), 271–73. For a full discussion of the ethical and epistemological problems inherent in the study of esoteric traditions, see EE introduction and Urban, "The Torment of Secrecy," 209–48.

4. Jeffrey J. Kripal, *Kālī's Child: The Mystical and the Erotic in the Life of Ramakrishna* (Chicago: University of Chicago Press, 1998). The major English newspaper in Calcutta, *The Statesman* (January 31, 1997), published a full-page review by Narasimha Sil, who accused Kripal of being a shoddy scholar who has "ransacked" another culture and produced a work that is, in short, "plain shit." Kripal has since written a thoughtful reflection on the aftermath of his book and its implications for the study of other cultures ("The Fearful Art of Writing Left-Handed: Some Personal and Theoretical Reflections on Translating the *Kathāmṛta* into American English," in *In the Flesh: Eros, Secrecy and Power in the Tantric Traditions of India,* ed. Hugh B. Urban and Glen A. Hayes [in progress]).

5. Jacques Derrida, *Des tours de Babel,* quoted in Venuti, *Rethinking Translation,* 7.

6. Venuti, *Rethinking Translation,* 8.

7. Rudolf Pannwitz, *Die Krisis der europäischen Kultur,* quoted by Walter Benjamin, "The Task of the Translator," in *Illuminations: Essays and Reflections* (New York: Schocken, 1981), 80–81.

Chapter I

1. The term *bhāva* is extremely difficult to translate, and can carry meanings as diverse as "birth, origination, existence, presence, essence, shape, condition, mood, love, friendship,"

and so on. Here I am following the lead of June McDaniel, who suggests that, in the case of Bengali mystical and devotional literature, it is best translated as "ecstasy" (*The Madness of the Saints: Ecstatic Religion in Bengal* [Chicago: University of Chicago Press, 1989], 21–22).

2. The oldest known manuscript of Karātabhāja songs that I have found is the "Kartābhajā Gīta," contained in the Bāṅgīya Sāhitya Pariṣat Library, Bengali Ms. 956. The most important publications of the songs are the *Bhāver Gīta*, ed. Rameścandra Ghoṣe (Goabagan: Aurora Press, 1882), and the recent edition printed by Śāntirañjan Cakravartī (Calcutta: Indralekha Press, 1993). Other Kartābhajā texts include: Manulāl Miśra, *Bhāver Gīta Vyākhyā Saha Sahaja Tattvaprakāśa Vā Sanātana Sahaja Satya Dharmer Ādi Itihāsa* (Calcutta: the author, 1911), and Miśra, *Kartābhajā Dharmer Ādivṛttānta Vā Sahajatattva Prakāśa* (Calcutta: the author, 1925).

One of the most important features of the Kartābhajā sect is the fact that we have a fairly large body of historical evidence for their growth in colonial Bengal. Apart from the mystical songs of the BG, the primary texts include these works of Manulāl Miśra, but there are also two important personal accounts by Kartābhajā devotees: that of Babu Gopāl Krishna Pāl, in J. H. E. Garrett, *Bengal District Gazetteers, Nadia* (Calcutta: Bengal Secretariat Book Stall, 1910), and that of Krishna Pāl, ed. William Ward, *A Brief Memoir of Krishna Pāl: The First Hindoo in Bengal Who Broke the Chain of Caste by Embracing the Gospel* (London: J. Offer, 1823).

Contemporary newspaper accounts include *Saṃvāda Prabhākara*, 18 Caitra 1254 B.S. [1848]; *Somaprakāśa*, 20 Caitra 1270 [1864]. Contemporary literary accounts include Dāśarathī Rāy, "Kartābhajā," in *Dāśarathī Rāyer Pāñcālī*, ed. H. P. Cakravartī (Calcutta: University of Calcutta Press, 1962); Nabīncandra Sen, "Ghoṣpāṛār Melā," part IV of "Āmār Jīvana," in *Nabīncandra Racanāvalī* (Calcutta: Baṅgīya-Sāhitya-Pariṣat, 1974), vol. 3; and the biographies of Rāmakṛṣṇa, such as *Śrī Śrīrāmakṛṣṇa-Kathāmṛta*, by Mahendranāth Gupta (Calcutta: Kathāmṛta Bhāban, 1987) and *Śrīśrīrāmakṛṣṇa-Līlāprasaṅga* of Swami Saradānanda (Calcutta: Udbodhan Kāryālay, 1986). Missionary accounts include William Ward, *Account of the Writings, Religion and Manners of the Hindus* (London: Black, Parbury and Allen, 1817–20), and James Long, *Handbook of Bengal Missions* (London: J. F. Shaw, 1848).

3. On the Sahajiyā tradition, see Edward C. Dimock Jr., *The Place of the Hidden Moon: Erotic Mysticism in the Vaiṣṇava-Sahajiyā Cult of Bengal* (Chicago: University of Chicago Press, 1966); Shashibhushan Dasgupta, *Obscure Religious Cults as a Background to Bengali Literature* (Calcutta: Firma KLM, 1968). On the Bāuls and their role as Bengali folk icons, made famous by Rabindranāth, see Charles Capwell, *Music of the Bāuls of Bengal* (Kent, Oh.: Kent State University Press, 1986); Carol Salomon, "Bāul Songs," in *Religions of India in Practice*, ed. Donald Lopez (Princeton: Princeton University Press, 1995), and Urban, "The Politics of Madness: The Construction and Manipulation of the 'Bāul' Image in Modern Bengal," *South Asia* 22, no. 1 (1999): 13–46.

4. Sukumār Sen, "Kartābhajā Kathā o Gān," in *Kartābhajā Dharmata o Itihāsa*, ed. S. Mitra (Calcutta: De Book Stores, 1977), 2:39.

5. When Rachel McDermott (Barnard College) told the Bengali historian Sukumār Sen that she wanted to write her dissertation on Kamalākānta Bhaṭṭācārya, Sen told her she ought to study something truly worthwhile like the Kartābhajās (personal communication, 1995).

6. See Urban, "The Extreme Orient: The Construction of 'Tantrism' as a Category in the Orientalist Imagination," *Religion* 29 (1999): 123–46.

7. D. C. Sen, "Kartābhajā Dal," *Baṅgabani*, 1 Barṣa, no. 4 (1951): 336. As Sen puts it, "The songs are composed in a very simple, beautiful form . . . which expresses deep philo-

sophical truth, but which cannot be understood by anyone apart from initiates. Although the language is simple, it is highly enigmatic. . . . Just as we can't understand the songs of birds, so, too, we can't understand these songs, but still our hearts are touched by their obscure beauty."

8. See Urban, "The Poor Company," 1–33, and Urban, "The Torment of Secrecy," 209–48.

9. My research was conducted under the generous auspices of the Social Science Research Council and the University of Chicago Committee on South Asia, from 1994 to 1997. During this time I translated roughly 300 Kartābhajā songs and interviewed several dozen gurus and devotees from West Bengal (chiefly Calcutta and Nadiya district) and Bangladesh (Jessore and Kushtia districts).

10. See Ranajit Guha, *Elementary Aspects of Peasant Insurgency in Colonial Bengal* (Delhi: Oxford University Press, 1983); Partha Chatterjee, *The Nation and Its Fragments: Colonial and Postcolonial Histories* (Princeton: Princeton University Press, 1993).

11. See Rosalind O'Hanlon, "Recovering the Subject: Subaltern Studies and Histories of Resistance in Colonial South Asia," *Modern Asian Studies* 22 (1988): 189–224; William Pinch, *Peasants and Monks in British India* (Berkeley: University of California Press, 1996). Two more promising attempts to understand the specifically religious dimension of subaltern consciousness are the works of David Hardiman, *The Coming of the Devi: Adivasi Assertion in Western India* (Delhi: Oxford, 1995), and Saurabh Dube, *Untouchable Pasts: Religion, Identity and Power among a Central Indian Community, 1780–1950* (Albany: State University of New York Press, 1998). As Dube argues, "religion is not . . . a hermetically sealed off domain of the sacred, a static repository of timeless traditions. . . . It is an inherently historical set of signifying beliefs and practices whose meaningful constructions . . . of the social world are at once tied to processes of domination and to strategies of resistance to authority" (6).

12. "The Kartābhajā religion is currently being practiced. This too is a path for reaching God—but it is a very filthy one. Just as there are various doors for entering a house—by some doors one enters the front room . . but there is a separate door for the sweeper [the latrine door]. The dirty path of the Kartābhajās is of this sort. Their habit is practice with a female partner" (Akṣaykumār Sen, *Śrī Śrī Rāmakṛṣṇa Puṅthi* [Calcutta: Udbodhana Kāryālaya, 1976], 116). See also Kripal, *Kālī's Child,* 274–75, 289–90.

13. Quoted in Debendranāth De, *Kartābhajā Dharmer Itivṛtta* (Calcutta: Jiggasa Agencies, 1968), 88–89.

14. Kālakūṭa (Samareś Basu), *Kothāy Se Jan Āche* (Calcutta: De's Pub., 1983), 34.

15. Jāhnavīkumār Cakravartī comments: "The people of Bengal have always been Tantrics and Sahajiyās. But in the Kartābhajā sect, this Tantric current has undergone many transformations and been conceived in a new form" ("Kartābhajāner Rūpa o Śvarūpa," in *Kartābhajā Dharmamata o Itihāsa,* ed. S. Mitra [Calcutta: De Book Stores, 1977], xxv). Other scholars who argue that the Kartābhajās are basically Sahajiyās, in continuity with the older Bengal Tantric tradition, include De, *Kartābhajā Dharmer Itivṛttā,* 7–10; Advaita Candra Dās, *Saṅgīta o Darśana* (Calcutta: Cayanikā, 1992); Dās, *Śrī Satīmā Candrikā* (Calcutta: Firma KLM, 1986); Tuṣār Caṭṭopādhyāy, "Ghoṣpāṛār Melā o Kartābhajā Sampradāy," in *Lālan Sāhitya o Darśana,* ed. K. R. Hāq (Dhaka: Bangla Academy, 1976); and Ratan Kumār Nandī, *Kartābhajā Dharma o Sāhitya* (Naihati: Asani Press, 1984). For general background on the Vaiṣṇava-Sahajiyā tradition, see Edward C. Dimock, *The Place of the Hidden Moon: Erotic Mysticism in Bengal* (Chicago: University of Chicago Press, 1966), and Shashibhushan Dasgupta, *Obscure Religious Cults* (Calcutta: Firma KLM, 1968).

16. As Manindra Mohan Bose explains, Sahaja is a Sanskrit term meaning "what one is born with . . . the natural tendency one possesses from birth . . . Love is a natural characteristic of the Supreme Being which is possessed by man by his origin from the Eternal Spirit" (*Post Caitanya Sahajia Cult of Bengal* [Calcutta: University of Calcutta Press, 1930], vi).

17. The question of the possible use of sexual rituals in Kartābhajā practice is an extremely controversial one. A few of the Kartābhajā songs do make cryptic references to sexual rites, similar to the related sect of the Bāuls. The Kartābhajās were, moreover, attacked and reviled throughout the nineteenth century for their alleged use of Tantric sexual techniques. Most "orthodox" members of the community, however, vehemently deny the presence of any kind of sexual rites—what they call the "stinking fruit" which crept into and corrupted the "Garden of Love." On this whole controversy, see EE chapter 6, "The Stinking Fruit in the Garden of Love," and Urban, "The Torment of Secrecy," 209–48.

18. Oddie, "Old Wine in New Bottles? Kartābhajā (Vaishnava) Converts to Evangelical Christianity in Bengal, 1835–1845," *Indian Economic and Social History Review* 32, no. 3 (1995): 329.

19. *Somaprakāśa,* 20 Caitra 1270 B.S. (1864). As Sumanta Banerjee argues, "almost all the contemporary records" show overwhelmingly that the Kartābhajā following came largely from "depressed castes, untouchables, Muslim peasants, and artisans, as well. as women" (*The Parlour and the Streets: Elite and Popular Culture in Nineteenth Century* Calcutta [Calcutta: Seagull, 1995], 44). For general descriptions of the social and economic context in Calcutta in the late eighteenth and early nineteenth centuries, see S. Chaudhuri, ed., *Calcutta, the Living City,* vol. 1: *The Past* (Calcutta: Oxford University Press, 1990), and T. P. Nair, ed., *Calcutta in the Nineteenth Century* (Calcutta: Firma KLM, 1984).

20. Banerjee, *The Parlour and the Streets,* 69.

21. KDA, cited in Bhāṭṭācārya, *Bāṅglār Bāul,* 62.

22. On the image of the "secret Caitanya" and secret Vṛndāvana, see Satyaśiva Pāl, *Ghoṣpāṛār Satīmā o Kartābhajā Dharma* (Calcutta: Pustak Bipaṇi, 1990): "This Madman was Śrī Bhagavān, the destroyer of doubt. From time to time he comes down to the earth. From age to age he takes the form of a great Person and engages in sport with human beings as his *avatār* on earth. . . . In the Kali yuga, he became manifest in the form of Śrī Caitanya. After that, he remained hidden for long time. But here, having arisen in Ghoṣpāṛā, the devotees of Vṛndāvana can know him if they see him secretly with their secret eyes" (246). In the words of the great poet of the Sāhebdhanī sect, Kubir Gosāiṅ (d.1879): "Ghoṣpāṛā has become the secret Vṛndāvana, manifest to both boys and girls, rays of red sun light" (cited in Pāl, *Ghoṣpāṛār Satīmā,* 83).

The image of the secret marketplace (*gupta hāṭ*) is a play on a famous but cryptic passage from the *Caitanya Caritāmṛta*: Advaita sends a secret message to his Master Caitanya, saying "tell the Madman that there is no need for anxiety; tell the Madman that the rice is not sold in the marketplace" (*Bāulke kahio—hāṭe nā bikay cāul. Bāulke kahio—kāye nāhik āul*) (*Antya Līlā,* 19.18–21). According to the mainstream Vaiṣṇava interpretation, this means that Caitanya's work is now complete and he no longer need worry; there is now sufficient love (i.e., "rice") for all living beings, so there is no more need to sell it in the "marketplace" of the world. See Edward C. Dimock, Jr., trans., *The Caitanya Caritāmṛta of Kṛṣṇadāsa Kavirāja* (Cambridge: Harvard University Press, 1999), 981.

However, according to the Kartābhajās' esoteric interpretation, this verse means on the contrary that the old Vaiṣṇava community begun by Caitanya has now become corrupt and filled with thieves, who are greedy and selfish and no longer distribute the "rice" of love and devotion to poor human beings. Therefore, it was necessary for Caitanya to reincarnate in the form of the Āul or madman—namely, the poor mad fakir, Āulcāṅd—and create a new "secret marketplace" in the "hidden Vṛndāvana" of Ghoṣpāṛā (see De, *Kartābhajā Dharmer Itivṛtta,* 5–6).

23. S. K. De, *Bengali Literature in the Nineteenth Century, 1820–1825* (Calcutta: University of Calcutta Press, 1919), 37.

24. See Pāl, *Ghoṣpāṛār Satīmā,* 190.

25. Ghoṣe, preface to BG (1882). Ghoṣe gives three reasons for the difficulty with the text: "(1). No original text can be found; (2). It is impossible to find all of the songs in any single text; those that can be found were copied from hand-written sources and many errors have occurred . . . (3) the manuscripts are very old and fragile . . . and written in colloquial dialects. It is difficult to determine which were written by Lālśaṣī, as many devotees gave the name to their own compositions."

26. Sen, "Āmār Jīvana," 187.

27. Cakravartī, *Vrātya Lokāyat Lālan* (Calcutta: Pustak Bipaṇi, 1992), 131. For a good discussion of other popular song forms in Calcutta at this time, see Rajyeshwar Mitra, "Music in Old Calcutta," in *Calcutta the Living City,* Vol. 1: *The Past,* ed. Sukanta Choudhuri (Calcutta: Oxford, 1990); Charles Capwell, "Musical Life in 19th Century Calcutta as a Component in the History of a Secondary Urban Center," in *Bengal Vaiṣṇavism, Orientalism Society and the Arts,* ed. Joseph O'Connell (East Lansing: Michigan State University Asian Studies Center, 1985); Dusan Zbavitel, *Bengali Literature* (Wiesbaden: Otto Harrassowitz, 1976); De, *Bengali Literature in the Nineteenth Century*; Rachel Fell McDermott, *Singing to the Goddess: Poems to Kālī and Umā from Bengal* (New York: Oxford University Press, 2001).

As Capwell suggests, nineteenth-century Calcutta was a unique place for music, precisely because it was an area of such intense change, rapid growth, and the confrontation of different cultures during the colonial era: "Like religious, educational, journalist, social . . . components in the development of culture in the 19th century, musical and related arts too were an area of change, development, self-reflection and controversy in the process of confrontation between native and imported traditions" (171–72).

28. The differences between the printed form of this song in the BG and its handwritten form in the KG manuscript are minor: Most are variations in spelling (most often in sibilants and vowel length), which probably reflect different regional dialects. It seems likely that these minor discrepancies are the result of the editor's attempt to standardize his diverse manuscripts and to eliminate as many colloquial variations as possible.

29. The *akṣaravṛtta* or *payār* system is the one of the three primary systems of scansion used in Bengali literature. According to this method, every line has an even number of units (typically 14, though not necessarily always the same in every line of the poem). An open syllable (vowel-final syllable) counts as one unit; a closed syllable (consonant final) counts as one unit when internal in a word and as two units when final.

30. For example, the following song of Kṛṣṇa to his beloved Rādhā: "You are the princess, the goddess of the Rāsa [dance]—come, beautiful Lady! Come, young lady Rādhā, my lover and desire! To the Rasika, you are the ocean of *rasa.* . . . Because of your qualities, I float in bliss!" (BG 463).

31. De, *Kartābhajā Dharmer Itivṛtta,* appendix I.

32. On the Sāhebdhanīs, see Sudhīr Cakravartī, *Sāhebdhanī Sampradāya, tāder Gān* (Calcutta: Pustak Bipaṇi, 1985), and chapter IV (this volume). Capwell includes several of Kubir's songs in his *Music of the Bāuls,* appendix A.

33. On the Vaiṣṇava *kīrtan,* see, e.g., Edward C. Dimock, *In Praise of Krishna: Songs from the Bengali* (New York: Anchor Books, 1967); on the Śākta songs of Rāmprasād, see McDermott, *Singing to the Goddess,* introduction.

34. For a good overview of the main forms of folk music (*prabandha),* as distinguished from classical music), see Rajyeshwar Mitra, "Music in Old Calcutta," in *Calcutta the Living City,* Vol. 1: *The Past,* ed. Sukanta Choudhuri (Calcutta: Oxford, 1990), 179–85; Sukumar Ray, *Music of Eastern India: Vocal Music in Bengali, Oriya, Assamese and Manipuri, with Special Emphasis on Bengali* (Calcutta: Firma KLM, 1973), 110–12; Sudhibhusan Bhattacarya, *Ethnomusicology and India* (Calcutta: Indian Publications, 1968), 15–16; and Sukumar Sen, *History of Bengali Literature* (New Delhi: Sahitya Academy, 1960), 170–75.

35. In the early nineteenth century, a list of all the popular song forms of Calcutta was compiled by a local Zamindār and poet, Rājā Jayanārāyaṇ Ghoṣāl—a man who in fact knew the Kartābhajās intimately and may even have been an initiate (*Karuṇānidhāna Vilāsa* [1820]). Jayanārāyaṇ's list includes, among others, the following major forms: *pāñcālī* (popular songs interspersed with recitation of short rhymes about Hindu divinities); *sāri* (boatmen's songs); *mālaśī* (songs about Kālī); *vijayā* (sung on the last day of Durgā Pūjā); *ākhṛāi* (a contest of songs); *jatra* (dramatic performances set to music); and *kīrtans* (sung in praise of divinities like Kṛṣṇa, Rādhā or the great Saint Caitanya) (summarized by Banerjee, *The Parlour and the Streets,* 90–93). In the same text, Ghoṣāl cites the first Kartā, Rāmśaraṇ Pāl, Kabīr, and Jesus Christ as the three of great *avatārs* of the modern age who will herald a new era of spirituality and peace. Many believe that Ghoṣāl was initiated by Dulālcāṅd himself (see Sen, "Kartābhajā Kathā o Gān," 37–38).

36. Chakrabarty, *Vaiṣṇavism in Bengal,* 368, 368n.

37. See EE, ch. 4–6, and Urban, "The Torment of Secrecy."

38. On the "exotericization" and "institutionalization" of tradition, see EE epilogue and Sumanta Banerjee, "From Aulchand to Satima: The Institutionalization of the Syncretist Kartabhaja Sect," *Calcutta Historical Journal* 16, no. 2 (1995): 29–59.

39. Akṣaykumār Datta, *Bhāratavarṣīya Upāsaka Sampradāya* (Calcutta: Karuṇā Prakāśanī, 1987), 224. On the Ghoshpara Melā, see EE, ch. 7; and Sudhīr Cakravartī, *Paścim Baṅger Melā o Mahotsava* (Calcutta: Pustak Bipaṇi, 1996), 158–77; for a more popular novelist's account of the Melā, see Kālakūṭa, *Kothāy Se Jan Āche.*

40. The Bāul songs belong to a group of village music (*pallīgīti*), which also includes forms such as *bhāoyāiyā* and *bhāṭiyālī* (Capwell, *Music of the Bāuls,* 33–42; Ray, *Music of Eastern India,* 110–15.)

41. On the problem of the origins of the Bāuls, see Urban, "The Politics of Madness," 13–46, and Capwell, *Music of the Bāuls of Bengal,* ch. 1.

42. The best discussion of the form and structure of the Bāul songs is Capwell's *Music the Bāuls,* especially ch. 3–5. For a comparison of the Bāul and Kartābhajā songs, see Cakravartī, *Vrātya Lokāyata Lālan,* 131–32.

43. See Praphulla Candra Pāl, *Pracīn Kaviwālār Gān* (Calcutta: University of Calcutta Press, 1958); Zbavitel, *Bengali Literature,* 205–208. In early-nineteenth-century Calcutta, two of the most outstanding Kobis were Haru Ṭhākur (1738–1824) and Rām Basu (1786–1828).

44. De, *Bengali Literature in the Nineteenth Century,* 38, 303, 311. "The spirit of this verse system is that of unbounded lawlessness bound only by a law of its own: that of resistance to the established verses like *payar* or *tripadi*" (339). See Banerjee, *The Parlour and the Streets,* 92–95.

45. See Pāl, *Pracīn Kaviwālār Gān,* 36–37.

46. Gupta, *Īśvara Gupta Racanāvali* (Calcutta, 1974), 110.

47. Banerjee, *The Parlour and the Streets*, 102.

48. Technically, *Mānuṣa* means "humanity" and can refer to both males and females. However, I have chosen to translate it as "Man" for two reasons: (1) because this is the way that the phrase *Maner Mānuṣa* has most often been rendered in modern scholarship and is probably most recognizable to readers today; and (2) because the Kartābhajā path is, in the end, largely a male-centered and male-dominated one. Despite the constant rhetoric of equality and egalitarianism, it is ultimately (as in most Tantric traditions) the male gurus who hold the most power. For a fuller discussion of this point, see EE ch. 2.

49. See Urban, "The Politics of Madness"; Capwell, *Music of the Bāuls,* ch. 1.

50. On the *Sahaja Mānuṣa,* see, e.g., Manindra Mohan Basu, ed., *Sahajiyā Sāhitya* (Calcutta: University of Calcutta Press, 1932), *pada* 21: "Everyone says, 'a Man is a Man'; but how is one a Man? Man is a Jewel, Man is life, Man is the heart's treasure. . . . Those Men who are dead while alive are the essence of Man."

51. Tuṣār Caṭṭopādhyāy, "Ghoṣpāṛār Melā, Kartābhajā o Lālan," in *Lālan Sāhitya o Darśana,* ed. K. R. Hāq (Dhaka: Bangla Academy, 1976), and "Śrī Caitanya o Lokāyata Uttarādhikāra," in *Gouṛaṅgasaṃskṛti o Śrīcaitanyadeva,* ed. S. Gosvāmi (Calcutta: Calcutta Publishers, 1988).

52. Cited in Caṭṭopādhyāy, "Ghoṣpāṛār Melā," 144. According to another song attributed to Lālan, "What bliss there is in Ghoṣpāṛā! It is the rescue of both sinners and renunciants. With Dulālcāṅd, Mā has sat at the base of the Dālim tree . . . Lālan offers homage to you with the earth of the Dālim tree" (ibid).

53. See Sen, "Kartābhajā Kathā o Gān," 41–42.

54. Translated by Salomon, "Bāul Songs," 199.

55. Chatterjee, *The Nation and Its Fragments,* 187.

56. Quoted in J. E. H. Garrett, *Bengal District Gazetteers, Nadia* (Calcutta: Bengal Secretariat Book Stall, 1910), 49–50. "A person of however low a social status he may be . . . is accepted as the spiritual guide by those who are socially his superiors . . . It is this highly liberal and democratic character of our sect . . . which induces outsiders to join our ranks" (ibid.).

57. Sen, "Āmār Jīvana," 184.

58. Cakravartī, *Sāhebdhanī Sampradāya,* 42.

59. *Trust deed of the Brāhmo Samāj,* cited in Sophia Collet, *The Life and Letters of Rammohum Roy* (Calcutta: D. K. Biswas, 1962), 147; cf. David Kopf, *The Brahmo Samaj and the Shaping of the Modern Indian Mind* (Princeton: Princeton University Press, 1979).

60. Caṭṭopādhyāy, "Śrī Caitanya o Lokāyata Uttarādhikāra," 280. There is no doubt that Rāmmohun was interested in many diverse religious sects, and it is quite plausible that he might have visited Ghoshpara from time to time. Rāmmohun's own guru Hariharānanda lived close to Ghoshpara, in Chakdoha village, and was undoubtedly familiar with the Kartābhajās (Nandī, *Kartābhajā Dharma o Sāhitya,* 131–32).

61. P. J. Marshall, *Bengal: The British Bridgehead* (Cambridge: Cambridge University Press, 1987), 178.

62. On this point, see Sanatkumār Mitra, "Kartābhajā: Saṃśaya o Samasyā," in *Kartābhajā Dharmamata o Itihāsa,* vol. 1, ed. S. Mitra (Calcutta: De Book Stores, 1977), 89: "Rāmmohun was a rationalist and established his ideals on the rational religion of the Upaniṣads. . . . But the Kartābhajās became a tremendous irrational force, based on the miraculous deeds of Āulcāṅd. This was the complete opposite of Rāmmohun's ideal."

63. Hyram Haydn, *The Counter-Renaissance* (New York: Grove Press, 1960); Robert S.

Kinsman, ed., *The Darker Vision of the Renaissance* (Berkley: University of California Press, 1974).

64. Banerjee, *The Parlour and the Streets,* 68, 69.

65. Rāy, *Dāśarathī Rāyer Pāñcālī,* 669 (chapter V, this volume).

66. Some 204 of these Mint Sayings were collected in the early twentieth century by the Kartābhajā master, Manulāl Miśra (STP; chapter III, this volume). On Tantric sandhābhāṣā, see Hayes, "Vaiṣṇava Sahajiyā Traditions," 334–35, and Urban, "The Torment of Secrecy."

67. De, *Kartābhajā Dharmer Itivṛtta,* 99–100.

68. Sen, "Conquest of Marketplaces," 229–30.

69. "Seventy percent of the songs of the Bhāver Gīta refer to such business terms as Company, merchants, agents, brokers, traders, porters, stockists, indigo traders, invoice, trade mark, etc" (Chakrabarty, *Vaiṣṇavism in Bengal,* 360).

70. Sen, "Conquest of Marketplaces."

71. Mikhail Bakhtin, *Rabelais and His World* (Bloomington: University of Indiana Press, 1984), 153.

72. Guha, *Elementary Forms of Peasant Insurgency,* 158.

73. "When the boat set sail over the waters of love, some clung on, eager to reach their destiny. . . . A market and post were set up by the quay and the flag went up, a warning to the sinful. Storehouses of four rasas in every direction, secured all around with the name of Hari. Guards sat chanting and chanting that name. One could buy or sell in this market at will" (*Hāṭ Pattan,* trans. Sudipta Sen, "Passages of Authority," 31).

74. Sen, "Passages of Authority," 32.

75. Śaktināth Jhā, *Phakir Lālan Sāiṅ: Deś, Kāl evaṃ Śilpa* (Calcutta: Saṃvād, 1995), 218. As Lālan sings, "O Madman, you've brought the Money-lender's wealth, and now you've lost it with the remaining debt, you'll go the world of the dead; your fate is sealed with indebtedness. . . . Come to the bazaar of bliss and engage in business" (63). In the late nineteenth century, Rāmakṛṣṇa would make similar ironic criticisms toward the dislocated urban mercantile in colonial Calcutta. As Sumit Sarkar has argued, Rāmakṛṣṇa often spoke in satirical terms of the pathetic lives of the poorer and lower-middle-class babus, particularly the cakris or clerks, who toiled in the mercantile and governmental offices of colonial Calcutta (see Sumit Sarkar, *An Exploration of the Ramakrishna-Vivekananda Tradition* [Simla: Institute of Indian Studies, 1993], 31).

76. Banerjee, *The Parlour and the Streets,* 84.

77. BG [1882] 124; paraphrased by Chakrabarty, *Vaiṣṇavism in Bengal,* 354; cf. Urban, "The Poor Company," 1–33.

78. BG [1882] 122, 138; paraphrased by Chakrabarty, *Vaiṣṇavism in Bengal,* 378.

79. Marshall Sahlins, *Culture and Practical Reason* (Chicago: University of Chicago Press, 1976), 169. Also: "All commodities have a social use and a cultural meaning. . . . Commodities are cultural signs. They have already been invested by the dominant culture with meanings, social connotations. . . . Because the meanings which commodities express are socially given—Marx called commodities 'social hieroglyphs'—their meaning can also be socially altered or reconstrued . . . things are imprinted with new meanings and values which expropriate them . . . and relocate them" (J. Clarke, S. Hall, T. Jefferson, and B. Roberts, "Subcultures, Cultures and Class: A Theoretical Overview," in *Resistance through Rituals,* ed. S. Hall and T. Jefferson [London: Routledge, 1993], 54–55).

80. Dick Hebdige, *Subculture: The Meaning of Style* (London: Metheun, 1979), 18.

81. Jean and John Comaroff, eds. *Modernity and Its Malcontents: Ritual and Power In Post-*

colonial Africa (Chicago: University of Chicago Press, 1993), xi–xii. Sahlins comments: "Western capitalism has loosed on the world enormous forces of production, coercion and destruction. Yet precisely because they cannot be resisted, the relations and goods of the larger system take on meaningful places in the local scheme of things" ("Cosmologies of Capitalism: The Trans-Pacific Sector of the World System," *Proceedings of the British Academy* 74 [1988]: 4). On this point, see also Michael Taussig, *The Devil and Commodity Fetishism in South America* (Chapel Hill: University of North Carolina Press, 1980).

82. The category of "Tantra" is notoriously difficult to define. Most authors agree that it cannot be defined in any simple, singular, or monothetic way but must be given a polythetic definition, which simply identifies a series of shared characteristics or family resemblances. See Douglas Brooks, *The Secret of the Three Cities: An Introduction to Hindu Śākta Tantrism* (Chicago: University of Chicago Press, 1990), 55–71; André Padoux, "Tantrism, an Overview," in *Encyclopedia of Religion*, ed. Mircea Eliade (New York: MacMillan, 1986), 14: 271–72. I have also traced the genealogy of "Tantrism" in Urban, "The Extreme Orient," 123–46, and Urban, "The Cult of Ecstasy: Tantrism, the New Age and the Spiritual Logic of Late Capitalism," *History of Religions* 39, no. 3 (2000): 268–304.

83. Sir Monier Williams, *Hinduism* (London: Society for Promoting Christian Knowledge, 1894), 122–23. On this point, see Urban, "The Extreme Orient," 123–46.

84. See Sen, *Śrī Śrī Rāmakṛṣṇa Puṅthi,* cited in note 12.

85. Pāl, *Ghoṣpāṛār Satīmā*, 246. "The Kartābhajā religion is utterly opposed to the *parakīyā* doctrine. It is based on the *svakīyā* doctrine" (ibid). A similar interpretation is suggested by some contemporary scholars, such as Chakrabarty, *Vaiṣṇavism in* Bengal, 379–80, and Bimalkumār Mukhopādhyāy, "Pravartakakendrik Sahajiyā," in *Kartābhajā Dharmamata o Itihāsa*, ed. S. Mitra (Calcutta: De Book Stores, 1977).

86. Dās, *Śrī Satīmā Candrikā* (Calcutta: Firma KLM, 1986), 71–72. This Tantric interpretation of the tradition is suggested by many contemporary scholars, including De, *Kartābhajā Dharmer Itivṛtta*, 7ff.; Chatterjee, "Some Observations on Guru Cult," 207ff.; and Nandī, *Kartābhajā Dharma,* 100ff. According to Sudhīr Cakravartī, the later Kartābhajā tradition split into two branches—one that developed into a popular devotional faith, largely in harmony with mainstream Vaiṣṇava theology, and one that continued the more transgressive Sahajiyā and sexual practices, largely in secrecy and on the margins of the mainstream tradition (*Sāhebdhanī Sampradāya,* 50–53).

87. Apurna Bhattacharya, *Religious Movements of Bengal, 1800–1850* (Calcutta: Vidyasagar Pustak Mandir, 1981), 47.

88. Rāy, "Kartābhajā," 668–69; translated in full in chapter V (this volume).

89. Sudhīr Cakravartī, *Paścim Baṅger Melā o Mahotsava* (Calcutta: Pustak Bipaṇi, 1995), 169.

90. Banerjee, "From Aulchand to Satima," 38–39.

91. Māṇik Sarkār, "Ghoṣpāṛār Melā o tār Prāṇbhomrā," in *Kartābhajā Dharmamata o Itihāsa*, ed. S. Mitra (Calcutta: De Book Stores, 1977), 6–7; see Urban, "The Poor Company," and Banerjee, "From Aulchand to Satima," 38–39.

92. J. N. Bhattacharya, *Hindu Castes and Sects* (Calcutta: University of Calcutta, 1896), 382.

93. Advaita Dās, *Ghoṣpāṛer Kartābhajā Sampradāya* (Calcutta: Kālī Press, 1983), 56.

94. Oddie, "Old Wine in New Bottles," 15.

95. Ibid., 15–16.

96. Chatterjee, "Caste and Subaltern Consciousness," in *Subaltern Studies VI*, ed. R. Guha (Delhi: Oxford University Press, 1988), 206–7. See also O'Hanlon's critique of the

subaltern work ("Recovering the Subject," 214, 223), and Pinch, *Peasants and Monks in British India*, 147–48.

97. Michel de Certeau, *The Practice of Everyday Life* (Berkeley: University of California Press, 1984), xi–xii. "Submissive, and even consenting to their subjection, the Indians nevertheless made of the representations . . . imposed on them something quite different from what their conquerors had in mind; they subverted them not by rejecting . . . them but by using them with respect to ends foreign to the system they had to accept" (ibid.).

98. Gerald Larson, *India's Agony over Religion* (Albany: SUNY, 1995), 41.

99. Guha, *Elementary Forms of Peasant Resistance*, 18.

100. Guha, "The Prose of Counter-Insurgency," in *Subaltern Studies II*, ed. R. Guha (Delhi: Oxford University Press, 1983), 34.

101. "One argument of subaltern studies, Gayatri Spivak comments, "has been that the subaltern . . . persistently translates the discourse of religion into the discourse of militancy" ("A Literary Representation of the Subaltern: Mahasweta Devi's *Stanadayini*," in *Subaltern Studies V*, ed. R. Guha [Delhi: Oxford University Press, 1987], 131).

102. On this point, see David Hardiman's discussion of the worship of the Goddess among the adivasis of Western India (*The Coming of the Devi*, 216–17), and Dube's discussion of Satnamis of Central India (*Untouchable Pasts*, 1–23).

103. Dube, *Untouchable Pasts*, 221–22.

Chapter II

1. Translated here from the 1992 edition of Śrī Śāntirañjan Cakravartī [BG] and the manuscript "Kartābhajā Gīta" [KG] (1228–33 B.S. [1821–26]).

2. *Gorib kompānī bāhādure.*

3. *Ādab kompānī. Ādab* is a Perso-Arabic term used to designate the qualities of refinement, distinction, and etiquette that characterize the aristocracy; for a fuller discussion of this term and the Kartābhajās' ironic appropriation of it to describe themselves, see EE chs. 4 and 6.

4. The song is referring to the wondrous fruit which the Divine Madman planted in the Garden of Love, which was just described in a previous song. See the following section entitled "The Stinking Fruit in the Garden of Love" (BG 154–59; II.84–89).

5. *Inbhāis.*

6. The term *rasa* is virtually impossible to translate into English, so I have left it untranslated in these songs. Literally, it means something like "flavor, taste, or juice"; however, in Sanskrit poetics, it has a more specialized meaning of aesthetic enjoyment or "savoring" a particular dramatic or poetic mood, and in Vaiṣṇava theology, it bears the sense of a particular devotional relationship to Lord Kṛṣṇa.

7. In Vaiṣṇava theology, the five *bhāvas* are the five primary relationships or modes of love of Kṛṣṇa: the peaceful, servant, friend, parent, and lover relations (Dimock, *The Place of the Hidden Moon*, 22–23).

8. *Guṇas*, or the three primary qualities that comprise all of existence.

9. The meaning of this difficult song seems to be as follows. Gold or silver is melted down and divided up when it is made into currency; however, it retains its true value once the stamp or seal of the company is placed on it, and it is minted as a legitimate coin. In the same way, the divine *rasas* are distributed throughout the world, but they retain their full value when the seal of the poor company—that is, the Kartābhajā sect—is stamped on them.

10. *Konṭrakṭ.*

11. On the meaning of *rasa*, see note 6. Here *rasa* means something like the juices of love or nectar of devotion in which the true devotee is immersed.

12. A *Rasika* is literally one who is capable of appreciating the meaning or flavor of something. In aesthetic terms, it is a connoisseur or an aesthete who can truly enjoy beauty; in erotic terms, it also refers to one who is versed in the art of love making. In religious literature, particularly in the Vaiṣṇava and Sahajiyā traditions, Rasika is also a term for Kṛṣṇa, as the supreme lover and enjoyer of beauty (see, e.g., SS 77, pada 83). In the *Bhāver Gīta*, the *Rasika*—like the *Nāgar* (Gallant Lover) and the *Pāgal* (Madman)—refers simultaneously to Kṛṣṇa, Caitanya, and Āulcāṅd.

13. This song clearly appears play on the double meaning of *gorā,* which suggests both "fair skinned" and "Englishman." In Vaiṣṇava literature it is traditionally an epithet of Caitanya, the fair-skinned one, but here, in the context of the image of the company it also seems to be a clever pun referring to the Englishmen of the British East India Company. The image of the "Three Madmen" is common in many Bāul songs and refers to Caitanya and his foremost disciples, Nityānanda and Advaita Ācārya; according to the following song recorded by Capwell, "That rosik madman came and created an uproar in Nodia. . . . Nitai is mad, Gowr is mad, Caitanya is the root of madness. Advaita became mad and sank into *ras*" (*Music of the Bāuls*, 190).

14. The line "bhor-jubatīr kol, haribol ār māgur mācher jhele " (literally, "the breast of the lady of the Dawn, Haribol, or catfish curry") is extremely odd. Carol Salomon has suggested that this may refer to Nityānanda's former life as a Tantric Avadhūta and the use of meat and sexual intercourse in Tantric ritual. I have found support for this view in at least one other later reading, but this is speculative at best. Capwell cites a similar Bāul song, which he translates as follows: "My Nitai has full knowledge of Brahma; he has seen the universe filled with Brahma. He said 'Catfish curry and the lap of a maiden.' This time, dying I will say Hari with all my strength" (*Music of the Bauls*, 195). Unfortunately, Capwell does not offer any explanation as to what this might mean.

15. The Bengali terms here are *advaita* and *dvaitabhāve*; the song is playing on the name of Advaita-Ācārya, which also means "nonduality."

16. *Gorā kompānī.*

17. The following two songs use the image of the "three Madmen," namely, Caitanya, Nityānanda, and Advaita, and the "fourth Madman," namely, the "poor wretched fakir" or the "heavy-bearded one," who is of course Āulcāṅd; together, these four madmen "complete the cycle" and fulfill the "company."

18. This difficult line contains the strange word *ādāṛe,* which has no clear meaning. I have read it as *ādare,* meaning with honor or respect.

19. June–July 1827.

20. The poor wretched one here, as elsewhere, is the poor madman Āulcāṅd. The phrase *nāgāṛa lāgilo* is literally "made it continuous"; as we learn in the next song, the meaning of this is that Āulcāṅd, the poor wretched one, is the fourth madman, who completes the cycle or finishes the task begun by the first three madman (Caitanya, Nityānanda, and Advaita). As a whole, these two songs offer an ingenious narrative that justifies the birth of the Kartābhajā sect: Āulcāṅd is called the fourth Madman, and he completes the work left unfinished by Caitanya and his companions.

21. The three men or three madmen are clearly identified as Caitanya, Nityānanda, and Advaita in several other songs (BG 414, 420–21).

22. *Ād kompānī. Ād* here could either be taken as *ādi*, "first, original," or more probably as *ādab*, which appears elsewhere in the Bhavār Gīta to mean "distinguished, good-mannered, polite;" either way, it refers to the old company of the original Gauḍīya Vaiṣṇava tradition founded by Caitanya.

23. The term *byāorā* here is probably the same as *bāorā*, which is glossed elsewhere in this text as *pāgal* (i.e., mad or crazy). Both are related to *bāul*.

24. *Ojor yadi gojore hay baṛo phāṃpar*. Elsewhere (BG 61 q.2), the editor glosses *gojore* as *atīt haiyāche*, that is, "has passed away, elapsed," but its meaning in this line is unclear.

25. The reference here is to the "fruit tree" of *rasa* which Āulcāṅd came to plant here in this world; see the following selections under the title "The Stinking Fruit in the Garden of Love."

26. *Kāṅgāler palṭan*.

27. The Madman here is Caitanya-Āulcāṅd.

28. Compare this line with the song of Lālan Shāh, "tin pāgale melā holo. . . ." Here is still further evidence of the connections between Lālan and the Kartābhajās, and the possible influence of the latter on the former. The three madmen here, as in the Bāul songs, are Caitanya, Nityānanda, and Advaita.

29. Here I am reading *khorāre* as *khoyāre*, "misery, distress, humiliation." The only other possible reading of *khorāre* might be *khorā*, a large cup without a stem, or a goblet.

30. *Nius pepār.*

31. The use of the Bengalicized English words *hāph moni* is somewhat unclear; here I have taken it as "some money," or a little money, though other readings are possible.

32. *Salā*.

33. *Pistal olḍ niu phyāsān*.

34. *Kāptenerā*.

35. The term *mahājan*—literally "great man"—has many meanings, which become particularly relevant in the context of colonial Bengal. A *mahājan* often refers to a moneylender or banker, in many cases with very negative connotations, but here it seems to be used in the positive sense of a wealthy merchant, stockholder, or foreign investor.

36. *Gourava ādab kompānī*.

37. In many songs (see BG 134–35; II. 44–50.) the *ḍhākā sahar* carries the dual sense of both the real city of Dhaka and also the mystical "Hidden City," which seems to be a metaphor for the womb and the state of the human being before birth.

38. *Mānoyārī*.

39. This refers to the conflict between the French and British in India, corresponding to their wars at home. Specifically, it probably refers to the military campaigns waged by the company against the French beginning in 1795, as dictated by the Revolutionary War in Europe.

40. *Mags* (i.e., Arakans and Burmese).

41. *Vakta*. Here I'm assuming this is a variant of *vaktā* or *vaktār*, a speaker or an orator.

42. *Parmiṭ*. The editor gives a footnote defining this term as "where import and export occurs"; however, it seems probable this could be the Bengali rendering of the English term "permit."

43. The reference here is to the Mājhī, the helmsman, who appears in the songs that precede this selection; the Mājhī is the symbol of God (Nirañjan), the helmsman who ferries us across the ocean of the world.

44. Here I am assuming that the printed text *śarīr* is a typo for *śaśīr*. Not only does this make more sense, but it is in keeping with the typical format of the songs, almost all of

which close with a statement by or about Śaśī (who is both the author, Lālśaśī, and the "moon").

45. Like many satirical songs of nineteenth-century Calcutta, this song appears to be poking fun at the plight of the Babu or middle-class Bengali who trails along on the coat-tails of the British East India Company, hoping to share in their wealth and prestige but often winning only their contempt and ridicule.

46. *Kāṅgāler melā*.

47. Literally, "if I had a bowl of *gāñjā*."

48. *Khojā*. Again, this seems to be a satirical portrait of the pathetic Babu who seeks to win favor and prestige by tagging along behind the British.

49. Literally, "who wants to open his mouth?"—that is, no one is impressed by the pseudomachismo of the weak Bengalis.

50. The words *ākṛā ghoṭā* are unclear; it may be *ākhṛā ghoṅṭā*, meaning "stirring up (or ransacking) the club or monastery."

51. *Khātirjamā*. It is tempting to render this with Bourdieu's phrase "symbolic capital."

52. It seems likely that the author is playing on the dual meaning of *paṇ*—as both a promise or a dowry and a unit of measure, hence an amount of money—and *buṛī*—as both an old woman and another unit of measure.

53. Here the author is using the metaphor of the world of *saṃsāra* as a giant market-place, in which all living things are constantly coming and going, selfishly engaged in business for their own interests.

54. *Lok ghar*. In this verse the author is comparing the mortal human body to a house, which will ultimately fall apart and die. A similar use of the body-house metaphor is found in many Bāul songs; see, for example, the song of Tinkori Das recorded in Capwell's *Music of the Bāuls*, 182. The "Broker" here, according to Ramakanta Chakrabarty, is a "religious broker" or leader of one of the various sects, who promises to save the human-house but only gives it temporary relief. Ultimately, the body-house will collapse and die (*Vaiṣṇavism in Bengal*, 377).

55. That is, a single broker arranges many business deals, just as a single body of water has many waves or ripples. And just as an elephant and his driver are brought together, so, too, the broker brings the buyer and seller together in a transaction.

56. According to Chakrabarty, these brokers with "packets from England" are Christian missionaries (*Vaiṣṇavism in Bengal*, 375).

57. *Komiṭe*.

58. Here I'm reading *kṛmata* as *kimata*, "of what sort, how."

59. *Āṭakpāle āpni khele hay meṭo*. This is a difficult line. Here I am reading *meṭo* as *meṭho*, meaning rustic or pertaining to agriculture or farming. Taken in this sense, Lālśaśī would seem to be making fun of the broker, who runs back and forth between the peasants and the merchant, and so becomes like a mere peasant himself. Other possible readings are *meṭ* (meaning mate or gangsman on a ship) or *muṭe* (meaning a porter or laborer).

60. *Kalpa*. A period of cosmic time in Hindu mythology equivalent to one day and night in the life of Brahmā, or 8 billion, 640 million human years.

61. *Dālālī dasturi jārijuri nāi kāro*.

62. *Byabsādārer samāje*. This seems to be a clear indication that Lālśaśī is making an explicit attempt to promote his teachings among the shopkeeper and petty merchant classes of the marketplace.

63. In this song, we get the Kartābhajās' curious sort of "mercantile cosmogony," in which the primordial void (*śūnyabhora*) is filled and gives rise to the warehouses, merchandise, clerks, and brokers who make up the marketplace of the world.

64. Here I'm reading *khadder* (*kharidār*, "buyer") for *khodder.*

65. The image of the "secret Caitanya" is a common one in Kartābhajā discourse. The story is that, after his death, Caitanya remained hidden for a time and then reappeared in the secret Vṛndāvana of Ghoshpara. His new task was to teach an easy and simple (*sahaja*) path for the poor and lowly people neglected by the mainstream Vaiṣṇava tradition (see Pāl, *Ghoṣpāṛār Satī Mā*, 82–83; STP 1–10.

66. The text referred to here, the *Caitanya Caritāmṛta* by Kṛṣṇdāsa Kavirāja, is the most famous biography of the sixteenth-century Bengali saint, Caitanya. See the new translation of the CC by Dimock.

67. The *bhāgyavān,* the fortunate or lucky ones are the rich and affluent men, in contrast to the poor and lowly (*gorib, kāṅgāl*) men, who are most in need of Caitanya's aid. More pointedly, the *bhāgyavān* here are probably also identified with the mainstream Gauḍīya Vaiṣṇava tradition, which, in the Kartābhajās' view, had corrupted and perverted the true teachings of Caitanya.

68. The two beings here appear to be angels or spiritual guides who bring the soul into the world at the time of birth.

69. In other words, the two angels who had brought him into the world now take him back into the void at the time of death.

70. Here I'm reading *mastakīn* as *masta-ākīrṇa*, widely scattered or distributed.

71. According to a popular belief, the soul's fate is written on one's forehead.

72. That is, the period of time spent in the womb

73. The mythical accountant of the land of the dead.

74. *Adhamā adhamādhamā.* The identity of this "lowest of the lowest of the low" is unclear; it could be taken in a negative sense, as the finite self or ego which binds the soul to the suffering world of rebirth, but it might also be taken in a positive sense as the Poor Wretched Madman, Āulcāṅd, or the Sahaja Mānuṣa, who is often described with derogatory epithets. The last line of the next verse, "he lies within the lotus of the heart," makes the interpretation very tricky.

75. That is, in the Satya, Tretā, and Dvāpara yugas, men used to live thousands of years, but now in the Kali yuga only live at best 120 years.

76. The mysterious jewel here is probably the "Jewel of Man," the *Sahaja* or *Maner Mānuṣa.*

77. As we learn in the third verse, the author is playing on the dual meaning of *varṇa* as both "color" and "class," in the sense of the four classes: Brāhmaṇ, Kṣatriya, Vaiśya, and Śūdra. Hence, to say that its splendor does not lie in its color also means that it is beyond social divisions, transcending caste.

78. This line is quite ambiguous: *bhāva sahe yā bhāvī janār sāthe, sei ojana jaharete.* Here I am taking the *bhāvī janā* as the "one possessing *bhāva*," or possibly even as *bhāvinī*, a woman or ideal image of a woman.

79. Kāma is the god of lust, the Indian Cupid.

80. Here I'm reading *Kandarpa* [the God of Love, Cupid] for *Kanda.*

81. That is, the living soul was forced to be born, live, and die in this world of Māyā.

82. *Janme keho marmme ye tār śeṣ, nā holo prabeś.* Another difficult line; this interpretation was suggested to me by Edward C. Dimock (personal communication, 1997), who reads it as "There is in life no entering into the secret which is his (or its) end (purpose)."

83. A *piṭulir ālpanā* is a drawing made of rice paste put on the floors or walls used to sanctify or render auspicious a given home, temple, or other building.

84. *Rati.*

85. *Bindu*, also semen.

86. On the meaning of *Rasika* see note 12. The supreme *Rasika* is Lord Kṛṣṇa.

87. *Rasika Nāgara*, or the connoisseur in the art of illict love, namely Kṛṣṇa.

88. This refers to Kṛṣṇa's reincarnation in Bengal as Caitanya.

89. This word *Sahaja* is virtually impossible to translate with a single English word. It literally means "together-born" (*saha-ja*), hence the inborn, natural, spontaneous, or easy state of all things in their original divnity and perfection. The *Sahaja Manuṣa* is our own innate, original state of divinity, or our true Self as identical with the absolute reality. Thus, there are many ways of translating this key phrase *Sahaja bhāva*: the "natural or inborn state," the "easy state," the natural emotion," and the "spontaneous ecstasy." Perhaps something like the "natural ecstasy" or "simple joy" is best here.

90. The Cakora is a bird said to drink moonbeams. In Kartābhajā and Bāul literature, it has erotic overtones, much like the image of the bee which drinks the nectar of the flower (the sexual fluids from the female partner).

91. *Ābhāse,* or in shadows, secretly.

92. The meaning of *supādi* is unclear; it may be a corruption in the text.

93. Types of sacred text, typically of the Tantric variety.

94. The two forms of love here are *prema* and *pirīti.*

95. In every cosmic age, Lord Viṣṇu-Nārāyaṇa incarnates himself in this world in order to uphold the cosmic order or *dharma.* Kṛṣṇa and Caitanya are two such incarnations.

96. *Bābājīs.*

97. The reference is to the traditional time of the Kartābhajā gathering on Friday evenings.

98. Literally, "the essence become particular"; here, I am taking this to mean that the divine essence, the *Sahaja Mānuṣa,* has assumed the finite, particular form of an individual human being.

99. The text here has *hrad*, "lake," but I am guessing that it may be a typo for *hṛd*, "heart." However, *hrad* would also make some sense in this passage.

100 *Bideśī jan.* This probably refers to the "fair-skinned man," Caitanya.

101. *Niścay louha parśe.* This line was explained to me by Carol Salomon, who pointed out its similarity to many Bāul songs that refer to iron and the alchemical touchstone (*paraśmaṇi*).

102. *Ati rati.*

103. *Saṅger saṅgī.*

104. *Sādhaka, siddha, sādhu, śūra.* According to many Sahajiyā traditions, these are the four stages on the spiritual path, leading from novitiate disciple to divine being (*śūra*).

105. Here I am reading *beorā* as *bāorā*, which appears several times elsewhere in the text and is glossed by the editor as *pāgal* or crazy, mad.

106. In the previous song (BG 306), we are told that in Phālgun month (February–March) of 1235 B.S. 1828), the questioning disciple asked Lālśaśī about the ocean of the world and how to cross over it.

107. Compare this with Lālan's song: "Just dive into the ocean of the heart and you'll see you can learn the deepest secrets . . . The mother of the world floats on the sea. Lālan says, the father is in her belly, and when he is born he drinks his wife's milk" (Salomon, "Bāul Songs," 206).

108. *Kuṭhī*

109. The meaning of the word *sātuyā* in this line is unclear.

110. Carol Salomon has pointed out to me that the image of the *nigam* (i.e., *nir-gam*, unenterable) room is used in Bāul songs to refer to the *yoni* or vagina of the female.

111. This line is reminiscent of a Sahajiyā song of Caṇḍīdās, refering to the two currents that flow through man and woman, which are united in their love: "There are two currents in the lake of love, which can be realized only by the *Rasikas*. When the two currents remain united together in one, the *Rasika* realizes the truth of union" (*Songs of Caṇḍīdāsa*, cited in Dasgupta, *Obscure Religious Cults*, 132).

112. This image of the seed or drop (*bindu*) of creation falling from God's forehead is reminiscent of the Sufi and Nāth-yogi conception of creation emerging from the drop of sweat on God's forehead. See Dasgupta, *Obscure Religious Cults*, 311–312. Similar imagery of the seed or semen—as both the source of the universe and as the inner essence of the human being—appears in many Bāul songs. For example: "On the other shore of the ocean of one's own self quivers a drop of fluid—as the origin of all. . . . The root of all is based in you. Explore the base to reach the essence" (Bhattacharya, *Songs of the Bards*, 70).

113. According to most commentaries, this verse is a reference to the yogic technique of retaining the semen (*bīja-rakṣaṇa*), which is believed to be the vessel of the Supreme Self or *Sahaja Mānuṣa*.

114. This song and the next one [75 and 76] use rich mythic imagery to describe the journey of the *sādhaka* in search of the *Sahaja Mānuṣa* or "Wealthy Man" upon the altar of the heart. According to most commentators, this is an account of the technique of Kuṇḍalinī yoga. The mythic serpent Vāsuki is the coiled Kuṇḍalinī; the seven rivers and oceans refer to the veins and *cakras* of the subtle body; the Wealthy Man is the *Maner Mānuṣa* on the throne of the heart. As Rājnārāyan. Caṭṭopādhyāy, explains: "Within the body there are seven heavens and seven hells. Among these, *Rasātala* is the lowest. There lies a foundation, upon which . . . there is a vein named the Brahmanāḍī. Within that vein, upon the lotus of the heart, there is a jeweled altar called the Svādisthāna. This is the seat of the Supreme Self . . . It is the seed-bearing flower which pervades all things and all directions. Just as Vāsuki holds up the earth with his head so too, in the Rasātola, below the navel, the serpent Kuṇḍalinī is the basis of this bodily universe. Three thousand subtle veins arise from this and pervade the entire body" (*Bhāver Gīta Vyākhyā*, 18–19).

115. *Bihaṅgam*

116. Rasātola is the lowest of the seven underworlds; in the Kartābhajās' mythical-bodily cosmology, it is also identified with the lowest of the seven cakras, the Mūlādhāra or root-cakra at the base of the spine where the serpent Kuṇḍalinī (here Vāsuki) dwells.

117. *Dhanī lok.*

118. Again, I suspect that the printed *hrad* ("lake") may be a typo for *hṛd* ("heart").

119. The word *man* bears the sense of both "mind" (mental state, mentality, memory, etc.) and "heart"(mood, devotion, attachment, etc.). Hence I have chosen to translate it as "mind" when it refers to the limited self or finite ego, and as "heart" when it refers to the indwelling Divine Self or *Maner Mānuṣa*.

120. Here, the images of the king and the throne appear to represent the human soul or finite ego who has been placed within the body [the throne] world of *saṃsāra* [the kingdom]; the ego thinks itself to be the ruler of the world, but in fact remains ignorant of its own true Self, the Man of the Heart.

121. This line contains the strange word *ārastula*, which I have failed to decipher. It may be a corruption in the text.

122. For a full discussion of this controversy, see EE ch. 6.

123. The images of the fish playing in the waters and "catching the fish" are common Bāul metaphors for catching the Man of the Heart, who swims in the female menstrual

flow for three days each month; see, e.g., Bhattacharya, *Songs of the Bards*: "I plunged into the water/ like a fisherman/ hoping to catch the fish of faith" (75).

124. The image of the male and female goose or swan appears in many Bāul songs as a key metaphor of sexual union and the technique of catching the Man of the Heart amidst the female menstrual flow: "The blood is white/ and on the lake of blood/ float a pair of swans/ copulating continuously/ in a jungle of lust and love" (song of Gopāl, in Bhattacharya, *Songs of the Bards*, 62).

125. Here Kṛṣṇa. On the meaning of *Rasika*, see note 12.

126. *Hita bhāvite biparīta*. This line is extremely important but difficult and obscure. Much hinges on the interpretation of this verse, which could be taken to mean either that *Parakīyā* love is transgressive and should be rejected or that it is valuable and to be employed on the path. Various Kartābhajās have read this line both ways. The rest of the song, however, appears to place a positive value on *parakīyā*.

127. In other words, the one who can charm Lord Kṛṣṇa is Lālśaśī ("the Moon"), that is, the Kartā; hence the disciple should be bound to the Kartā just as the Cakora bird is freely bound to the moonlight.

128. The terms here are *pravṛtti* and *nivṛtti,* the first and last stages of the Kartābhajā path. Like other Sahajiyā schools, the Kartābhajās typically divide the path into the stages of *pravarta* or novice, *sādhaka* or practitioner, *siddha* or perfected, and *siddher siddha* or *nivṛtta*, cessation and extinction.

129. This seems to suggest that both *parakīyā* and *svakīyā rasas* are necessary on the spiritual path.

130. This series of songs (84–89) presents a mythological narrative describing the problem of *parakīyā* love, or intercourse with another man's wife, which was a central topic of debate and controversy within the Vaiṣṇava and Sahajiyā communities of the seventeenth and eighteenth centuries (see EE ch. 6). The central image is the "fruit tree" of *parakīyā* which the divine madman (Caitanya) planted within the garden of love; the fruit of the tree, however, became foul smelling and intoxicating to any who tasted it and therefore had to be uprooted by the "good-mannered" or "distinguished company."

131. The madman here, as elsewhere, is Caitanya-Āulcāṅd.

132. The reference here is to the fruit tree of *parakīyā* love [intercourse with another man's wife] as explained in the songs 86–89—see especially BG 159.

133. Again, this is the "foul-smelling fruit" of *parakīyā* described in the songs 86–89.

134. See note 3. It is tempting here to translate it as "Hon'ble Company."

135. *Tumi eman galpa karo nā kakhan jeno kāro sākṣāte*. This seems to be a clear indication that this is a highly esoteric, secret affair.

136. *Khepā bāul*.

137. Again, the foul-smelling fruit here is *parakīyā* love.

138. The *tophā* (wondrous, excellent, delicious thing) is the sweet fruit of *parakīyā* love (which later becomes foul smelling) mentioned in the previous songs.

139. The "three" here probably refers to the three madmen, namely, Caitanya, Nityānanda, and Advaita Ācārya, mentioned in other songs (BG 415–16). The two kinds of company (*du-rakam kompānī*) refer to the "rich company" (which seems to be both the *real* East India company *and* the "old Company" of the Gauḍīya Vaiṣṇava tradition) and the "poor company," that is, the Kartābhajās.

140. *Kompānīre thāko cāpā*

141. The reference is to Āṣāṛ month of 1232 B.S. [1826], the date mentioned in the previous song, when Lālśaśī first sang the songs of the *Bhāver Gīta* (BG 156–57).

142. *Saṅgśaya-bhañjana tama.* Here the Madman is clearly Caitanya-Āulcāṅd.

143. The lowest hell here is *Rasātala.* The term *kal-nidhi,* the treasury or store of the mill or factory, is mysterious. It probably refers to the secret place of the *Sahaja Mānuṣa.* which is often described with the imagery of an "office" (*kuṭhi*) or a "fortress."

144. *Atisāri hay;* literally, "suffer morbid looseness of the bowels; diarrhea or dysentary."

145. *Meoyār bāgicer piche kompānīre abirām.* This line is extremely ambiguous and has been interpreted in different ways by Kartābhajā authors. According to the more orthodox and conservative faction, it means that the company continues in a purified form, free of the foul smell of *parakīyā* love; according to the more Tantric or esoteric faction, it means that *parakīyā* love continues to be practiced, though now in a more secretive, hidden form. See EE ch. 6.

146. Here I am reading *usus* as *usul* (avengement, realization of a bill).

147. The implication is that the true teachings are esoteric and hidden, but when they were revealed openly, in exoteric form, they became the Vedas.

148. *Bellik.*

149. *Sereste,* typically a business office.

Chapter III

1. From Manulāl Miśra's *Sahaja Tattva Prakāśa* (Calcutta: Author, 1309 B.S. [1902]), 58–71.

2. Elsewhere Miśra provides an explanation of the meaning of the "Mint": *"The Essential Meaning of Ṭeṅkśālī [the Mint]*: Out of compassion for the lower-class people, and in order to give a taste of this pure heavenly teaching to common people who are sunk in delusion, Dulālcāṅd revealed the Sahaja path. And he made the path of this very rare *sādhanā* free from danger. Out of desire to teach people of little intelligence, he revealed the teachings of the Vedas and Vedānata and the most secret practices in a very brief form. But not everyone can understand the essential meaning of these secret teachings. All these divine teachings which have issued from the mouth of Dulālcāṅd are called 'the Mint.' This is because, just as by means of the Mint—that is, that device by which coins are fashioned—gold, silver, etc., are stored up in vast amounts, so, too, in this precious treasury, many valuable meanings are hidden within each word" (*Satyadharma Upāsana,* 66–67). On this point, see EE, ch. 3, and Urban, "The Torment of Secrecy."

3. Miśra explains this saying as follows: "The Word itself is Brahma! At the primordial time of creation, when the world was sunk in depthless waters, the all-pervading sound OṂ arose. In the Christian Bible it is written that 'in the beginning was the Word.' Therefore, the Word is . . . the supreme Brahma and the primordial Kartā. . . . By means of the Word, human life . . . can pierce through the worldly darkness of *māyā*'s delusion. . . . Thus there is no difference between the devotee and God. This is because, like the full moon amidst the pure sky, the Master [*mālik*] is manifest day and night within the heart of the devotee. To convey this teaching to his devotees, Dulālcāṅd said, 'one is oneself both the Master [*Kartā*] and the servant'; that is, there is no difference between the Master and the devotee" (*Satyadharma Upāsana,* 70).

4. *Tāmāśā,* "a farce, an amusing spectacle."

5. Miśra's commentary: "Man comes into this world for just a few days, and becomes firmly enmeshed within it; but after only a short time he will die. . . . He sees with his own eyes hundreds of people die, but he never remembers that this, too, will one day be his own fate—thus how could he be any more like a jest [*tāmāśā*]? Infinite numbers of worldly

minded men have been dissuaded from these difficult teachings, but if one begins with a firm mind, all the deeds of this world become easy. That's why the name of his work is called *Sahaja,* and it appears to be manifold" (*Satyadharma Upāsana,* 70–71).

6. Being born in the house of one's mother and father probably means being spiritually reborn through initiation at the hands of one's spirtual parents, the Mahāśay and Mā Gosāiṅ.

7. The curious term *svāvyasta* appears numerous times in this text; by context, it always seems to have the meaning of "one's self-nature" or "true status." I am taking it as a compound comprised of *sva* (self) + *a-vyasta* (without anxiety or worry; not distracted or scatterd), thus meaning something like "self-contentment" or "self-fulfillment."

8. The term *mahājan* appears in this text with the meanings of both a "virtuous man" (i.e., a guru or *mahaśāy*) and a "merchant" or moneylender (cf. saying number 204).

9. *Ekāṅga*; literally, single-bodied.

10. *Sa-aṅgī*; literally, of the same body.

11. *Kono mate Kartā hāoyā nā hay.* This is an extremely odd and cryptic line, which appears to contradict the basic theology of the Kartābhajās. My own reading of this line is that it expresses the mystical and exoteric ideal that (1) the Kartā is beyond existence or nonexistence, and (2) at the highest level of spiritual realization, there is neither disciple nor guru, but the seeker realizes the presence of the abolsute reality—the Kartā or supreme Self—within himself. Hence it is perhaps not unlike Meister Eckhart's statement that one must "go beyond God." Miśra offers a similar interpretation of saying number 1, where "one is oneself both Master and disciple."

12. The implication is that one need not receive spiritual knowledge secondhand, from someone else's speculations (*anumāna*); rather, spiritual knowledge can be experienced directly for oneself (*vartamāna).*

13. The meaning of *Ātābak* is quite unclear, and I have found no commentary that explains it. My only speculation is that it might be *Ātmā-vak*, meaning something like true to one's own words, or speaking from the divine Self. Thus the meaning of this saying would be something like "those who speak the words of the Self [or those who are true to their own word] don't need to ask for anything else." This curious term appears again in saying number 140.

14. *Sarkāri.*

15. The scum-covered pond here may well be a reference to the Hīmasāgara pond in Ghoṣpāṛā.

16. The father and mother here are the spiritual father and mother, the Mahāśay and Mā Gosāiṅ, at whose hands the disciple is reborn into the family of the Kartābhajās.

17. Miśra's commetary: "If one is born in terrible distress and tears come to his eyes, and yet he does not become very ardent in his desire for the Master [*Mālik*], and if he does not wash away the darkness of life with the tears of love, he cannot be a true devotee" (*Satyadharma Upāsana*, 72).

18. The import of this seems to be basically "go with the flow"—that is, if you are free of egotism (*ahaṃkāra*), you will go along naturally and easily with the current of life.

19. The Man here, as elsewhere in these sayings, is most likely the Man of the Heart or *Sahaja Mānuṣa*, Kṛṣṇa-Caitanya-Āulcāṅd.

20. See note 7 to saying number 10.

21. *Sarkāri*, that is, in conformity with the rules and regulations of exoteric society.

22. Or in the name of God. The meaning of this is unclear. It could be taken either in a positive sense (i.e., that sharing food and going with others is like stealing for a good rea-

son, or with God's grace); or it might be taken negatively (i.e., that this is hypocritical, like stealing while invoking the name of God).

23. *Nicu dharma.*

24. This probably means that one cannot cross over to the other (heavenly) world with even a trace of worldly desires or possessions (i.e., you can't take it with you).

25. The meaning of *charāhāṛi* is unclear, but I am reading it as an urn-shaped pot (*hāṛi*) for sprinkling (*chaṛā*) (i.e., sprinkling holy water to purify a place).

26. I am taking *patra* (receptacle, vessel) as the vessel of physical form, or the body.

27. *Jāhāke loiyā colite habe.* The meaning is unclear, but I am reading the *jāhāke* as the *Maner Mānuṣa* or inner Self, who should always be one's spiritual companion.

28. The terms here are *eihik* and *paramārthik.*

29. *Sa-aṅgī.*

30. Probably grief-stricken with the love for Kṛṣṇa in separation from him.

31. *Sambhoga.*

32. *Gupta je, mukta se, bepardā byabhicāriṇī.*

33. Alternatively, "nothing is but the moment" (*tilārdha chāṛā nāi*).

34. *Ei je teṅkśālī bol bājārer janya nahe athabā dāyer janya nahe, kebal kāṅgāler janya.*

35. *Ādabe.* On the meaning and importance of the Perso-Arabic term *ādab,* see EE ch. 6.

36. *Thāke na thāke vastu anya-sahabāse;* literally, "whether or not the substance dwells with another." my reading of this line is admittedly rather loose.

37. The meaning of *ātābak* is unclear; it may be from *ātmā-vāc*, meaning something like the "word of the Self," or one who is true to his word. See note 13, to saying 32.

38. *Ādab.*

39. This saying is quite obscure; the "both" referred to here may mean both the Master or Great Man mentioned in saying number 140 and the subject or servant. In the first sense, it would be similar to the saying that "one is both guru and disciple," [saying number 1] or the idea that, ultimately, there is no distinction between master and disciple, because the *Maner Mānuṣa* dwells in every human heart.

40. The term *baśībhūta* here is tricky, meaning simultaneously "brought under control, attached or addicted to, enchanted, and fond of or obedient to." Hence it can have both negative connotations (in the sense that the world is controlled by Māyā) and positive connotations (in the sense that God is devoted to and fond of his devotees).

41. *Pirīta,* which usually refers to secret or illicit love, as opposed to purely spiritual love (*prema*).

42. *Tattva;* Reality, God, Essence.

43. *Nivṛtti,* the final stage of the spiritual path. The stages of the Kartābhajā path are(1) *pravarta* or novice, (2) *sādhaka* or practitioner, (3) *siddha,* "perfect" or accomplished, and (4) *siddher siddha* or *nivṛtti,* the state of cessation and extinction in Sahaja. The threefold union here may refer to the "conquering of space, time, and the vessel [of the body]" mentioned in saying number 178.

44. *Bhāva.*

45. *Mahābhāva.*

46. *Vihāra vilāsa.*

47. *Śṛṅgāra.*

48. The term *śṛṅgata* is unusual; it seems to be a kind of past passive participle from *śṛṅgāra,* meaning the object of sexual love, hence my gloss as "beloved."

49. See note 25 to saying number 72.

50. That is, if he hasn't been reborn through initiation at the hands of the Mahāśay and Mā Gosāiṅ.

51. *Gorib kompānī.*

52. Again, probably the *Maner Mānuṣa* or God.

53. *Hālāl.* Permissible according to Muslim scriptures; killed in the prescribed way.

54. If one is joined with God, everything in this world seems like a divine miracle or a wondrous magical display.

55. Rational argument and intellectual gymnastics can be manipulated by anyone into any shape, to justify any argument; what is truly needed on the spiritual path is faith and fortitude.

56. *Prakṛti.* "Natural," the first stage of the path.

Chapter IV

1. The twenty-two fakirs are the first disciples of Āulcāṅd. Rather significantly, this list (unlike most lists of the twenty-two) does not include the first Kartā, Rāmśaraṇ Pāl.

2. *Hāṭer pattan.* This notion of "founding the marketplace" of Bhakti is almost certainly a reference to—as well as an appropriation and subversion of—the image of the "Foundation of the Marketplace" in Vaiṣṇava texts such as the *Hāṭ Pattan,* attributed to Narottam Dās.

3. *Kartā bhajā.*

4. This song is often cited as part of the *Bhāver Gīta*; however, it does not appear in either the 1882 or 1992 editions.

5. *Bhāver Mānuṣa* (i.e., Āulcāṅd).

6. The *Rasika* here is probably the *Maner Mānuṣa,* also identified with Kṛṣṇa/ Caitanya/ Āulcāṅd.

7. These ten oarsmen are probably the five sense organs and five organs of action.

8. The Dervish here is Āulcāṅd.

9. Kṛṣṇa.

10. Caitanya.

11. This song is clearly an allegory for the act of sexual intercourse, in which the *sādhaka* attempts to withhold his semen and is in constant danger of losing control and ejaculating (here "unloading his cargo"). The Triveṇī here is clearly the *yoni* of the female partner.

12. In other words, if he ejaculates, he can save his partner from reaching orgasm if he remains motionless.

13. That is, he is in danger of shedding his semen.

14. This is clearly a description of the subtle physiology of the human body, following in the Bāul tradition. The son of Śacī or Caitanya here is the indwelling *Maner Mānuṣa,* who dallies in the Triveṇi or the meeting place of the three *naḍīs* each month.

15. That is, in his incarnation in the form of Kṛṣṇa.

16. The *Iḍā* and *Piṅgalā nāḍīs,* on either side of the central *Suṣumnā* vein.

17. The term *alek* or *alakṣya* is frequently used in Bāul songs to refer to the formless or imperceptible nature of the *Maner Mānuṣa.*

18. *Aleker premer kale.*

19. The crooked vein here is the *Suṣumnā nāḍī;* causing the water to flow in the reverse direction means retaining the semen and causing it to flow upward through the subtle body.

20. *Kahabo tomar ṭhākrī.* The meaning of *ṭhākrī* is unclear, but I am reading it as *ṭhānchī,* a variant of *ṭhāi,* meaning place, room, space; hence, "I'll tell you your [proper] place."

21. The indwelling guru, or Self.

22. *Siddha rati.*

23. *Sthāyī bhāva* ("foundational emotion") is an aesthetic term used to refer to the basic emotional state that serves as the basis for the primary *rasas* or aesthetic moods.

24. That is, love is mixed with lust.

25. The terms here are *kāma, akāma*, and *Mahākāma,* which could also be read as "when lust becomes free of lust, the Great Lust arises."

26. *Ati gopane.*

27. *Śūnyatā.*

28. See Nandī, *Kartābhajā Dharma*, 41–43; Pāl, *Ghoṣpāṛār Satīmā,* 173–74.

29. According to tradition, Kubir composed 1,209 songs, which were recorded by his disciple in 1893. Sudhīr Cakravartī has published 90 songs from the various manuscripts and oral sources he discovered in West Bengal (*Sāhebdhanī Sampradāya,* 157–223).

30. See Cakravartī, *Sāhebdhanī Sampradāya*, 28–59; Nandī, *Kartābhajā: Dharma o Sāhitya.*

31. Ghoṣpāṛā and Jangipur are, respectively, the centers of the Kartābhajā and Sāhebdhanī sects.

32. That is, the Kartābhajā and Sāhebdhanī traditions

33. *Dolete caṛeche dulāl.* The Dulāl is clearly Dulālcāṅd, a.k.a. Rāmdulāl Pāl or Lālśaśī. The gist is either that he literally mounted the swing (playing the part of Kṛṣṇa among the *gopīs*), or that he arose or mounted the throne at Ghoshpara.

34. I owe my reading of this line to Ed Dimock, who suggested that *dhomār* may be a form of *dhūm*, smoke; hence, a steamship and *phanās* as a form of *phenā*, froth.

35. *Ingrājer khaṛi* would mean literally the "chalk" or "silt" of the English, but here I am taking "chalk" in the wider sense of education, mathematical knowledge, or learning of the British.

36. *Kale niśānete kaylā puti base kalye jhāṇḍā gāṛi.* My reading of this line is admittedly rather loose and speculative. It makes little sense if taken literally.

37. A *poyā* is a measure equaling either a half mile or one quarter of a *ser* (= 2 lbs.).

38. In other words, you're stuck with the human body-machine.

39. The meaning of *kyāsiyār* is unclear, but I'm assuming it to be a Bengali rendering of the English term "cashier."

40. *Ṭikiṭ māsṭār.*

41. The ten here are the five sense organs (*jñānendrīya*) and the five physical organs or (*karmendrīya*); the six enemies are the six passions.

42. The two main train stations in Calcutta.

43. *Iskurup.*

44. The implication here seems to be that only a few fortunate human beings get to "go first class in life"—that is, lead a wealthy and high-class life; and that is why the True Religion of the Sāhebdhanīs is established, so that the poor "second-class" people can also ride the train of salvation.

45. The author is playing off the dual meaning of *hābrā* as both the physical place Haora and its sense of old or decrepit.

46. This probably refers to the menstrual flow in the female.

47. Here I'm reading *luncha* as *luccā.*

48. Literally, "he swims in a forest of wool" (*uler bane*).

49. The author is playing on the word *nīl,* "blue" or "indigo," and the epithet of Lord Śiva, the "blue-throated."

50. The meaning of *bichanbeśe* is unclear; here I'm reading it as either *bicibeśe*, "in the form or guise of seeds," or *bicchinnabeśe,* "in sporadic, scattered form."

51. *Kompānī.*

52. A *poyā* is a measure equaling about a half mile. Fourteen *poyās* appears frequently in these songs as the measure of the human body.

53. *Ḍepuṭi kālekṭar.*

54. The term *rasika* is virtually untranslatable. See chapter II, note 12.

55. Kālī.

56. *Pyāri*, the Lover.

57. Jaṭādhārī; "having matted hair."

58. *Kartā.* An interesting and ironic play on the term.

Chapter V

1. From Haripad Cakravartī, ed., *Dāśarathī Rāyer Pāñcālī* (Calcutta: University of Calcutta Press, 1962).

2. For a good discussion of Dāśarathī and the *Pāñcālī* form, see Cakravartī's introduction to *Dāśarathī Rāyer Pāñcālī,* and Banerjee, *The Parlour and the Streets*, 107–114.

3. This is Rāmśaraṇ Pāl, who married Sarasvatī [Satī Mā], daughter of Gopāl Ghoṣe.

4. The holy food offered to the deity and then shared as "leftovers" by devotees.

5. *Ekādaśī,* or the eleventh day of the lunar fortnight, is the traditional day when widows fast.

6. The Līlā here is the Kṛṣṇa-līlā, or the dramatic reenactment of scenes from Kṛṣṇa's life in Vraja—his play with the *gopīs*, the *rāsa*-dance, stealing the clothes of the *gopīs*, slaying the serpent Kāliya, and so on.

7. Paramahaṁsa.

8. This may refer specifically to the five Ms of Tantric ritual.

9. The author is playing off the multiple meanings of *bāj/bāje*, with the basic meaning that the words of worthless, ignorant people are often taken the most seriously and generate the most commotion.

10. Agni.

11. *Bhāva.*

12. Puri, in Orissa, the seat of Lord Jagannāth.

13. The author is playing on the dual meaning of *gollā* as both a "globular sweetmeat" and as "zero, a spoiled or ruined state."

Bibliography

BENGALI SOURCES

Editions of *Bhāver Gīta* (in chronological order)

Kartābhajā Gīta. Bengali manuscript no.964. Bāṅgīya Sāhitya Pariṣat Library, Calcutta, 1228–33 B.S. (1821–26).

Kartābhajār Gītāvalī Ed. Navīncandra Cakravartī. Calcutta: Caitanya Candrodaya, 1277 B.S. (1870).

Bhāver Gīta. Ed. Romeścandra Ghoṣe. Calcutta: Aurora Press, 1389 B.S. (1882).

Śrī Śrī Juter Pada. Ed. Bhuvanamohan Gaṅgopādhyāy. Calcutta: Author, 1894, 1900, and 1905.

Bhāver Gīta. Ed. Manulāl Miśra. Calcutta: Author, 1313, 1325, 1329 B.S. (1906, 1918, 1922).

Bhāver Gīta. Ed. Govardhan Cakravartī. Calcutta: Indralekha Press, 1950.

Bhāver Gīta. Ed. Indrabhūṣan Cakravartī. Calcutta: Indralekha Press, 1977.

Bhāver Gīta. Ed. Śāntirañjan Cakravartī. Calcutta: Indralekha Press, 1399 B.S. (1992).

Other Bengali Sources

Basu, Manindramohun (ed.). *Sahajiyā Sāhitya*. Calcutta: University of Calcutta Press, 1932.

Bhaṭṭācārya, Upaendranāth. *Bāṅglār Bāul o Bāul Gān*. Calcutta: Oriental Book Co., 1981.

Cakravartī, Jāhnavīkumār. "Kartābhajāner Rūpa o Śvarūpa." In *Kartābhajā Dharmamata o Itihāsa,* Vol.2, ed. S. Mitra. Calcutta: De Book Stores, 1977.

Cakravartī, Sudhīr. *Sāhebdhanī Sampradāya*. Calcutta: Pustak Bipaṇi, 1985.

———. *Vrātya Lokāyata Lālan*. Calcutta: Pustak Bipaṇi, 1992.

———. *Paścim Baṅger Melā o Mahotsava*. Calcutta: Pustak Bipaṇi, 1996

Caṭṭopādhyāy, Tuṣār. "Ghoṣpāṛār Melā, Kartābhajā o Lālan." In *Lālan Sāhitya o Darśana*, ed. K. R. Hāq. Dhaka: Bangla Academy, 1976.

———. "Śrī Caitanya o Lokāyata Uttarādhikāra." In *Gouraṅgasaṃskṛti o Śrīcaitanyadeva*, ed. S. Gosvāmi. Calcutta: Calcutta Publishers, 1988.

Dās, Advaita. *Ghoṣpāṛār Kartābhajā Sampradāyā*. Calcutta: Kālī Press, 1983.

Datta, Kedarnāth. *Sacitra Guljār Nagar*. Calcutta: Pustak Bipaṇi, 1982.

Datta, Rāmcandra. *Tattvasāra*. Calcutta: Śaśadhar Prakāśanī, 1983 [1885].

De, Debendranāth. *Kartābhajā Dharmer Itivṛtta*. Calcutta: Jiggasa Agencies, 1968.

Ghoṣe, Bholanāth. *Canda-alaṃkāra-dīpikā*. Calcutta: S. Banerjee and Co., 1963.

Gupta, Mahendranāth. *Śrīśrīrāmakṛṣṇa-Kathāmṛta*. Calcutta: Kathāmṛta Bhavan, 1987.

Jhā, Śaktināth. *Phakir Lālan Sāiṅ: Deś, Kāl evaṃ Śilpa*. Calcutta: Saṃvāda, 1995.

Kālakuṭa (Samareś Basu). *Kothāy Sen Jan Āche*. Calcutta: De's Publishing, 1983.

Kavirāj, Kṛṣṇadās. *Śrī Śrī Caitanya Caritāmṛta*, ed. Rādhāgovinda Nāth. Calcutta: Bhakti-pracāra-bhāṇḍar, 1355 B.S. (1948).

Miśra, Manulāl. *Sahaja Tattva Prakāśa*. Calcutta: Author, 1309 B.S. (1902).

———. *Bhāver Gīta Vyākhyā Saha Sahaja Tattvaprakāśa Vā Sanātana Sahaja Satya Dharmer Ādi Itihās*. Calcutta: Author, 1911.

———. *Kartābhajā Dharmer Ādivṛttānta Vā Sahajatattva Prakāśa*. Calcutta: Author, 1925.

Mitra, Sanatkumār. 1976. "Kartābhajā: Saṃśaya o Samasyā." In *Kartābhajā Dharmamata o Itihāsa*, vol. 1, ed. S. Mitra. Calcutta: De Book Stores.

Mukhopādhyāy, Bimalkumār. 1977. "Pravartakakendrik Sahajiyā: Kartābhajā." In *Kartābhajā Dharmamata o Itihāsa*, Vol. 2, ed. S. Mitra. Calcutta: De Book Stores.

Nandī, Ratan Kumār. 1984. *Kartābhajā Dharma o Sāhitya*. Naihati: Asani Press.

Pāl, Praphulla Candra. *Pracīn Kaviwālār Gān*. Calcutta: University of Calcutta Press, 1958.

Pāl, Satyaśiva. 1991. *Ghoṣpārār Sātī Mā o Kartābahajā Dharma*. Calcutta: Pustak Bipaṇi.

Rāy, Dāśarathī. 1962. "Kartābhajā." In *Dāśarathī Rāyer Pāncālī*, ed. Haripad Cakravartī. Calcutta: University of Calcutta Press.

Saṃvāda Prabhākara. 18 Caitra, 1254 B.S. (1848). Reprinted in Subhāṣ Bandyopādhyāy, "Sekāler Saṃvādapatre Ghoṣpāṛār Melā." In *Kartābhajā Dharmata o Itihāsa*, Vol. 1, ed. S. Mitra. Calcutta: De Book Stores, 1976.

Sarkār, Māṇik. 1976. "Ghoṣpāṛār Melā o tār Prāṇbhomrā." In *Kartābhajā Dharmamata o Itihāsa*, Vol. 2, ed. S. Mitra. Calcutta: De Book Stores.

Sen, Akṣaykumār. *Śrī Śrī Rāmakṛṣṇa Puṅthi*. Calcutta: Udbodhana Kāryālaya, 1976.

Sen, Dineścandra. *Bṛhat Baṅga*. Calcutta: University of Calcutta Press, 1935.

———. "Kartābhajā Dal," *Baṅgabani*, 1 Barṣa, no. 4 (1358 B.S. [1951]): 457–466.

Sen, Nabīncandra. "Ghoṣpāṛār Melā," part 5 of *Āmār Jīvana*. In *Kabibār Nabīncandra Sen, Granthāvalī*. Calcutta: Basumati, 1974.

Sen, Sukumār. "Kartābhajā Kathā o Gān." In *Kartābhajā Dharmata o Itihāsa*, Vol. 2, ed. S. Mitra. Calcutta: De Book Stores, 1977.

Somaprakāśa. 20 Caitra 1270 b.s (1864). Reprinted in Subhāṣ Bandyopādhyāy, "Sekāler Saṃvādapatre Ghoṣpāṛār Melā." In *Kartābhajā Dharmata o Itihāsa*, Vol. 1, ed. S. Mitra. Calcutta: De Book Stores, 1976.

English Sources

Bakhtin, Mikhail. *Rabelais and His World*. Bloomington: University of Indiana Press, 1984.

Banerjee, Sumanta. *The Parlour and the Streets: Elite and Popular Culture in Nineteenth-Century Calcutta*. Calcutta: Seagull, 1989.

———. "From Aulchand to Sati-Ma: The Institutionalization of the Syncretist Karta-Bhaja Sect of Bengal." *Calcutta Historical Journal* 16, no. 2 (1995): 29–59.

Benjamin, Walter. *Illuminations: Essays and Reflections*. New York: Schocken, 1981.

Bhattacharya, Apurna. *Religious Movements of Bengal, 1800–1850*. Calcutta: Vidyasagar Pustak Mandir, 1981.

Bhattacarya, Sudhibhusan. *Ethno-musicology and India*. Calcutta: Indian Publications, 1968.

Bose, Manindra Mohan. *The Post-Caitanya Sahajiyā Cult of Bengal*. Calcutta: University of Calcutta Press, 1930.

Capwell, Charles. "Musical Life in 19th-Century Calcutta as a Component in the History of a Secondary Urban Center." In *Bengal Vaiṣṇavism, Orientalism Society and the Arts*, ed. Joseph O'Connell. East Lansing: Michigan State University Asian Studies Center, 1985.

———. *Music of the Bāuls of Bengal*. Kent, Ohio: Kent State University Press, 1986.

Chakrabarty, Ramakanta. *Vaiṣṇavism in Bengal, 1486–1900.* Calcutta: Sanskrit Pustak Bhandar, 1985.

Chatterjee, Partha. "Caste and Subaltern Consciousness." In *Subaltern Studies VI*, ed. R. Guha. Delhi: Oxford University Press, 1988.

———. *The Nation and Its Fragments: Colonial and Postcolonial Histories.* Princeton: Princeton University Press, 1993.

Chaudhuri, S. (ed.). *Calcutta, the Living City.* Vol. 1: *The Past.* Calcutta: Oxford University Press, 1990.

Clarke, J. Hall, S. Jefferson, T., and Roberts, B. "Subcultures, Cultures and Class: A Theoretical Overview." In *Resistance through Rituals*, ed. S. Hall and T. Jefferson. London: Routledge, 1993.

Collet, Sophia. *The Life and Letters of Rammohun Roy.* Calcutta: D. K. Biswas, 1962.

Comaroff, Jean, and Comparoff, John (eds.). *Modernity and Its Malcontents: Ritual and Power in Postcolonial Africa.* Chicago: University of Chicago Press, 1993.

Conze, Edward. *Buddhist Thought in India: Three Phases of Buddhist Philosophy.* Ann Arbor: University of Michigan Press, 1967.

Dasugupta, Shashibhushan. *Obscure Religious Cults as a Background to Bengali Literature.* Calcutta: Firma KLM, 1968.

De, S. K. *Bengali Literature in the Nineteenth Century.* Calcutta: Firma KLM, 1961.

de Certeau, Michel. *The Practice of Everyday Life.* Berkeley: University of California Press, 1984.

Dimock, Edward C., Jr. (trans.). *Caitanya Caritāmṛta of Kṛṣṇadāsa Kavirāja. A Translation and Commentary.* Cambridge: Harvard University Press, 1999.

Dimock, Edward C., Jr. *The Place of the Hidden Moon: Erotic Mysticism in the Vaiṣṇava-Sahajiyā Cult of Bengal.* Chicago: University of Chicago Press, 1966.

Dube, Saurabh. *Untouchable Pasts: Religion, Identity and Power among a Central Indian Community, 1780–1950.* Albany: *State University of New York Press*, 1998.

Garrett, J. E. H. *Bengal District Gazetteers, Nadia.* Calcutta: Bengal Secretariat Book Stall, 1910.

Guha, Ranajit. *Elementary Aspects of Peasant Insurgency in Colonial Bengal.* Delhi: Oxford University Press, 1983.

———. "The Prose of Counter-Insurgency." In *Subaltern Studies II*, ed. R. Guha. Delhi: Oxford University Press, 1983.

Hardiman, David. *The Coming of the Devi: Adivasi Assertion in Western India.* Delhi: Oxford, 1995.

Haydn, Hyram. *The Counter Renaissance.* New York: Grove Press, 1960.

Hebdige, Dick. *Subculture: The Meaning of Style.* London: Methuen, 1979.

Kelly, John. *A Politics of Virtue: Hinduism, Sexuality and Countercolonial Discourse in Fiji.* Chicago: University of Chicago Press, 1991.

Kinsman, Robert (ed.). *The Darker Vision of the Renaissance.* Berkeley: University of California Press, 1974.

Kopf, David. *The Brahmo Samaj and the Shaping of the Modern Indian Mind.* Princeton: Princeton University Press, 1979.

Kripal, Jeffrey J. *Kālī's Child: The Mystical and the Erotic in the Life of Ramakrishna.* Chicago: University of Chicago Press, 1998.

———. "The Fearful Art of Writing Left-Handed: Some Personal and Theoretical Reflections on Translating the *Kathāmṛta* into American English." In *In the Flesh: Eros, Secrecy and Power in the Tantric Traditions of India,* ed. Hugh B. Urban and Glen A. Hayes (in progress).

Larson, Gerald. *India's Agony over Religion.* Albany: State University of New York Press, 1995.

Long, James. *Handbook of Bengal Missions*. London: J. F. Shaw, 1848.

Marshall, P. J. *Bengal: The British Bridgehead: Eastern India, 1740–1828*. Cambridge: Cambridge University Press, 1987.

McDaniel, June. *The Madness of the Saints: Ecstatic Religion in Bengal*. Chicago: University of Chicago Press, 1989.

McDermott, Rachel Fell. *Singing to the Goddess: Poems to Kālī and Umā from Bengal*. New York: Oxford University Press, 2001.

Mitra, Rajeshwara. "Music in Old Calcutta." In *Calcutta, the Living City*, Vol. 1, ed. S. Chaudhuri. Calcutta: Oxford University Press, 1990.

Monier-Williams, Monier. *Hinduism*. London: Society for Promoting Christian Knowledge, 1894.

Oddie, Geoffrey A. "Old Wine in New Bottles? Kartābhajā (Vaishnava) Converts to Evangelical Christianity in Bengal, 1835–1845," *Indian Economic and Social History Review* 32, no. 3 (1995): 327–43.

O'Hanlon, Rosalind. "Recovering the Subject: Subaltern Studies and Histories of Resistance in Colonial South Asia" *Modern Asian Studies* 22, no.1 (1988): 189–224.

Padoux, André. "Tantrism, an Overview." In *Encyclopedia of Religion*, ed. M. Eliade. New York: Macmillan, 1986.

Pinch, William. *Peasants and Monks in British India*. Berkeley: University of California Press, 1996.

Ray, Sukumar. *Music of Eastern India: Vocal Music in Bengali, Oriya, Assamese and Manipuri, with Special Emphasis on Bengali*. Calcutta: Firma KLM, 1973.

Sahlins, Marshall. *Culture and Practical Reason*. Chicago: University of Chicago Press, 1976.

———. "Cosmologies of Capitalism: The Trans-Pacific Sector of the World System." *Proceedings of the British Academy* 74 (1988): 1–20.

Salomon, Carol. "Bāul Songs." In *Religions of India in Practice*, ed. D. Lopez. Princeton: Princeton University Press, 1995.

Sarkar, Sumit. *An Exploration of the Ramakrishna-Vivekananda Tradition*. Simla: Institute of Indian Studies, 1993.

Schulte, Rainer, and Biguenet, John (eds). *Theories of Translation: An Anthology of Essays from Dryden to Derrida*. Chicago: University of Chicago Press, 1992.

Sen, Sukumar. *History of Bengali Literature*. New Delhi: Sahitya Academy, 1960.

Sen, Sudipta. "Conquest of Marketplaces: Exchange, Authority and Conflict in Early Colonial North India." Ph.D. diss., University of Chicago, 1994.

———. "Passages of Authority: Rulers, Traders and Marketplaces in Bengal and Benaras, 1700–1750." *Calcutta Historical Journal* 17, no. 1 (1996): 1–40.

Spivak, Gayatri. "A Literary Representation of the Subaltern: Mahasweta Devi's *Stanadayini*." In *Subaltern Studies V*, ed. R. Guha. Delhi: Oxford University Press, 1987.

Taussig, Michael. *The Devil and Commodity Fetishism in South America*. Chapel Hill: University of North Carolina Press, 1980.

Urban, Hugh B. "The Poor Company: Economics and Ecstasy in the Kartābhajā Sect of Colonial Bengal." *South Asia* 19, no. 2 (1996): 1–33.

———. "The Torment of Secrecy: Ethical and Epistemological Problems in the Study of Esoteric Traditions." *History of Religions* 37, no. 3 (1998): 209–48.

———. "The Extreme Orient: The Construction of 'Tantrism' as a Category in the Orientalist Imagination." *Religion* 29 (1999): 123–46.

———. "The Politics of Madness: The Construction and Manipulation of the 'Bāul' Image in Modern Bengal." *South Asia* 22, no. 1 (1999): 13–46.

———. "The Cult of Ecstasy: Tantrism, the New Age, and the Spiritual Logic of Late Capitalism." *History of Religions* 39, no. 3 (2000): 268–304.

———. *The Economics of Ecstasy: Tantra, Secrecy and Power in Colonial Bengal.* New York: Oxford University Press, 2001.

Venuti, Lawrence. *Rethinking Translation: Discourse, Subjectivity, Identity.* New York: Routledge, 1992.

———. *The Translator's Invisibility: A History of Translation.* New York: Routledge, 1995.

Ward, Rev. William. *Account of the Writings, Religion and Manners of the Hindus.* 4 vols. Serampore: Mission Press, 1811.

———. (ed). *A Brief Memoir of Krishna Pal, the First Hindoo in Bengal Who Broke the Chain of Caste by Embracing the Gospel.* London: J. Offor, 1823.

Zbavitel, Dusan. *Bengali Literature.* Wiesbaden: Otto Harrassowitz, 1976.

Index

business, 24, 58–63, 118
business office, 42, 89, 170n.143

Caitanya, Śrī, 6, 10, 26, 44–7, 69–71, 77, 129, 147, 149, 156n.22
Secret Caitanya, 69–71, 129, 132, 156n.22, 166n.65
See also gorā
Caitanya Caritāmṛta, 70, 156n.22
Cakora bird, 81, 99, 167n.90
cakras, 123, 124, 168n.114
Calcutta, 8, 10, 12, 17, 20–1, 24, 30, 32, 34, 53–4, 132, 135, 141, 150, 157n.27
and Kartābhajās, 17, 20, 24
and marketplaces, 17, 24, 132, 137
metaphor for human body, 132, 137
Caṇḍīdās, 127–28, 168n.111
Caṇḍīmaṅgal, 22, 143
capital (*jamā*), 12, 40, 43, 44, 58, 62–5
capital of honor (*khātirjamā*), 12, 63
capitalism, 8, 29
cargo, 26, 39, 51–3, 69
unloading the cargo (i.e., ejaculation), 123–4, 173n.11
castes and classes, 18–20, 33, 42–3, 76, 84, 141
See also varṇa
Chatterjee, Partha, 8, 35
Chitragupta, 73
Christianity, 29, 34, 148
Kartābhajā conversions to, 34
Christian missionaries, 165n.56
colonialism, 8, 10, 22–4, 28–9, 36–7
commodities, 26, 28–9, 51–4, 160n.79
company. *See* British East India Company; *kompānī*
corporeal taxation (*daihik khajanā*), 34

dālāl (broker, middle-man), 12, 25, 52, 64–7, 144
religious brokers, 165n.54
See also marketplace
death, 112, 113, 138, 143, 144, 147, 166n.69
de Certeau, Michel, 36
debt, 58–9, 62, 63, 72, 90
deha, 13, 131, 134
See also body
Derrida, Jacques, 4–5, 153n.2
dervish, 122, 137
devotion. *See bhakti*
Dhaka, 54, 57
dhākā sahar (Hidden City) 57, 71
dharma, 77, 92, 137, 139, 144, 146, 148, 167n.95
Dulālcāṅd, x, 11, 34, 159n.52
See also Lālśaśī

ecstasy, 4, 6, 16, 70, 77–8, 83, 117, 121, 130
See also bhāva
Englishmen, 26, 55–6, 134, 137
eunuch. *See khojā*
excrement, shit, 104, 116, 170n.144

factory, 49, 83, 104
of *rasa*, 83
fakir, 6, 9, 24, 30, 49, 115, 119, 120–2
See also Āulcāṅd
fish, 98, 168n.123
catching the, 168n.23
fort, Company's, 42, 101, 170n.143
Freemasonry, 12

garden of love, 31, 100–4
Ghoshpara, 33, 131–3, 141, 159n.52
Ghoshpara Melā, 16, 19–20, 131–2
as Secret Vṛndāvana, 131–2 156n.22
Good-Mannered Company, 42, 46, 101, 104
See also ādab
gopīs, 99, 143, 147, 175n.6
gorā, 26–7, 45, 163n.13, 163n.16
gorā kompānī, 26–7, 44–5, 163n.13, 163n.16
gorib, *gorīb*, x, 28, 40–4, 166n.67
gorib kompānī, 7–8, 22, 28, 40–4, 118, 173n.51
See also kāṅgāl; kompānī; poverty
gour, 26, 44–5, 70, 79, 129, 147, 163n.13
Guha, Ranajit, 8, 23, 36–7
gunas, 8, 162n.8
gupta, 11, 156n.22
gupta Caitanya, 11
gupta hāṭ, 11, 25, 120, 156n.22
gupta Vṛndāvana, 11, 19, 132, 156n.22
See also secrecy
guru, 84, 113, 116, 117, 119, 123, 136, 145–6
as Self, 128
See also Kartā; *mahāśay*

Haora Railway Station, 135–6
Hari, 69–70, 147
hāṭ, 11, 22–3, 25, 120–1
See also gupta

secret marketplace, 11, 25, 120, 156n.22
See also gupta
seed, semen, 78, 92, 119, 127–8, 136, 173n.11
retention of semen, 173n.11, 173n.12
seed of creation, 92
See also bīja; bindu
Self, 81, 124, 125, 129, 130
Sen, Nabīncandra, 11, 20
Sen, Rāmprasād, 15, 22, 158n.33
sex, 7, 14, 30–3, 87, 97–8, 115, 118, 119, 128, 156n.17, 167n.90, 173n.11
and Kartābhajā practice, 7, 100–4
in Tantric practice, 161n.86, 173n.11
See also parakīyā; *rati*; stinking fruit; *svakīyā*
shopkeepers (*dokāndār*), 22, 40, 52, 63, 79. *See also bājār; hāṭ*; merchants
siddha, 167n.104, 169n.128
sikka, 43, 139
Śiva, 98, 125, 137, 142
Spivak, Gayatri, 162n.101
stinking fruit, 30, 100–4
See also parakīyā,
Subaltern Studies, 8, 35–7, 155n.11, 162n.101
śūdras, 20–1, 43, 76, 166n.77
suṣūmnā, 124, 173n.16, 173n.19
svādiṣṭhāna, 168n.114
svakīyā, 97, 99–100, 161n.85

Tagore, Rabindranath, 7, 16, 18
ṭākās, 115, 134
Tantra, 7, 9, 11, 16, 29–33, 35 80, 97–8, 144, 160n.82, 163n.14
in colonial Bengal, 7, 31–3, 97–8
and five M's, 29, 175n.9
and Kartābhajās, 7, 16, 29–33, 97–8, 155n.15
as problematic category, 161n.82
tantras, 40, 82, 95, 148
Tantrasāra, 148
Tantric practice, 97–8, 123–4, 163n.14
See also kuṇḍalinī, sādhana, sex
taxation, 10, 34, 68, 138–9
corporeal, 34
tripadī, 15, 158n.44
triveṇī, 123–5, 173n.14
truth. *See satya*
ṭyāṅkśālī, 22, 111–9, 170n.2

Untouchables, 142, 144
Upaniṣads, 84

Vaiṣṇava-Sahajiyās, 9, 97, 154n.3, 155n.15
Vaiṣṇavas, 10, 14, 23, 28, 30, 83, 97, 123, 161n.86
vaiṭhakī, 12
varṇa (class or color), 42, 75–6, 166n.77
Vāsuki, 93, 145, 168n.114
metaphor for *kuṇḍalinī*, 168n.114, 168n.116
Vedānta, 82, 126
Vedas, 108, 121, 126, 130, 146, 149
Victoria, Queen, 140
Vidyāpati, 128
Viṣṇu, 125, 167n.95
Vṛndāvana, 14, 19, 132, 135, 149, 156n.22
Secret Vṛndāvana, 11, 19, 132–3, 156n.22
See also Ghosphara, *gupta*

womb, 140, 166n.72
women, 14, 77, 79, 81, 83, 87, 104–5, 115, 121, 127–8, 140, 141–2, 150, 168n.111
in Kartābhajā practice, 87, 97, 127–8, 141–2, 159n.48, 167n.90,
mysteries of, 139–40

yantra, 144
yoga, 123, 124, 129, 146
yoni, 123, 167n.110, 173n.11
yugas, 133
See also Kali yuga

zamindār, 23, 34